Autonomous Bidding Agents

Intelligent Robotics and Autonomous Agents
George A. Bekey, Henrik I. Christensen, Edmund H. Durfee, David Kortenkamp, and Michael Wooldridge, Associate Series Editors

Robot Shaping: An Experiment in Behavior Engineering, Marco Dorigo and Marco Colombetti, 1997

Behavior-Based Robotics, Ronald C. Arkin, 1998

Layered Learning in Multiagent Systems: A Winning Approach to Robotic Soccer, Peter Stone, 2000

Evolutionary Robotics: The Biology, Intelligence, and Technology of Self-Organizing Machines, Stefano Nolfi and Dario Floreano, 2000

Reasoning about Rational Agents, Michael Wooldridge, 2000

Introduction to AI Robotics, Robin R. Murphy, 2000

Mechanics of Robotic Manipulation, Matthew T. Mason, 2001

Strategic Negotiation in Multiagent Environments, Sarit Kraus, 2001

Designing Sociable Robots, Cynthia L. Breazeal, 2002

Introduction to Autonomous Mobile Robots, Roland Siegwart and Illah R. Nourbakhsh, 2004

Autonomous Robots: From Biological Inspiration to Implementation and Control, George A. Bekey, 2005

Principles of Robot Motion: Theory, Algorithms, and Implementations, Howie Choset, Kevin M. Lynch, Seth Hutchinson, George Kantor, Wolfram Burgard, Lydia E. Kavraki and Sebastian Thrun, 2005

Probabilistic Robotics, Sebastian Thrun, Wolfram Burgard, and Dieter Fox, 2005

Autonomous Bidding Agents: Strategies and Lessons from the Trading Agent Competition, Michael P. Wellman, Amy Greenwald, and Peter Stone, 2007

Autonomous Bidding Agents

Strategies and Lessons from the Trading Agent Competition

Michael P. Wellman, Amy Greenwald, and Peter Stone

The MIT Press
Cambridge, Massachusetts
London, England

This book was set in Times Roman by the author using the LaTeX document preparation system. Printed on recycled paper and bound in the United States of America.

Library of Congress Cataloging-in-Publication Data

Wellman, Michael P.
Autonomous bidding agents : strategies and lessons from the trading agent competition / Michael P. Wellman, Amy Greenwald, Peter Stone.
p. cm. — (Intelligent robotics and autonomous agents series)
Includes bibliographical references and index.
ISBN 978-0-262-23260-9 (hardcover : alk. paper)
1. Electronic commerce. 2. Intelligent agents (Computer software)
I. Greenwald, Amy II. Stone, Peter, 1971– III. Title.
HF5548.32.W465 2006
338.4'3—dc22 2006034223

to Erika, Justin, and Tammy

Contents

Preface

This book distills the experiences and lessons learned from the international Trading Agent Competition (TAC) series. Motivated by TAC, a community of academic and industry researchers has been inventing and polishing techniques for autonomous bidding by software agents. We, the authors, have been both organizers of TAC and successful participants. As such, we have tackled the problems posed by TAC with our own independent efforts, and we have closely observed the evolution of approaches developed by the community as a whole.

TAC is a stylized setting exemplary of the rapidly advancing domain of electronic marketplaces. It is also a benchmark, motivating researchers to apply innovative approaches to a common task. A key feature of TAC is that it provides an academic forum for open comparison of agent bidding strategies in a complex scenario, as opposed to, for example, automated trading in real-world securities markets, in which practitioners are less inclined to share their technologies. As the product of sustained focus and cross-fertilization of ideas over time, TAC provides a unique case study of the current capabilities and limitations of autonomous bidding agents.

Throughout the text, we balance the contextual reporting of results from the specific TAC scenario with the desire to generalize to the broader problem of autonomous bidding. To ground the discussion, we include substantial data from controlled TAC experiments and TAC tournaments, methods employed by particular TAC agents, and anecdotes from TAC events. To generalize these lessons and techniques, we develop a generic trading agent architecture unifying the approaches observed, define abstract versions of trading agent subproblems, and highlight important properties of these problems and proposed solutions through theoretical and experimental analysis.

We consider this dual approach—intensive design focused on a concrete scenario, interleaved with abstraction and analysis aimed at drawing general lessons—essential for deriving principled trading agent designs. Real-world markets are too complex to rely solely on abstract modeling, and specific markets are too idiosyncratic to admit direct transfer of techniques. By testing general ideas in particular scenarios, we are forced to work through operational details that tend not to arise in more abstract models. Through careful evaluation of proposed designs, we can achieve some confidence in their viability, and gather evidence about their limitations. Lifting the methods back up to more generic market scenarios enables adaptation to similar environments, and even transfer across qualitatively different market domains.

The main contributions of this book are (i) the story of the development and evolution of the TAC research initiative, including anecdotal accounts of

TAC agent interactions over the years; (ii) detailed analyses of specific TAC agent designs and bidding techniques; and (iii) development of some general engineering foundations for trading agent design. Our intended audience includes individuals interested in developing TAC agents, but we expect most readers are primarily motivated by other trading domains. By inviting all to immerse yourselves in the TAC domain, we lead you on the very path we have taken in developing our understanding of the current best practices for designing autonomous bidding agents.

Acknowledgments

By its very nature, the Trading Agent Competition is a collective enterprise, and this book would not have been possible without the contributions of scores of developers who have implemented TAC agents over the years. We would especially like to thank the people central to the design and operation of the TAC Travel game servers: Peter Wurman and Kevin O'Malley (University of Michigan) and Sverker Janson, Joakim Eriksson, and Niclas Finne (Swedish Institute of Computer Science). Individuals serving as GameMaster over the years are listed in Appendix A. Other volunteers who have served important roles enabling the TAC Travel tournaments include Eric Aurell, Maria Fasli, Nick Jennings, David Parkes, Norman Sadeh, and Shihomi Wada.

Many of the results presented herein were produced collaboratively with our colleagues and students. In most cases, specific attribution is provided by citations throughout the book to articles previously published in various journals and conference proceedings. The contributions of these coauthors and others listed below are to a great extent inseparable from our own.

ATTac was developed by Peter Stone in collaboration with colleagues at AT&T Labs—Research: Michael Littman (ATTac-00 and ATTac-01); Michael Kearns and Satinder Singh (ATTac-00); and János Csirik, David McAllester, and Robert Schapire (ATTac-01). Many of the ideas described in connection with ATTac, particularly in Chapter 6 would not have come about without their cooperation. Stone's research related to this book was supported in part by the National Science Foundation under Grant No. IIS-0237699, and by an Alfred P. Sloan Foundation research fellowship.

RoxyBot was developed by Amy Greenwald, initially in collaboration with Justin Boyan (2000–2002), and later in collaboration with her students at Brown University, specifically Jesse Funaro (2003), Jonathan Bankard (2004),

Bryan Guillemette (2005), Seong Jae Lee (2006), and Victor Naroditskiy (2003–2006). Victor deserves our sincerest gratitude for his substantial contributions to the theoretical development in Chapter 3 (Theorems 3.2 and 3.4) and for creating the series of examples of the stochastic bidding problem presented in Chapter 5. Seong Jae also deserves special thanks for conducting the experiments reported in Chapter 5. Greenwald's research related to this book was supported in part by the National Science Foundation under Grant No. IIS-0133689, and by an Alfred P. Sloan Foundation research fellowship.

The Walverine team, supervised by Michael Wellman, has engaged many graduate and undergraduate students at the University of Michigan. Participants from 2002–present included Shih-Fen Cheng, Evan Leung, Kevin Lochner, Daniel Reeves, Julian Schvartzman, and Yevgeniy Vorobeychik. Kevin O'Malley, Christopher Kiekintveld, Daniel Reeves, and William Walsh were instrumental in the operation of the first two TAC events. Daniel Reeves, Kevin Lochner, and Rahul Suri provided indispensable testbed and analysis tools. Wellman's research related to this book was supported in part by the National Science Foundation under Grant Nos. IIS-9988715, IIS-0205435, and IIS-0414710.

1 Introduction

Trade is a quintessential human activity. Throughout history, the institutions and artifacts of trade, such as markets and currency, have evolved hand in hand with major technological advances, such as the printing press and telecommunication networks. The rise of the Internet in the past decade is another transformative advance. In the new online markets, buyers and sellers have unprecedented opportunities for trade through a wide array of novel mechanisms. For example,

- Consumers navigate the Internet through general search engines, specialized search services (e.g., online travel agencies), and customized shopping facilities (e.g., price comparison sites). These discovery tools quickly compile information about goods and services provided by a multitude of online vendors, allowing consumers to make more informed choices [Wan et al., 2003].
- Individuals sell idiosyncratic goods (e.g., baby clothes, collectibles) through online channels, on a one-off basis or as a regular business. The largest online auction site, eBay [Cohen, 2002], is alone responsible for creating viable markets for goods previously harder to trade, and providing a medium where hundreds of thousands of small businesses earn their livelihood.[1]
- Investors trade financial securities through online brokers. Brokerage firms and institutional investors in turn route orders through new electronic trading mechanisms, such as ECNs (electronic communications networks), which automate the matching of compatible offers. According to Stoll [2006], electronic trading has reduced transaction costs and improved the accuracy of price signals, contributing to an overall increased efficiency of stock markets.
- Corporate officers procure goods and services through electronic reverse auctions. Such auctions (popularized by Freemarkets—now Ariba) enable buyers to negotiate with multiple suppliers simultaneously on a global scale. Sophisticated techniques optimize over numerous alternatives of suppliers in large-scale procurement events [Sandholm et al., 2006].

Before the advent of the Internet, trades were negotiated by people: face-to-face, over the phone, or by mail. Some conventional negotiations follow a structured process, such as choosing listed-price items from a catalog or

1. A 2005 study by AC Nielson, reported by *ECommerce Guide* (`http://ecommerce-guide.com`), found that 724,000 eBay sellers rely on eBay for their primary or secondary source of income, and another 1.5 million individuals supplement their income there.

bidding on fine art at auction, and others proceed informally, such as haggling at a flea market. Online negotiation similarly includes both structured and unstructured modes. By automating some key operations in negotiation (e.g., calculation, record-keeping, and messaging), the online medium fosters the deployment of structured trade mechanisms.

A structured trade mechanism is one that operates according to clearly defined rules. Those rules govern who may participate and when, and specify allowable actions, generally in terms of an interface for communicating market activity. Market interfaces tend to be relatively simple. Traders' messages are typically limited to offers to exchange quantities of standardized goods for standardized currency using standardized exchange processes. For example, the action of bidding for an item on eBay involves specifying the item number and the offer price, and sufficient information (e.g., a user login and password) to authenticate the sender as an authorized account holder. Because of this simplicity, automated bid submission on eBay is straightforward using standard web protocols [Krishnamurthy and Rexford, 2001]. Other electronic marketplaces also facilitate bidding through simple, thus reliable, published protocols. For example, the Small Order Execution System (SOES) allows retail investors to automatically execute trades of Nasdaq securities.

Automating the negotiation process naturally leads to opportunities for automating the traders' tasks. Although online negotiations are still carried out primarily by humans, the trend toward automation is well underway. On eBay, for instance, sellers can avail themselves of a variety of online services and software tools to automate their posting of items for sale, manage transactions, communicate with buyers, and obtain information relevant to timing and pricing their offerings. Buyers can employ specialized third-party services (e.g., `eSnipe.com`) to monitor auctions and submit their bids at prespecified times or on the basis of other auction results. In financial markets, programs have been created that suggest particular trades based on known or proprietary criteria. Retail stock market investors can employ readily available software or electronic brokerage services to specify complex rules to trigger buy and/or sell orders in response to designated price patterns. Major brokerage houses employ sophisticated and highly secret algorithms to generate trades [Bass, 1999], which often get executed automatically or with minimal human involvement.

Compared to other interactive decision-making domains, the trading task is particularly amenable to automation. Successfully automating trading, however, depends not only on reliable software interfaces but also on being able to render effective *decisions* about which trading actions to take (e.g., which goods to bid on, when, and at what price). The topic of effective decision making is paramount to many disciplines, including psychology, economics, operations research, philosophy, and computer science. The field of *artificial intelligence* (AI) [Russell and Norvig, 2003] draws on principles from these subjects and others to develop techniques for decision making by *autonomous agents*.

Autonomous agents are software programs that make decisions (generally on behalf of some person or organization) without direct human intervention. Even though computer software is conceived of by (human) designers and implemented by (human) programmers, we refer to programs as autonomous to the extent that their decisions are not rote implementations of instructions spelled out by a human. For example, a program that carried out the direction "bid $99 for eBay item 123" would not be considered an autonomous bidder. But a program that submitted this bid based on the direction "buy a digital camera at a good price" could be credibly attributed a meaningful degree of autonomy. Henceforth, we employ the term *agent* as shorthand for autonomous agent, taking as understood that these computational entities act beyond the direct control of humans.

The central topic of this book is how to design agents that make effective trading decisions in online markets.[2] Even within this narrower scope, this *trading agent problem* can be arbitrarily complex. Making decisions about how to bid to achieve stated trading objectives entails consideration of numerous factors, including estimating the value of goods to the agent and predicting prices at which goods will ultimately trade. Arbitrary complexity is difficult to handle for any trader, even human. The premise of our enterprise is that competent trading by autonomous agents is often attainable. That is, in many domains, a substantial portion of decision making for trading can be effectively automated.

As with many computer-based activities, trading agents come equipped with some inherent advantages over humans. They can monitor many markets simultaneously; they can process immense amounts of information in real time; and they can perform complex numerical calculations instantaneously. However, on the surface, they might also appear to be hindered by inherent disadvantages. Demonstrating that trading agents can competently perform functions not typically attributed to computers, such as learning from past

2. We do not address some other relevant questions, such as how an agent could determine from the eBay web site that item 123 constitutes a digital camera. Such inference can be performed reliably in many cases, because many goods are unambiguous or described in standard ways.

experience and evaluating tradeoffs by making complex value judgments, is the subject of current trading agent research, including this book.

1.1 Trading Agent Research

The foremost aim of trading agent research is to develop a body of techniques for effective design and analysis of trading agents. Contributions to trading agent design include the invention of trading strategies, together with models and algorithms for realizing the computations entailed by those strategies, and methods to measure and evaluate the performance of agents characterized by those strategies. Researchers seek both specific solutions to particular trading problems and general principles to guide the development of trading agents across market scenarios.

Beyond understanding just how effective trading agent strategies can be, a secondary goal of trading agent research is to understand how characteristics of a market environment can affect the performance of various trading agent designs. Of related interest is how the presence of automated traders might affect the distribution of goods in electronic markets. Just as the automation of market functions has expanded options for deployed market mechanisms [MacKie-Mason and Wellman, 2006], automated traders may potentially introduce patterns of behavior qualitatively different from those observed in markets with only human participants. Understanding such phenomena in an increasingly automated world is crucial to improving designs of markets themselves.

In principle, knowledge that would contribute to such understanding could be generated from nascent efforts in automated trading (e.g., programmed traders in financial markets). Unfortunately, data about real-world trading agents is difficult to obtain. Designers of successful trading agents are naturally reluctant to reveal their automation techniques, since doing so could compromise their proprietary advantages. Bass's [1999] account of the Prediction Company is an unusually forthcoming story of one significant effort, yet still stops short of technical and strategic precision. Designers of unsuccessful agents may also be reluctant to discuss their experience, albeit for different reasons. This lack of public information about trading agent strategies has led interested researchers to study their own designs, often applied to hypothetical market scenarios. These studies have generated useful ideas and observations, contributing to the goals of the trading agent research community.

However, markets constitute multiagent environments, where the performance of a particular agent strategy depends on the other agents' behaviors. Consequently, solitary research on trading agents (or indeed on agent design for any multiagent environment) has a serious limitation. Since an agent's effectiveness depends on the strategies of others, having one designer choose all strategies introduces a great source of fragility to the research exercise. There is an important circularity in multiagent research for which we must account: principled agent design requires a model of other agents, but these other agents' designs should be informed by principles from multiagent research.

Of course, particular researchers may avail themselves of ideas from the trading agent research literature, and thus attempt to evaluate their designs in the context of designs published by others. Doing so can be difficult, however, as trading agent designs developed for particular market scenarios may not easily transfer to other, equally relevant, market scenarios. Thus, much of the research literature (properly) focuses on abstract and stylized markets, such as sealed-bid auctions and other canonical market mechanisms.

Another natural approach to trading agent research is for researchers to cooperate by addressing their design energy toward solving a common problem. The common environment would be conducive to comparing approaches and sharing ideas, eliminating the arduous task of translating across domains merely to compare agent strategies. If separate research groups were to develop agents to participate in a common market environment, the aggregate result might be similar to a real market economy, thus supporting the generation and dissemination of answers to core questions about trading agent research.

This supposition was the primary motivation for organizing the international Trading Agent Competition (TAC) [Wellman and Wurman, 1999], a series of annual research tournaments where agent designers from around the world put forth their best efforts at automated trading for a specified market scenario. The hope was that by providing the software infrastructure, designers could be induced to cooperate (by competing!) in furtherance of broad research goals.

1.2 Trading Agents Competing

The first TAC tournament [Greenwald and Stone, 2001; Wellman et al., 2001b], held in July 2000 in Boston, attracted 16 entrants from six countries in North America, Europe, and Asia. Excitement generated from this event led to refinement of the game rules, and continuation of regular tournaments with increasing levels of competition over the next six years. Year by year entrants improved their designs, developing new ideas and building on successful techniques from previous tournaments. Published accounts of TAC agents and TAC-based experimental studies now amount to a substantial literature (much of which is referenced in this book), fulfilling the original aim of promoting progress in trading agent research. The distilled experience from seven years of competition provides the basis for this book.

TAC dresses in a familiar narrative several realistic features of trading in electronic markets. The choice of the travel domain was somewhat arbitrary, but shopping for airline flights and hotels is a routine activity for many people, and assembling trips for clients is a plausible application for agent technology. The key feature captured by this domain is that goods are highly interdependent (e.g., flight and hotel reservations must be coordinated), yet the markets for these goods operate independently. We consider this interdependence to be a central challenge in trading agent strategy, and many of the techniques we develop are designed expressly to deal with this problem. A second important feature of the game is that agents trade via three different kinds of market mechanism—posted price, ascending auction, and continuous double auction—each of which presents distinct challenges. In grappling with all three while constructing their agent strategies, participants are confronted by an ample set of interesting problems.

These two features distinguish TAC from related competitions, such as the Santa Fe Double Auction Tournament [Rust et al., 1994], which focus on one auction mechanism for trading a single abstract good. Yet further removed are popular contests for stock market trading,[3] which measure skill (or luck) in picking financial securities and forecasting external market movements. The TAC scenario, in contrast, compels agents to reason about complex tradeoffs in a dynamic market, depending on their individual situations: clients' preferences, holdings of goods, outstanding commitments, and so on.

Agent interactions are another noteworthy feature of TAC. In an instance of the TAC game, eight agents compete to assemble trips for their respective clients. Since there are only eight agents (as opposed to, say, hundreds), each exerts a nonnegligible influence on the markets for travel goods. At the same time, since each agent is on equal footing, no agent can control singlehandedly the overall market conditions. This qualitative balance is a common feature of

3. For example, at the time of this writing, MarketWatch's Virtual Stock Exchange (`http://vse.marketwatch.com`) is running 1492 public games, several of which have attracted over 1000 players.

real-world markets. Trading agents can deal effectively in such environments by reasoning strategically about individual agents and about the market as a whole.

1.3 Book Overview

To claim that TAC research contributes to the more general aims of trading agent research requires that we lift the lessons learned from the TAC scenario to the broader context. To a great extent we can do so, drawing on the TAC experience to propose a general trading agent architecture, and characterizing core subtasks faced by trading agents in their endeavors (Chapter 3). For example, high-level subtasks include *price prediction*—forecasting the eventual prices at which goods will trade—and *bid construction*—deciding what prices to bid for goods. Defining subproblems facilitates generalization, and it enables researchers to separately evaluate techniques developed for trading subtasks. Although interesting tasks tend not to be strictly separable in a complex trading problem, carefully designed experimental analyses can often support robust conclusions about the efficacy of design ideas.

Chapter 4 presents one such analysis, of the important problem of predicting prices. Although the case study focuses on a particular instance of the price-prediction problem as it arises in TAC, the ultimate lessons are more general in nature, bearing on the categories of techniques and kinds of information that might be employed for price prediction, and the factors that determine their efficacy. Whereas the eventual explanation is qualitative and general, a quantitative study in a concrete scenario provides credence to the conclusions, something that might be difficult to obtain from a more stylized model.

In Chapter 5 we frame what we consider to be the core problem in trading agent design: how to bid in interdependent markets in the face of uncertain prices. We develop a series of bidding "heuristics"—reasonable rules of thumb that an agent might employ in a complex trading scenario where the computation of an optimal trading strategy is intractable. We highlight the strengths and limitations of each of these heuristics, supported by examples, general analytical results, and simulation experiments performed within the TAC domain. The key ideas developed in this chapter were implemented over the years in successive modifications of the agent RoxyBot.

The role of machine learning in trading agent design is the subject of the next chapter. In many markets, the effects of an individual agent's bids may be highly uncertain because they depend on the other agents' (unknown) bids. This uncertainty renders the effectiveness of general bidding strategies an empirical question. When, in the context of a specific economy of other agents, repeated measurements are possible, the opportunity arises for an agent to autonomously improve its performance over time. Chapter 6, which highlights the agent ATTac, illustrates effective uses of adaptivity and learning by a trading agent.

Chapter 7 returns to the specific markets embodied in the TAC scenario. We provide an overview of each generic market type (posted-price mechanisms, simultaneous ascending auctions, and continuous double auctions). We also exhibit specialized trading strategies customized for the particularities of TAC markets, relating bidding insights between the respective realms.

Chapter 8, the last technical chapter of the book, steps back from particular strategy ideas to methodological issues in experimental trading agent research. Through a case study of Walverine, we show how to introduce game-theoretic analysis to trading agent design, employing empirical methods to overcome the inherent intractability of the underlying game.

The above summary mentions three specific agents, each of which was created by one of us in collaboration with colleagues and students, but independently from one another: RoxyBot (Greenwald), ATTac (Stone), and Walverine (Wellman). These case studies play an important role in the book, serving to illustrate concretely how the general approaches to autonomous bidding presented can be applied in a complex, specific market domain, namely TAC. While we do present lessons learned from other TAC agents as well, we prominently feature our own agents both because we are most familiar with their inner workings, and because they have been among the most successful.

Throughout the book, our aim is to present ideas in trading agent design and analysis that we consider to be broadly applicable. Some of these ideas are developed and justified in general terms, but most are inspired and vetted in the context of the TAC scenario. We thus begin in the next chapter by presenting the TAC travel market game (Section 2.1), and by recounting some interesting history from the annals of the Trading Agent Competition.

2 The TAC Travel-Shopping Game

At the nucleus of TAC is a challenging *market game*. We use the word *game* both in the colloquial sense—a competitive event based on a contrived scenario, usually played for amusement—and in the game-theoretic sense of a *multiagent* interaction with formally specified actions and rewards. Because it is embedded in a *market* environment, the TAC travel-shopping game emphasizes the exchange of goods and services at dynamically negotiated prices. Like most markets, TAC requires that players make decisions under uncertainty. Like most games, it is rife with strategic complexity. And like most market games, the severely incomplete information and huge space of possible strategies renders it well beyond the threshold of analytical tractability, meaning that it cannot be solved in practice by available mathematical methods.

In this chapter, we describe the TAC market game and give an historical account of the TAC research tournaments. The specification of game rules serves as background for subsequent chapters on specific game elements. The historical overview shows why we identify certain issues as key to trading agent design and at the same time it provides a perspective for measuring progress and assessing new ideas.

The TAC travel-shopping game is referred to in the literature variously as "TAC", "TAC Travel", and even (once subsequent games were introduced in the competition) "TAC Classic". Here we also call it "the TAC market game", or simply "the game".

2.1 TAC Market Game

TAC *agents*, playing the role of travel agents, strive to arrange itineraries for a group of *clients* who wish to travel to a common destination and home again during a five-day period. For example, the clients might all wish to attend a particular conference or festival. Although they have the same target location and dates, individual clients may differ in their preferred travel days, in their priorities for luxury hotel accommodation, and in their taste for entertainment.

TAC agents construct trips for their clients by assembling travel goods from an array of markets that run for the course of the game. Agents interact with the markets by submitting *bids* to *auctions*. A bid represents an agent's offer to buy or sell specified quantities of goods at designated prices. The auctions determine a set of exchanges consistent with their received bids, according to the market rules (customized for each good type, as described below).

An agent's objective is to procure goods serving the particular desires of its clients as inexpensively as possible. The score for an agent in a game instance is the difference between the value, or *utility*, it earns for its clients (which can be thought of as the price the clients are willing to pay for the trips arranged by the agent) and its net expenditure in the travel markets.

Although the basic game structure has persisted since the game was introduced in 2000, some details of its definition were revised in 2001 and again in 2004. The specification below corresponds to the 2004 rules. Following the main explanation we describe how the rules differed in previous incarnations of the game.

Trading Travel Goods

Each game instance lasts nine minutes, during which time eight agents trade three types of travel goods: (i) flights to and from the destination city, (ii) room reservations at two available hotels, one of higher quality than the other, and (iii) tickets for three kinds of entertainment events. Each type is traded according to distinct market rules, mediated by simultaneous auctions running throughout the game instance. As shown in Figure 2.1, there are separate auctions corresponding to every combination of good type and day. For the five-day scenario, this yields 28 auctions in total: eight flight auctions (there are no inbound flights on the fifth day and no outbound flights on the first day), eight hotel auctions (two hotel types and four nights), and 12 entertainment ticket auctions (three entertainment types and four days). All 28 auctions operate simultaneously, communicating price and transaction information to the agents according to the defined interface. We describe the auction rules for each good type in turn.

Flights An effectively infinite supply of flights is offered by TACAir (a built-in seller in the flight market) at continuously clearing auctions. Agents may buy whatever flights they want at any time at the posted price but are not permitted to resell or exchange flights.

The seller's offers follow a random walk, initialized independently for each flight from the uniform distribution $U[250, 400]$. Every ten seconds the seller perturbs the offer price by a random value that depends on t, the number of seconds after the start of the game, with a final perturbation bound x_f specific

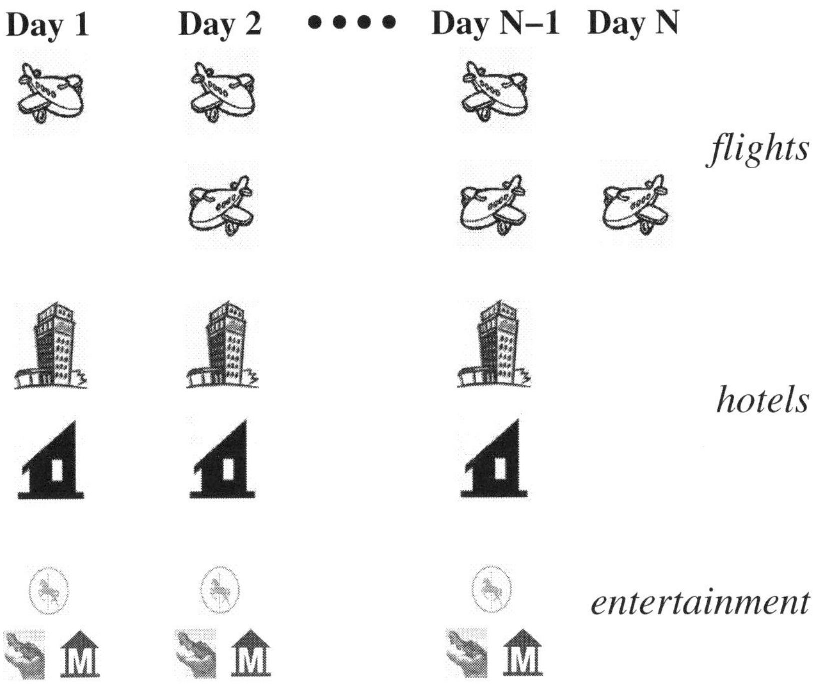

Figure 2.1
Configuration of markets in the TAC travel game, for an N-day horizon. In the actual scenario, $N = 5$. Each icon represents an auction for a good type and day.

to each flight f. The values x_f are drawn from $U[-10, 30]$ and are not revealed to the agents. The bound on perturbations is a linear function of time,

$$x_f(t) = 10 + \frac{t}{540}(x_f - 10). \tag{2.1}$$

The perturbation is then selected uniformly from

$$\begin{array}{ll} [-10, x_f(t)] & \text{if } x_f(t) > 0, \\ [-10, 10] & \text{if } x_f(t) = 0, \\ [x_f(t), 10] & \text{if } x_f(t) < 0. \end{array} \tag{2.2}$$

Finally, prices are confined within the bounds [150,800]; any perturbations taking prices outside this range are overridden by the boundary condition.

This pricing process is designed to exhibit significant variability, with an expected upward drift. The hidden state information (x_f) gives the agents the opportunity to forecast price movements based on observed patterns, albeit with substantial uncertainty and delay.

Hotels The TAC seller also has available 16 rooms per night in each hotel: *Towers*, the premium quality hotel, and *Shanties*, the lower quality lodging option.[1] The seller allocates rooms through simultaneous, ascending, multiunit auctions. In these auctions, agents place multidimensional bids for varying quantities of rooms, specifying the price offered for each incremental unit. These incremental unit offers can be collected across their respective bids and sorted, from highest to lowest. When the auction *closes*, the 16 highest unit offers are declared winners, and each bidder gets the rooms it won, at a price equal to that of the lowest winning (i.e., 16th highest) unit offer. As all winners pay the same, TAC hotel auctions are *uniform price*. Once the auction is closed, agents may no longer bid for this good.

Each minute while they remain open, the hotel auctions issue *price quotes*, indicating the 16th highest (*ASK*) and 17th highest (*BID*) prices among the currently active unit offers maintained in the auction's *order book*. To ensure that prices are ascending, hotel bidders are subject to a *beat-the-quote rule*: any new bid must seek to purchase at least one unit at a price of $ASK + 1$, and at least as many units at $ASK + 1$ as the agent was previously winning at ASK. No bid withdrawal or resale is permitted in hotel auctions.

It is commonly observed that bidders in such auctions (e.g., eBay [Cohen, 2002]) generally prefer to wait until the end to bid, both to avoid undue commitment and to withhold information from competing bidders (see Section 2.3). To induce agents to place realistic bids early, the hotel auctions are set to close at unknown times. Specifically, one randomly selected hotel auction closes after one minute, a second after two minutes, and so on, until the last auction closes after eight minutes. From the agents' point of view, the order of auction closings is unknown and unpredictable.

Entertainment TAC agents buy and sell tickets for three types of entertainment events: Amusement Park (AP), Alligator Wrestling (AW), and Museum (MU). Entertainment is traded through *continuous double auctions* (CDAs), one dedicated to each type of entertainment event on each day. Each agent

1. The names *Tampa Towers* and *Shoreline Shanties* were introduced for TAC-01, held in Tampa, Florida. We commonly refer to these by the shorthand *Towers* and *Shanties*, respectively.

receives an initial endowment of tickets and may bid to buy or sell at its own specified quantities and prices. If a new bid matches an offer present in the auction's order book (a unit buy offer priced above the lowest sell offer or a unit sell offer priced below the highest buy offer), the exchange executes immediately, at the price of the incumbent bid. The corresponding bids are deleted from the order book (or quantities are decremented, if the match is partial). A new bid that does not match is simply added to the order book. In either case, the auction posts a revised price quote reflecting the updated order book. In a CDA, the BID and ASK quotes represent respectively the highest buy offer and lowest sell offer currently outstanding.

In TAC, each agent is initially endowed with 12 entertainment tickets, partitioned as follows: for day 1 or day 4, four tickets of one type and two tickets of a second type; for day 2 or day 3, four tickets of one type and two tickets of a second type. A total of eight tickets is thus available in the market for each entertainment event on each day. Since each agent's tickets are concentrated on a subset of the type-day combinations, there are typically substantial potential gains available through trading.

Trip Value

Eight trading agents compete for travel goods in a TAC game instance, with each agent representing eight clients. The market demand is thus determined by the 64 clients' preferences, which are randomly generated from specified probability distributions. A client's preference is characterized by

1. *ideal arrival and departure dates* (IAD and IDD), which range respectively over days 1 through 4 and days 2 through 5;
2. *hotel premium* (HP), its value for staying in the higher quality hotel, uniformly distributed between 50 and 150;
3. *entertainment value* (EV_{type}), uniformly distributed between 0 and 200, for each of the three types of entertainment: AP, AW, and MU.

The IAD and IDD values are drawn so that each of the ten feasible combinations ($IAD < IDD$) is equally likely. A sample set of client preferences is shown in Table 2.1.

The value of travel goods (flights, hotels, entertainment) depends on how they are packaged into *trips* for clients. A package represents a *feasible trip* iff (i) the arrival date is strictly earlier than the departure date, (ii) the same hotel is reserved during all intermediate nights, (iii) at most one entertainment event

Table 2.1
A sample set of client preferences.

Client	IAD	IDD	HP	AP	AW	MU
1	1	2	99	134	118	65
2	1	3	131	170	47	49
3	1	1	147	13	55	49
4	3	3	145	130	60	85
5	1	3	82	136	68	87
6	2	3	53	94	51	105
7	1	2	54	156	126	71
8	1	4	113	119	187	143

per night is included, and (iv) at most one of each type of entertainment ticket is included. Note that given these rules, there are 392 feasible trips for clients. There are four possible flight combinations that lead to trips of length one day, each of which has four different possible entertainment ticket assignments (including the null assignment), and two possible hotel assignments for a total of 32 possible one-day trips. Similarly, there are 78 possible two-day trips, 136 possible three-day trips, and 146 possible four-day trips.

Clients accrue a baseline value of 1000 for a feasible trip, minus 100 for each day of deviation from ideal travel dates, plus applicable bonuses for staying at the premium hotel or attending entertainment. Formally, a feasible client trip r is defined by an inflight day in_r, outflight day out_r, hotel type (H_r, which is 1 if the premium hotel and 0 otherwise), and entertainment types (E_r, a subset of $\{\text{AP, AW, MU}\}$). The value of trip r to client c is given by

$$v_c(r) = 1000 - 100(|IAD_c - in_r| + |IDD_c - out_r|) + HP_c \cdot H_r + \sum_{t \in E_r} EV_{t,c}. \quad (2.3)$$

Given these preference distributions, there is typically contention for hotels. On average, clients prefer to stay two nights, so accommodating all 64 clients for their desired trip requires 128 hotel rooms. This is exactly the number available: two hotels $\times$ four nights $\times$ 16 rooms per night. But the desired nights are not uniform. Clients are 1.5 times as likely to prefer a stay that includes a middle night (2 or 3) as an end night (1 or 4). Moreover, even when there are enough rooms to satisfy all clients, there will generally be contention to stay in the premium hotel. Similarly, there are generally enough entertainment tickets to occupy all clients in aggregate, but particular events on particular days (differing among game instances) are likely to attract greater demand.

Allocating Goods to Clients

In the original version of the game, TAC agents were responsible for assigning goods to clients. Each agent attempted to determine an optimal configuration of feasible client trips given the goods on hand at market close, and reported its allocation of goods to clients to the server at the end of the game. This task is an instance of the more general *allocation problem*, which arises whenever agents' value for goods depends on how they allocate them to alternative uses. By 2001, the allocation problem for TAC was considered well understood. Thus, since then, the TAC server has computed and reported each agent's optimal allocation.

Previous Rules

2001 From 2001 to 2003, the rules remained constant and differed from the 2004 definition in only two respects. First, the game lasted 12 minutes rather than nine, with hotels closing each minute starting at minute four.

Second, the stochastic process governing flight prices was somewhat different. As in the 2004 rules, initial prices are distributed $U[250, 400]$. However, the 2001 scheme perturbs prices only every 30–40 seconds, and the perturbation bounds x_f for flight f are drawn from $U[10, 90]$. The actual perturbation at time t is drawn uniformly from the range $[-10, x_f(t)]$, with

$$x_f(t) = 10 + \frac{t}{720}(x_f - 10).$$

The changes from 2001 to 2004 reflect the reduced game duration from 720 to 540 seconds and the possibility of negative values for $x_f(t)$.

2000 The first offering of the tournament exposed some anomalies in the rules, which were fixed in subsequent years. Our presentation of the original 2000 rules (differences from 2001) enables interpretation of the 2000 results, and evokes some lessons for market and game design.

Games in 2000 ran for 15 minutes. Flight prices started from the same uniform distribution as in subsequent years, but in the first incarnation were perturbed every 30–40 seconds by a value from $U[-10, 10]$. (This can be viewed as a special case of later rules, with $x_f(t) = 10$ for all f and t.) Flight prices were constrained to remain in the range [150,600].

One major qualitative difference between 2000 and subsequent TAC rules lies in the timing of hotel auctions. TAC-00 hotel auctions provided continual price quotes (i.e., quotes updated whenever a new bid was admitted) and could remain open for bidding until the end of the game. To provide some incentive for agents to bid early, hotel auctions were subject to close after a random period of inactivity (undisclosed to participants, but actually uniform from 30 seconds to five minutes).

Entertainment auctions behaved as in subsequent years, but the initial distribution of entertainment tickets was somewhat different: for each event on each night, each agent received zero tickets with probability 1/4, one with probability 1/2, and two with probability 1/4. The revised distribution in 2001 resulted in less uniform allocations, thus increasing the expected gain from entertainment trading.

The final substantive rule difference for 2000 (already mentioned) was that agents were required to determine their own configuration of client trips. Once the markets closed, the agents had four minutes to compute an allocation of travel goods to clients and report it to the game server.

A cosmetic difference apparent in reports about the TAC-00 game is that the names of the hotel and entertainment events were different. For the original competition (held in Boston), entertainment options were symphony, theater, and Red Sox (baseball) games; the available hotels were called the Grand Hotel and le Fleabag Inn. The names were changed in 2001 to refer to local attractions, but kept constant thereafter for simplicity.

2.2 Game Operations

TAC games are played over the Internet, with agents running on entrants' own computers, connecting to markets implemented on the TAC game server. Agent computational platforms are unrestricted, and entrants have employed a variety ranging from relatively slow PCs to the fastest available machines, or even multiple computers.

To serve a TAC game instance, the system generates client preferences for each agent, and initiates the 28 auctions covering the associated flight, hotel, and entertainment goods. The server also spawns a system agent, to submit sell bids for flight and hotel auctions. For hotels, the seller simply offers 16 rooms at a price of zero, and for flights, it bids periodically to sell arbitrary quantities priced according to the specified stochastic process. During a game, the server provides status information, which can be displayed by an applet for real-time viewing of a game in progress (see Figure 2.2). At the end of the game, the server assembles transaction data and computes optimal trip allocations for each agent based on its client preferences and final holdings. It then calculates scores and records the information for posting and for compiling tournament records.

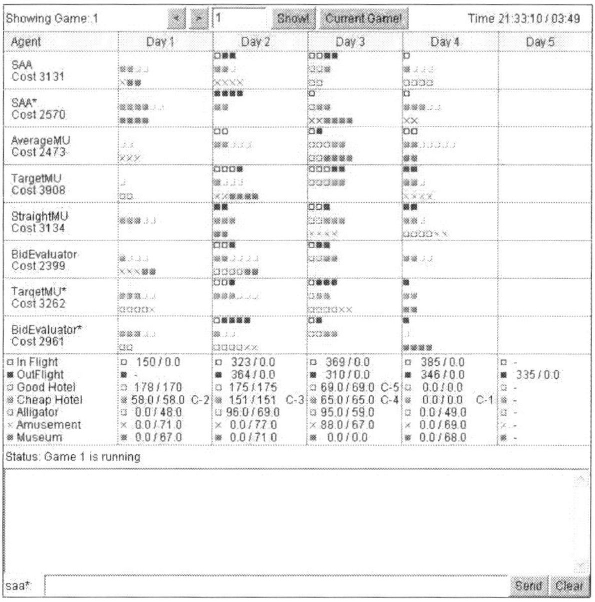

Figure 2.2
A TAC game in progress. Color-coded shape symbols (shown here in gray scale) indicate current holdings of each type of good on each day. Tentative allocations of hotels are indicated by flashing on screen. Price quotes are displayed below the agent/good matrix. Below the price quotes, a chat screen enables real-time communication among the observers.

TAC Software Infrastructure

For the first two years, TAC was operated by the University of Michigan, employing a game server based on the Michigan Internet AuctionBot [Wurman et al., 1998b]. The AuctionBot was designed to support configurable auctions, with a general bidding application programmer interface (API) [O'Malley and Kelly, 1998], and so required only minimal extension to handle the three types of TAC markets. The main development effort was therefore in ancillary game management functions (preference generation, spawning and killing auctions, visualization, allocation and scoring), and optimizing performance to handle the large load of agent bids [O'Malley, 2001]. Despite the attention to performance, the AuctionBot could not always keep up with the bidding, leading sometimes (especially in 2000) to long delays in bid response.[2] This presented yet another source of uncertainty to the agents, requiring them to anticipate such latencies in timing their bids [Stone et al., 2001].

Since 2002, TAC has been operated by the Swedish Institute of Computer Science (SICS). The SICS group implemented a new version of a game server, specialized to TAC, with improved performance [Eriksson and Janson, 2002]. In addition to speeding performance (effectively removing response latency as an issue), the new SICS server was made available for download and local operation. The SICS developers also provided a convenient agentware library, providing a higher-level interface for Java programmers encapsulating the more generic bidding API.

Background Rules

In addition to rules governing the behavior of the travel market mechanisms, TAC specifies general background policies for proper behavior by tournament participants. Although these policies cannot be enforced by technical means, they define activities that violate the spirit of the game and fair play in general. Ultimate arbitration of the policies (including possible disqualification of misbehaving agents) is up to the TAC *GameMaster*, appointed by tournament organizers, who also resolves any other general issues arising during the tournament.

Specific behaviors prohibited by TAC policy include:

- Trading designed to benefit some other agent at the expense of the trader's own score.
- Any form of communication between tournament participants and agents during a game. Agents may obtain runtime game information only via the specified API defined by the game server software.
- Denial-of-service attacks. Agents may not employ API operations for the purpose of occupying or loading the game servers.

Note that collusion in general is allowed; the policy rules out only *sacri-*

2. Most of the performance bottlenecks can be traced to the persistent database and transaction integrity safeguards implemented in the AuctionBot. As these are not required for simulated markets, successor game servers omitted such facilities for dramatically improved performance.

ficial collusion whereby one agent hurts itself to help another. For example, if agent A bought an entertainment ticket from agent B for a million dollars, B would achieve a score unbeatable by compliant agents. A would lose a like amount, but since it is not real money, such a sacrifice is easy to take. Because it is not possible to formulate a precise definition of actions that would constitute sacrificial collusion, TAC policy describes the improper behavior in general terms and leaves its interpretation to the judgment of the GameMaster.

The rule limiting agent communication to the API is well-defined but not closely monitored nor completely enforceable. In general, observers have more information about game state than do the participating agents, and on occasion may wish to share some of what they observe with their agents.

In recent years, organizers have also prohibited changes to agent software during a one-day (semi)final round, though modifications from one day to the next are allowed. Software changes are difficult to detect, however, especially since agents may automatically and legitimately adapt their strategy from game to game, possibly exhibiting qualitatively distinct behavior.

As with sacrificial collusion, denial-of-service attacks are defined by intent, so determining such behavior is in general a matter of judgment. If unintentional contention for game-server communication is an issue, the operators can set limits on connections or otherwise mandate "nice" behavior.

We describe these issues to emphasize some of the practical concerns in conducting an open research tournament. Obtaining scientifically useful observations while maintaining loose, distributed control can be challenging. We believe the TAC approach achieves a reasonable balance. In actual experience, rogue agent behavior has not been an apparent problem. GameMasters have never had to disqualify participants on such grounds.

2.3 Competition History

We conclude this chapter by recounting experience from the history of the competition's tournaments. For each year, we report observations on selected developments, illustrating both the general competitive dynamic and specific strategic innovations. Our intent here is to describe particular episodes at a high conceptual level, with forward references to subsequent chapters containing more comprehensive technical treatments of the significant methods and ideas. Full year-by-year details of the TAC tournaments (including participants and scores) are provided in Appendix A.

TAC 2000

Approaching the first TAC event, entrants and organizers little knew what to expect. Whereas previous research competitions[3] had provided inspiration for this contest [Wellman and Wurman, 1999], the TAC travel game was distinct from the games of prior exercises. Although the designers had their own ideas about what would be the pivotal issues in the game [Wellman et al., 2001b], there was little basis to predict what understanding and techniques the participants would bring to the competition. No existing strategy from the literature could be identified as a model or benchmark.

In retrospect, perhaps the most important results from the inaugural TAC-00 event were the following qualitative observations:

- There was indeed a critical mass of enthusiastic trading agent researchers willing to test their techniques on challenging problems, and able to produce competent and robust agents.
- Despite lack of open discussion (organizers as well as entrants tended to be secretive about their analysis of the TAC travel game prior to the first tournament), most participants grasped the key game properties and focused on the game's pivotal issues.

Several of these pivotal issues are discussed at length elsewhere in this book, as well as in articles describing TAC-00 and participating agents [Fornara and Gambardella, 2001; Greenwald and Boyan, 2005; Greenwald and Stone, 2001; Stone and Greenwald, 2005; Stone et al., 2001]. Here we focus on one of these—the problem of *last-moment hotel bidding*.

All else being equal, bidders in an auction face an incentive to submit their bids as late as possible. The primary advantage of bidding late is that an agent maximizes the information available at the time of bidding. When relevant features of the environment are changing, the agent can use its latest observation of these features to decide how to bid. For example, an assessment about how much a given hotel room is worth generally depends on the price of flights on various days, as well as the prices of alternative rooms. Since

3. At the time TAC was initiated (and to this day), the RoboCup competitions [Noda et al., 1998] were the most prominent example. AAAI had held robot competitions at its National Conference since 1992 [Bonasso and Dean, 1997], and the AI Planning Systems Conference commenced a biannual series of planning competitions at its 1998 meeting [McDermott, 2000]. And of course, computer game-playing tournaments have been commonplace for years. Especially relevant were prior competitions in trading domains, most notably the *Santa Fe Double Auction Tournament* [Rust et al., 1994].

information bearing on these prices is continually updated, one would like to accumulate as much information as possible before committing one's own bid. Even for an isolated good, it may be advantageous to wait and let others' bids form the initial prices. Such behavior was observed in the Santa Fe Double Auction Tournament. The two top-scoring agents, by Kaplan and Ringuette, adopted a strategy described by Rust et al. [1994] as "wait in the background and let the others do the negotiating, but when *BID* and *ASK* get sufficiently close, jump in and steal the deal".

Waiting until it is too late for other bidders to respond can also have the advantage of keeping down final prices. Roth and Ockenfels [2002] have documented and explained the tendency of last-moment bidding on eBay (commonly called *bid sniping*), where—as in TAC hotel auctions—prices ascend until a fixed closing time. If all bids are snipes, mechanisms like this effectively reduce to *sealed-bid auctions*, since no meaningful price quotes are issued in time for response.

Cognizant of this phenomenon, the TAC-00 designers attempted to discourage last-moment bidding by subjecting hotel auctions to early closing after random periods of inactivity; otherwise, the auctions closed simultaneously at the end of the game. However, this countermeasure proved ineffective, as clever agents merely entered minimal increments at measured intervals in order to ensure the auctions stayed alive. Most meaningful bids were submitted in the last moment after all, thus reducing the hotel market to an array of sealed-bid 16th-price auctions.

Due to this last-moment bidding, not only were final hotel prices unpredictable but they often *skyrocketed* (see Figure 2.3). Treating all current holdings of flights and entertainment tickets as sunk costs, the marginal value of an as-yet-unsecured hotel room reservation is precisely the value of the package itself.[4] During the preliminary competition, few agents bid their marginal values (upwards of 1000) on hotel rooms. Those that did, however, tended to be quite successful: always winning their target hotels but paying far less than their bids. Having observed the success of high bidding during the preliminary rounds, most agents adopted this strategy during the actual competition. The result: many negative scores, as there were often high prices for 16 or more hotel rooms.

For example, assuming no entertainment, a one-night package in which the

4. As stated, this observation holds only when the length of stay is exactly one night; for longer stays it relies on the further assumption that all other hotel rooms in the package are secured.

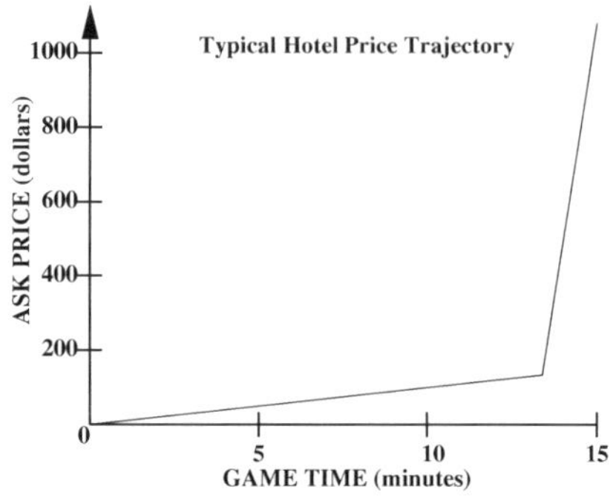

Figure 2.3
A typical hotel price trajectory in TAC 2000. The price increases gradually until near the end of the game, at which point it skyrockets.

hotel room is purchased at its marginal value yields a negative score equal to the price of flights; however an agent cannot do better than to bid its marginal value, since bidding any lower and therefore not purchasing the hotel room yields precisely the same negative value,[5] whereas bidding any higher could potentially yield an even more negative score.

In the TAC-00 finals, the top-scoring agents were those who not only bid aggressively on hotels but who also incorporated risk and portfolio management into their strategy in order to reduce the likelihood of buying highly demanded and highly priced hotel rooms. The top-scoring agent in TAC-00, ATTac, actively predicted which hotels would skyrocket in a given game, as detailed in Section 6.1.

TAC 2001

The degree of last-moment hotel bidding in the first tournament prompted significant rule changes for 2001. The new rules were designed to induce earlier bidding on hotels by removing the agents' knowledge of, or ability to control, when the auctions would close. Specifically, the second tournament introduced the mechanism whereby hotel auctions closed randomly at one-minute intervals. In this mechanism, agents must balance their preference

5. Technically, this claim is true of an $m+1$st price auction of m goods when the agent demands only a single unit, but is not true of an mth price auction of m goods [Wurman et al., 1998a]. Thus, in the case of TAC hotel auctions, the claim holds true only so long as the bid in question is *not* the mth highest, or the difference between the mth highest and the $m+1$st highest bids is sufficiently small.

to postpone commitment against the risk that the hotel auctions will close, eliminating further opportunities to procure rooms.

The revised hotel mechanism was indeed successful in deterring last-moment bidding. With random closing, agents generally placed bids each minute as if all hotel auctions were to end at that point, perhaps adopting a slightly conservative posture to account for the beat-the-quote constraint on subsequently reducing bids. One way to understand the agents' behavior is by examining the pattern of bids submitted throughout the game. Figure 2.4 presents a visualization of just such a data set, for a particular game in the TAC-01 finals. This image was generated using a tool designed and developed by Healey et al. [2001], which allows three-dimensional exploration of bidding patterns. In the visualization, time is left to right, and each row represents an individual auction. The eight rows closest to front are flight auctions, followed by 12 entertainment auctions, and furthest back by the eight hotel auctions. Although the picture is somewhat cluttered with bids from all agents shown, we can discern qualitatively different patterns for the respective market types. For flights, we see a flurry of purchases at the beginning, followed by a lull of a few minutes, then more sporadic flight purchases as information about hotel prices and allocations starts to flow in. The hotel auctions also receive some initial bids, but then fall into a periodic pattern, as agents submit batches of new bids each minute for the remaining hotels, at steadily increasing prices.

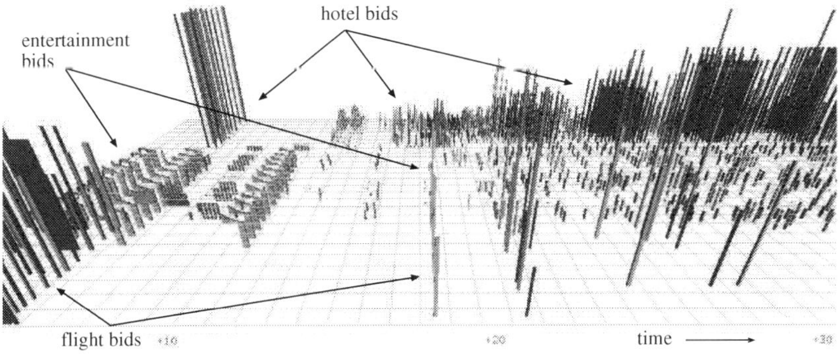

Figure 2.4
Visualization for Game 7321 of the TAC-01 finals. Bars represent bids, with height proportional to offer price and varying shades encoding the respective bidding agents.

The absence of skyrocketing hotel prices cleared the way for other strategic issues to come to the fore in TAC-01. We focus on one particularly interesting contrast [Wellman et al., 2003b] between the approaches taken by the two agents finishing at the top of the standings in the TAC-01 finals, ATTac and livingagents.

ATTac predicts prices using a data-driven approach and bids average marginal utilities (defined in Section 5.4) on all available goods. ATTac's price-prediction module uses machine-learning techniques (see Chapter 6) to generate distributions over hotel closing prices. As the game proceeds, the predicted price distributions change in response to the observed price trajectories, causing the agent to continually revise its bids. Figure 2.5 displays a visualization of the same game as Figure 2.4, selecting ATTac's bids.

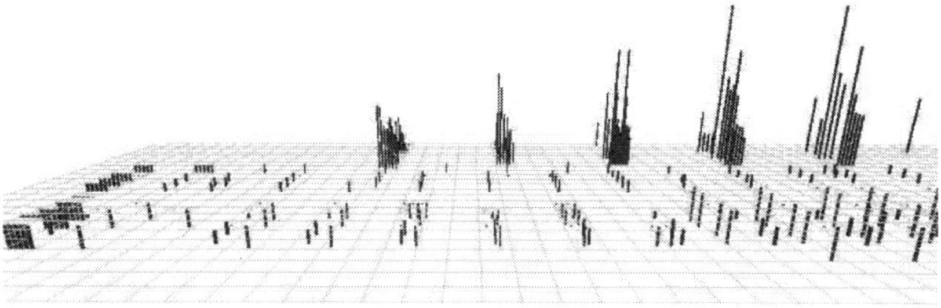

Figure 2.5
Bids of ATTac in Game 7321.

From Figure 2.6, it is strikingly apparent that the strategy of livingagents [Fritschi and Dorer, 2002] is quite different. livingagents calculates the optimal client trips based on initial flight prices, assuming hotel prices will be at their historical averages.[6] It then purchases the corresponding flights immediately, and places offers for the requisite hotels at prices high enough to ensure successful acquisition. These choices are never reconsidered; the flight and hotel auctions are not monitored at all. livingagents similarly makes a fixed decision about which entertainment to attempt to buy or sell, assuming they

6. For this estimate, livingagents used data from the preliminary rounds. As the designers note [Fritschi and Dorer, 2002], hotel prices in the finals turned out to be significantly lower than during the preliminary rounds, presumably because the more successful agents in the finals were better at keeping these prices down. Apparently, their performance did not suffer unduly from this difference.

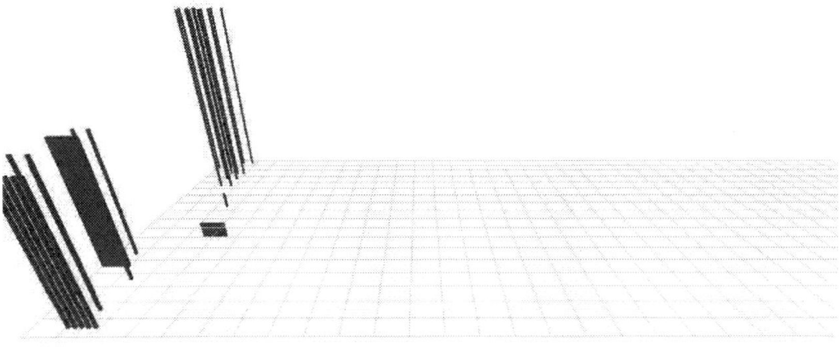

Figure 2.6
Bids of livingagents in Game 7321.

will be priced at their historical average of 80. It does monitor the entertainment auctions, accepting offers opportunistically until putting in final offers at reservation prices at the seven-minute mark.

At first glance, it is surprising that an effectively open-loop strategy such as that employed by livingagents could be so successful. In general, the optimal configuration of trips depends on hotel prices, yet the open-loop strategy ignores all the predictive information about them that is revealed as the game progresses. Moreover, the behavior is risky. If the initial hotel buy offers were not sufficiently high, the agent would fail to complete some trips and thus lose substantial value. But by placing bids that are sufficiently high to ensure purchase, there is a danger that the agent will have to pay a price at which the trip is undesirable (or less desirable than an alternative).

In particular, if all agents followed the strategy of livingagents, the result would have been disastrous. With all eight agents placing very high bids for the hotels, prices would skyrocket and most trips would be undesirable. Indeed, experiments with analogous behaviors for a version of the ATTac-00 agent bear out this result (see Section 6.1).

But of course, livingagents was *not* competing with copies of itself. Most of the other agents, like ATTac, employed closed-loop, adaptive strategies that condition their behaviors on the evolution of prices. By steering away from goods that are expensive (or predicted to become so), these agents also attenuate the forces raising those prices. Thus, these agents "stabilize" the system, keeping prices lower, and less variable, than they would be without such tight monitoring. This stabilization provides benefits to the monitoring agents, but it also provides benefits to those who are not monitoring, like livingagents.

All else being equal, the open-loop strategy has several advantages. It is simple, and avoids the expected tangible costs of waiting (e.g., letting flight prices rise) and hedging (e.g., buying contingency goods that may not be used). Considering these advantages, it seems that predictability of the closing prices is the largest factor determining whether it is worthwhile to monitor the markets and adapt bidding behavior accordingly.

- If prices are perfectly predictable from the start of the game, then there is no benefit to an adaptive strategy. (Indeed, the optimal closed-loop strategy would degenerate to an open-loop behavior.)
- With large price variances, a closed-loop strategy should do better. It places midrange bids in most auctions and ends up buying the cheapest goods. At the end of the game, it may have to pay some high prices to complete itineraries, but it should largely avoid this necessity. The open-loop strategy picks its goods up front and pays whatever the prices turn out to be, which in some cases will be quite high.
- With small price variances, an *optimal* closed-loop strategy would in principle still be as good as any open-loop strategy. Nevertheless, the increase in complexity may be great for a small potential benefit, and even small miscalculations (e.g., underconfidence in predicted values, leading to excessive waiting and hedging) can prevent the agent from achieving this benefit. Thus, the relative simplicity of the open-loop approach may more than compensate for its suboptimality in this case.

The foregoing argument suggests that there is some natural equilibrium between adaptive and open-loop behavior in the TAC game. We return to this question of strategic equilibrium in Chapter 8.

TAC 2002

Our discussion of TAC-01 makes clear that predicting hotel prices is a central problem for trading agents in the TAC market game. Whether the agent monitors state continually (as does ATTac), or only at the beginning (livingagents), expectations about eventual hotel prices play a key role in deciding what trips to assemble. Agents may employ a variety of methods to construct such expectations, and we devote Chapter 4 to a case study of price-prediction techniques from the 2002 TAC tournament.

TAC-02 featured a new game server developed by SICS [Eriksson and Janson, 2002], and a diverse agent pool [Greenwald, 2003a] comprising both new agents and refinements of contenders from the first two years. Two of the repeat entries, WhiteBear [Vetsikas and Selman, 2003] and SouthamptonTAC [He and Jennings, 2003], were the first- and second-place finishers, respectively, in the TAC-02 finals.[7] The designers of both of these entries reported building on the prior year's designs, tuning the agent's parameters based on extensive experimentation and analysis prior to the tournament.

Although all participants engage in some process of experimentation to improve their designs, Vetsikas and Selman [2003] were the first to employ a systematic and comprehensive methodology. To structure their exploration, they first identified parameterized components for separate elements of WhiteBear's overall strategy. They then defined extreme (boundary) and intermediate values for these strategy components. In their experiments, they fixed a particular number of agents playing intermediate strategies, varying the mixture of boundary cases across the possible range. In all, the WhiteBear experiments comprised 4500 game instances. This experience was further informed by 2000 games in the preliminary tournament rounds. The designers credit this effort with improving WhiteBear's standing from third in TAC-01 to first in TAC-02. We return to the issue of experimental methodology in Chapter 8.

TAC 2003

TAC observers perceived steady progress over the first three competitions. Participants continued to report new techniques and incremental improvements on methods employed by predecessor agents. Whereas many of the top performers in TAC-02 were familiar from TAC-01, the quality of the field as a whole was improving as intelligence about strategy effectiveness propagated through the community.

However, the case in support of this impression of progress has been largely anecdotal. Given the scientific objectives of the TAC enterprise, it would be far more satisfying to document progress in a more rigorous, quantitative manner. One way to measure progress over time is to track benchmark

7. The top-scoring agents from TAC-01, ATTac and livingagents, also competed—with no changes—in TAC-02. livingagents remained competitive, finishing in sixth place. If we scratch two games that livingagents missed due to a bug, it would have come in second or third place. ATTac also suffered from technical difficulties, due to a change in computational environments. Some errors were apparently introduced in the process of retraining its price-prediction module with TAC-02 preliminary-round data, causing its elimination in the semifinals.

levels of performance by keeping some agents constant. For example, in the CADE ATP (automated theorem proving) series of competitions [Sutcliffe, 2001], the best systems from a given year typically enter unchanged in the next year's event (along with improved versions, of course). This provides a direct measure, in comparable terms, of the relative performance across years. In a game setting, where other agents are part of the environment, it is not strictly fair to judge an agent with respect to a different field. Therefore, such benchmarks would provide an instructive albeit limited measure of progress in the TAC context.

Informally, we observe every year significant learning during the preliminary rounds, as agents being actively developed steadily progress up the ladder against agents remaining constant. Year to year, as noted above, the TAC-02 experience partially confirmed progress, as the top agents were incrementally improved versions of solid performers from TAC-01.

By the same token, TAC-03 was viewed as evidence of a stall in progress. One of the top two TAC-01 agents, ATTac (this time with its price prediction module as originally trained from the 2001 data), returned to the top of the field in 2003. Three of the top four TAC-02 agents (WhiteBear, Thalis, and umbctac) had adjusted scores (see Section 8.3) above or within a few points of ATTac's. It was becoming more difficult to distinguish one's performance from the pack.

With the perception of diminishing returns to strategic innovations, the community was already looking for new challenges. In 2003, one was readily provided by a new and exciting TAC market game in the domain of supply chain management (TAC/SCM) [Arunachalam and Sadeh, 2005]. Many of the regular TAC Travel competitors designed and developed agents for the new TAC/SCM event, apparently distracting from further improvement of their TAC Travel entries.

A different gauge of agent effectiveness is how well they allocate resources, *in the aggregate*, through their market interactions [Wellman et al., 2003a]. This is an indirect measure, at best, since the objective of each agent is to maximize its own surplus, not that of the overall system. Nevertheless, such a *social welfare* analysis can provide a benchmark, and shed light on the allocation of resources through an economy of interacting software agents.

We measured aggregate effectiveness by comparing actual TAC market allocations with ideal global allocations, calculated centrally assuming knowledge of all client preference information. Consider the total group of 64 clients, and the set of available resources: 16 hotel rooms of each type per day, plus eight entertainment tickets of each type per day. The global optimizer calculates the allocation of resources maximizing total client value, net of expenditures on flights assuming they are available at their initial prices. We take initial prices to be the relevant inherent cost (exogenously determined, independent of TAC agent demand) of flights, treating the expected stochastic increase in flight prices during the game as a cost of decision delay that would be avoided by an idealized optimizer. Note that the global optimizer completely neglects hotel and entertainment prices, as these are endogenous to the TAC market. Monetary transfers affect the distribution of surplus across TAC buyers and sellers, but not the total amount. We formulated the global optimization problem as an integer linear program, and solved it using CPLEX.

The average idealized net value, per client, in the various years of the TAC tournament (final round only) as determined by global optimization is reported under the heading "Global" in Table 2.2. The percentage of this net value achieved in the actual TAC games (also neglecting hotel and entertainment expenditures, but counting actual payments for flights) is reported under "TAC (%)". The results for 2001–03 are qualitatively consistent with the anecdotal account above: relative agent efficiency increased from TAC-01 to TAC-02, with a drop-off in competitiveness for TAC-03. The table also measures separately the efficiency in entertainment trading (entertainment value received by the actual TAC market compared to the globally optimal allocation).

Table 2.2
The efficiency of the TAC market compared to the global optimum—overall and specifically with respect to entertainment.

Year	Global	TAC (%)	Entertainment (%)
2001	637	85.7	85.5
2002	609	89.1	85.3
2003	614	85.1	86.1
2004	723	79.7	90.8
2005	723	83.2	89.3
2006	727	83.4	85.5

Results from 2004 are not comparable to 2003 and before, since the rule modification necessitated that we change from initial flight prices to minimum flight prices in measuring global welfare. However, we can see a modest resumption of progress according to the relative efficiency measure from TAC-04 to TAC-05 and TAC-06.

TAC 2004

The 2004 tournament featured rule changes, after three straight years under 2001 rules. The new game was shortened to nine minutes, enabling faster simulation by closing the first hotel at minute 1 rather than minute 4. The eliminated three minutes had been mostly dead time, when agents tracked flight quotes and updated price predictions, with occasional flight and entertainment transactions but relatively little compared to the dynamic activity once hotels start closing.

Most significantly, the TACAir flight pricing behavior changed to provide greater variability of pricing patterns, including the possibility that some flights would have expected decreases over part of the game. The rationale for the change was that most agents were resolving the flight purchase tradeoff (see Section 7.1) by purchasing most flights right at the beginning. Under the revised rules, this behavior would be clearly suboptimal, as shown analytically and experimentally by Vetsikas and Selman [2005]. Indeed, the TAC-04 agents responded by spreading flight purchases throughout the game.

With delayed flight commitments, agents maintain greater flexibility regarding the trip dates for their clients. This in turn affects the dynamics of hotel markets, since agents who delay flight purchases can more easily shift their room demands across days.

The designers of WhiteBear responded to the new rules by reconsidering key strategic choices based on an extensive new set of simulations [Vetsikas and Selman, 2005]. This experimental methodology apparently paid off, as WhiteBear came out on top again, by a convincing margin.

TAC 2005

The 2004 outcome underscored the value of experience. Over time, agent developers have the opportunity to refine their agent designs by solidifying their core operations and tuning their strategy to maximize performance. Thus, it would appear that entrants from prior years, who can build on their existing strategic ideas and software implementations, have an inherent advantage in TAC tournaments. However, the ability to learn from experience is not limited to those who actually participate in a tournament. The publication of algorithms, designs, analyses, and other TAC-derived knowledge means that outside observers can also access lessons learned from previous tournaments.

Mertacor, a first-time entrant in TAC-05, eagerly took advantage of this opportunity [Toulis et al., 2006]. For example, the Mertacor designers reported adopting the approach of SouthamptonTAC to hotel price prediction through fuzzy rule-based techniques [He and Jennings, 2004]. In the process, they modified the rule-set, and customized it for the context of their own agent's design. In addition to extending versions of techniques employed by previous TAC agents, the Mertacor design also includes completely new methods of their own (e.g., their entertainment trading strategy). In some respects, starting anew can be beneficial, as it allows the designers to flexibly choose the most appealing elements of a variety of prior efforts. Moreover, coming at the game from a fresh perspective can promote generation of new ideas.

By 2005, veteran competitors WhiteBear and Walverine had refined their approaches through systematic experimentation. (The empirical analysis methodology employed by Walverine designers is described in detail in Chapter 8.) This made for an unusually competitive tournament in 2005, with Mertacor emerging as the official winner.[8] As Mertacor demonstrated by its first-place finish in TAC-05, even after six years of competition the TAC community had not exhausted the possibilities for the "best" way to play this game.

TAC 2006

TAC 2006 turned out to be a very close competition between two of the agents featured in this book, RoxyBot and Walverine. Both agents had participated for many years—RoxyBot since the beginning in 2000 and Walverine since 2002—but neither had yet achieved a clear first-place finish.

In TAC-00, RoxyBot demonstrated the effectiveness of a general trading agent strategy designed for applicability in a wide array of markets. At the core of RoxyBot-00's architecture was a deterministic optimization problem, namely how to bid given price predictions in the form of point estimates. A weakness of this design is that it does not explicitly account for variance within auction clearing prices. In the years since 2000, RoxyBot's designers explored several different approaches (e.g., Greenwald and Boyan [2004]) to recast their agent's problem from a deterministic to a stochastic bidding problem, exploiting price predictions in the form of distributions. Although such a generalization should in principle improve performance, there was some question over the years (e.g., [Stone et al., 2003]) as to whether distributional price predictions were necessarily beneficial (see Section 4.3).

After 2000, RoxyBot fared unimpressively in tournament conditions year

8. As described in Appendix A, the final ranking depends on whether a subset of games marred by errant agent behavior is included.

after year, in spite of its designers' perseverance. Until 2006. In contrast with some of its previous incarnations, RoxyBot-06 [Lee et al., 2007] was a solid piece of software. In the qualifying and seeding rounds (each run continuously over a week), RoxyBot ran uninterrupted missing no games during either round. RoxyBot dominated this stage of the competition, in part because of its software stability, but even more so because of its new approach to bidding based on distributional price information.

The final outcome confirmed the preliminary results. Half a decade in the laboratory spent searching for bidding heuristics that can exploit stochastic information at reasonable computational expense finally bore fruit, as RoxyBot emerged victorious in TAC-06. The "secret" of RoxyBot-06's success, namely the SAA* bidding heuristic, is revealed in Chapter 5. But before we get to that point, we must present some prerequisite concepts and techniques, themselves the ingredients of success for RoxyBot-00 and several other TAC agents throughout the years.

3 Bidding in Interdependent Markets

The core technical question faced by trading agents in the TAC travel game boils down to: *How do I manage my bids in the separate travel markets, given that travel goods are highly interdependent*? Interdependence means that agents cannot decide how to bid for each good on an individual basis, because the ideal bid for each good depends on what happens in other markets.

We employ a simple two-good example (not from the TAC travel domain) to illustrate some of the issues in interdependent markets. Suppose an agent is interested in buying a camera and flash, and these goods are to be auctioned off separately. The agent values the items together at \$200, but the camera alone at only \$110, and the flash alone at only \$20. In such a case we say the agent has *complementary preferences* for the goods. If the agent bids for each good according to its independent value, it might not acquire the package even if the total price is well under \$200 (e.g., the camera may go for \$120 and the flash for \$30). If it bids above a good's independent value, however, the agent risks winning only that good, and getting stuck paying more than it is worth by itself. For example, the agent might win the camera for \$150, but then see the price of the flash rise above \$50.[1]

This example illustrates the classic *exposure problem*, which arises whenever complementary goods are traded in separate markets. TAC agents face the exposure problem, for example, in hotel markets, where in order to assemble a multiday trip they must bid for rooms on individual days—thereby exposing themselves to the risk of acquiring only a partial trip. Similar problems arise when an agent has *substitutable preferences*, as it might for two alternative camera models, or for two alternative entertainment tickets to different events on the same night or to the same event on different nights. The agent values each good individually, but once it obtains one, its marginal value for the other diminishes or even vanishes. If it bids on both, it risks obtaining both goods at a total cost more than its value for the pair. But if it bids on only one, it may miss an opportunity to get the best deal—or any deal at all, if its lone bid fails.

Given a configuration of interdependent markets, such risks are often unavoidable. However, one of the main points of this book is to demonstrate that

1. Once the agent wins the camera, its *marginal value* for the flash becomes \$200 − \$110 = \$90: the increment in value associated with obtaining the flash. Treating the camera expenditure as a sunk cost, the agent should be willing to pay up to this marginal value of \$90 for the flash. However, it would rather not win the camera for \$150 in the first place if the eventual price of the flash is going to be greater than \$50.

through careful design a trading agent can assess and manage these risks. We present and compare a variety of techniques, employed in TAC and elsewhere, that explicitly model the interdependence of markets, leading to bidding strategies that handle complementary and substitutable preferences as well as the uncertainty underlying market dynamics.

The aim of this chapter is to present a basic architecture for trading agents, which applies to TAC and other market domains. In the following section, we briefly describe the component tasks of this architecture, with references to subsequent parts of the book where we treat the associated techniques in detail. For example, price prediction is a key module, studied in detail in Chapter 4. Although treatment of the bidding task as a whole must wait until Chapter 5, in this chapter we formulate a series of *bid determination problems* that identify relevant goods on which to bid. We also define the fundamental concept of *marginal value*, which can guide the agent in identifying prices at which to bid on those goods. These core ideas serve as building blocks for the comprehensive trading agent strategies developed throughout this book.

3.1 A Generic Bidding Cycle

Although each TAC agent design includes its own special features, given their common objective it is not surprising that many share important elements. We attempt to unify the various approaches by describing a basic architecture, or skeletal procedure, that is common to many TAC agents.

Table 3.1 presents the canonical agent *bidding cycle*. According to this procedure, agents execute a continual loop of gathering and updating information, making projections, and deciding how to bid. Each step in this cycle represents a decision task in support of the overall bidding problem. Naturally, different agents may frame these steps somewhat differently, or even in an implicit way. Nevertheless, this skeletal structure provides a convenient organization for a discussion of characteristic strategic features.

At this skeletal level, the generic bidding cycle applies well beyond TAC, indeed to any market environment comprising multiple interdependent goods with auctions operating simultaneously (or overlapping in time). The remainder of this section expands on each of the steps in this generic bidding cycle, as labeled in Table 3.1.

Table 3.1
Trading agent bidding cycle: a skeletal view.

While at least one auction remains open, do:

1. Update current prices and holdings for each auction.
2. Predict, or project, future prices and holdings based on a model of the market environment.
3. Construct and place bids, for example employing an optimization process with the following steps:
    (a) Determine target holdings: which goods to attempt to buy or sell.
    (b) Decide which target goods to bid on now and which to bid on later.
    (c) Calculate bid prices for the target goods to be bid on now.

After markets close: transact goods, and allocate holdings to their respective uses.

Step 1: Update Prices and Holdings

At the start of each bidding cycle, the agent *updates* its view of the market by gathering the latest available information. TAC auctions provide price quotes and transaction notifications upon request. Flight price quotes are updated every ten seconds, hotel quotes every minute, and entertainment quotes every time a new bid is received. Typically, the bidding cycle reflects these frequencies: for example, it is unnecessary for an agent to compute hotel bids more than once per minute, since no hotel information can change within that period. Agents may adopt separate, more frequent cycles for flights and entertainment, but given their interdependence it is important to consider the latest information from *all* the markets in making bidding decisions for each.

In principle, short-term changes in flight and entertainment markets *could* cause an agent to want to reconsider its hotel bids. Consequently, the agent may choose to wait until near the end of its one-minute cycle to determine its bids for hotels. On the other hand, if price projection involves complex computation or if bid determination involves difficult optimization, the agent may devote nearly the whole minute to these tasks, ignoring changes in other markets that occur during the computation. In general, agent designers trade off between the length of computation and the timeliness of information; or they construct flexible procedures that accommodate information updates within the computation process.

Step 2: Model-Based Prediction of Prices and Holdings

The update step defines the agent's view of the current market state. Computing effective bids also requires anticipation of future states, which is the role of the *prediction* step. Broadly speaking, agents form expectations for the future based on some model of the market environment. We discuss the nature of such models and the range of prediction methods in full detail in subsequent chapters. Specifically, since hotel price prediction has turned out to be a major component of the game, we devote Chapter 4 to an in-depth study of this problem. Flight price estimation, also important but analytically more straightforward, is the subject of Section 7.1.

Few would disagree with the notion that predicting future prices is relevant to bid construction. It may seem strange, though, to predict one's *holdings*, since that is something one controls through the bids under consideration. However, at any (noninitial) point in TAC bidding, an agent may already be tentatively committed through outstanding bids. In particular, the hotel auctions prohibit withdrawing or decreasing bids (via the beat-the-quote rule). Therefore, even if an agent would choose not to buy a hotel room at the current price (given what it knows now), it may end up doing so based on its prior decisions. An agent can account for these commitments by projecting its future holdings under the various possible price outcomes.

Step 3a: Determine Target Holdings

Given its view of current market state and projection for the future, what goods does the agent want to buy or sell? The answer to this question defines a configuration of *target holdings* that the agent would choose given its market projections. However, since the ideal configuration of goods depends on (uncertain) future prices, agents need not make a definitive determination based on current projections. Rather, the target can be provisional (subject to change), or contingent on prices or specific events in other markets. In the extreme, an agent could consider all goods to be targets insofar as there may be *some* price at which they would be desirable to purchase. For example, ATTac and Walverine consider as targets any open hotel room for which there is some potential use by some client.

The *completion problem*, described formally in Section 3.2, represents a special case of the general problem (i.e., determining target holdings) where the agent optimizes with respect to a fixed array of market prices. Although a more general prediction would take the form of probability distributions over future prices, the simpler deterministic version of the problem is often a useful approximation. We consider approaches to bidding under uncertainty that employ both forms of prediction in Chapter 5.

Step 3b: Bid Timing

The target holdings define what goods to bid on. The question of when to bid can be reduced to the question of which of these target goods to bid on *now*.

The three TAC auction types present agents with distinct timing concerns. Flights are offered continuously on a posted-price take-it-or-leave-it basis, so during each iteration of the cycle, the agent's decision is simply whether to commit at that time. Since flight prices are expected to increase over time, TAC agents face the tradeoff of buying early for less, or paying more later with the benefit of gaining information about other goods (e.g., hotel prices and winnings). Different approaches to timing flight purchases are discussed in Section 7.1.

Hotels, in contrast, are exchanged through ascending auctions with periodic revelation of price quotes and one-time clearing. Specifically, once per minute, each hotel auction releases a price quote and one is randomly selected to clear and close. Since no information is revealed during these one-minute intervals, hotel bidding is effectively organized into discrete rounds.[2] TAC agents typically spend the bulk of each round calculating their bidding decisions, placing bids at round end. Exactly what time constitutes the "end", though, depends on an agent's assessment of network latency and the ensuing risk of placing a late bid. Note that agents should maintain active bids for all open hotels, since the next hotel to close is unknown and unpredictable.

Like flights, entertainment is exchanged in continuous auctions, giving agents the opportunity to time their offers based on strategic considerations. Many agents (e.g., livingagents, 006) explicitly maintain separate control threads for entertainment-bidding decisions.

Step 3c: Compute Bid Prices

Once an agent determines the set of goods on which it intends to bid now, it faces the final choice: at what price to make its offer for each good in the set. Some agents further decompose this choice into the problems of first

2. This was not the case in TAC-00, where price information was revealed continually, and, in practice, all hotel auctions cleared at the end. Consequently, most TAC-00 agents placed their serious hotel bids at or near the end and prices often rose dramatically at that point (see Section 2.3).

establishing a *reservation value*, that is, a good's inherent worth to the agent, and then computing a bid based on that value. It is not straightforward to assign reservation values to individual goods, however, due to the interdependencies among them (recall the camera example). Perfectly complementary goods (e.g., an inflight and outflight for a particular client) are worthless in isolation, and perfectly substitutable goods (e.g., rooms in different hotels for the same client on the same day) provide added value only in isolation.

We formally define the marginal value of a unit of a good g as the incremental value that could be obtained by an agent if it were to own that unit in addition to its current holdings. Let C be a collection of goods, and let $v(C) \in \mathbb{R}$ represent the value of C to the agent.

DEFINITION 3.1 MARGINAL VALUE: The marginal value, $\mu(g, C)$, of a good g with respect to a (fixed) collection of goods C is defined as follows:

$$\mu(g, C) = v(C \cup \{g\}) - v(C), \tag{3.1}$$

where $C \cup \{g\}$ is the collection obtained by adding the good g to C.

Taken literally, each good necessary for trip feasibility (e.g., a hotel room on a particular night, once flights have been purchased assuming no alternative rooms are available) has a marginal value equal to the value of the whole trip. (Recall the camera and flash example at the start of this chapter and see Footnote 1.) As described in Section 2.3, several TAC-00 agents entered bids on this basis, causing hotel prices to escalate wildly in that tournament. This phenomenon was less common following the TAC-01 rule change whereby hotel auctions closed successively at one-minute intervals, although many agents continued to base their bids on marginal values.

Since it is defined with respect to a fixed collection of other goods, marginal value accounts for complementarity or substitutability among the goods. When an agent bids for a particular good, however, it is generally uncertain about the outcome of bidding in other markets, and so a marginal value with respect to a particular set of *projected* holdings is an estimate at best. Moreover, even if those estimates were correct, it would not necessarily be optimal to simply bid for each good independently based on its marginal value (see Section 3.3). Nevertheless, it is often useful to employ such marginal values in bidding—at least as a baseline reservation value.

As alluded to above, agents typically evaluate marginal value with respect to *projected holdings*: its current actual holdings plus net transactions of other goods it intends to execute in the market. An extended definition of marginal value appears in Section 3.3 below. Definition 3.7 relaxes the restriction to a fixed set of holdings, making the dependence on predictions explicit.

The Final Step: Allocate Holdings

When an agent is acting on behalf of multiple clients (as in TAC), or otherwise has alternative uses for goods, it must eventually decide how to allocate its final holdings to packages corresponding to these clients or "uses". Although it is not strictly part of the bidding cycle (since it occurs after markets close), determining this final allocation is an important component of the overall trading task.[3] Moreover, when constructing bids during the bidding cycle, an agent should consider how it would allocate any hypothetical holdings. For instance, in order to assess the marginal value of a good, as in Equation (3.1), the agent must determine the value of holdings with and without the good. These values can be computed by determining suitable allocations. Thus, many agents solve the allocation problem (or some variant thereof) many times during the bidding cycle, as well as at the conclusion of trading.

3.2 Bid Determination Problems

The question of how to bid (Step 3 in Table 3.1) lies at the core of trading agent design. We devote Chapter 5 to a detailed technical treatment of this problem. Before tackling this core problem head-on, however, it is helpful to define some subproblems that play a useful role in the overall process of bid construction.

In reasoning about how to bid in interdependent markets, agents may pose and solve various subproblems, using the results to construct their ultimate bids. We define four key *bid determination problems* [Boyan and Greenwald, 2001; Greenwald, 2005], applicable to TAC and many other market environments:

Allocation: "Given only the set of goods I already own, how can I allocate those holdings to packages so as to maximize my valuation?"

Acquisition: "Given my holdings, as well as market prices and supply in all open auctions, what set of additional goods should I buy?" The objective is to

3. In TAC, the game server now computes final allocations for the agents under the assumption that they would be able to do so optimally. But in the original game formulation (2000 rules), final allocation was the responsibility of the agents.

augment current holdings to maximize *surplus*, defined as value of the optimal feasible allocation minus procurement costs.

Completion: "Given my holdings, as well as market prices, supply, and demand in all open auctions, what set of goods should I buy and sell?" The objective is the same as in acquisition, but since selling is allowed, surplus is defined as allocation value plus sales revenue minus procurement costs.

Arbitrage: "Given market prices, supply, and demand in all open auctions, what set of goods should I buy and sell so as to maximize sales revenue less procurement costs?" Unlike acquisition and completion, in arbitrage we are concerned about surplus from the transactions only, without considering allocation value.

We refer to acquisition as a *one-sided* (or *single-sided*) problem, since it involves decision making about only the buy side of the market. Completion and arbitrage, in contrast, are *two-sided* (or *double-sided*) problems, addressing both buy and sell decisions. Allocation could be called "zero-sided", since it does not deal with market actions at all.

These bid determination problems, and variants thereof, have been important since the TAC series began. Indeed, the first competition (TAC-00) *required* agents to solve an allocation, that is, to construct their own trips from their holdings at the end of the game. Approximate solutions to completion—the most general of these bid determination problems—were essential components of the architectures of the two top-scoring TAC-00 agents, ATTac and RoxyBot [Stone and Greenwald, 2005]. In subsequent competitions most agents have included modules solving some version of these problems.

In what follows, we formally define the bid determination problems listed above. Based on these definitions, we show that arbitrage is "easy" (i.e., it can be solved in linear time), but that allocation, acquisition, and completion are NP-hard. We also show that completion is no harder than acquisition, in the sense of polynomial-time reducibility.

Basic Concepts

We start by introducing some basic concepts, and associated formal notation. These concepts are useful for defining the bid determination problems, and discussing other elements of trading agent strategy throughout the book.

Packages and Values

Throughout this book, we let G denote an ordered set of n distinct goods. In addition, we let $N \in \mathbb{N}^n$ represent the multiset of these goods in the marketplace, with N_g denoting the number of units of each good $g \in G$. We write $|N| = \sum_{g \in G} N_g$ to indicate the total number of units summed across all goods in the marketplace. We also write $g.k$ to identify the kth unit of good g.

A *package* M is a collection of goods, that is, a "submultiset" of N. We write $M \subseteq N$ whenever $M_g \leq N_g$ for all $g \in G$, and $g.k \in M$ whenever $k \leq M_g$. Also, we let $\emptyset \subseteq N$ denote a vector of $|G|$ zeros.

Given $A, B \subseteq N$, we rely on the following basic operations: for all $g \in G$,

$$(A \oplus B)_g \equiv A_g + B_g$$
$$(A \setminus B)_g \equiv A_g - B_g$$

For example, if $G = \{\alpha, \beta, \gamma\}$ and $N = \langle 1, 2, 3 \rangle$, then $A = \langle 0, 1, 2 \rangle \subseteq N$ and $B = \langle 1, 1, 1 \rangle \subseteq N$, but neither $A \subseteq B$ (because $A_\gamma > B_\gamma$) nor $B \subseteq A$ (because $B_\alpha > A_\alpha$). Moreover, $(A \oplus B)_\alpha = 1$, $(A \oplus B)_\beta = 2$, and $(A \oplus B)_\gamma = 3$, whereas $(A \setminus B)_\alpha = 0$, $(A \setminus B)_\beta = 0$, and $(A \setminus B)_\gamma = 1$.

It is instructive to interpret this notation in the TAC Travel domain. The flights, hotel rooms, and entertainment events up for auction in TAC comprise an ordered set of 28 distinct goods. In principle, the multiset of goods in the TAC marketplace is

$$N^{\text{TAC}} = \langle \underbrace{\infty, \ldots, \infty}_{\text{8 flights}}, \underbrace{16, \ldots, 16}_{\text{8 hotels}}, \underbrace{8, \ldots, 8}_{\text{12 events}} \rangle \in \mathbb{N}^{28}.$$

In practice, however, since each agent works to satisfy the preferences of only eight clients, it suffices to consider the multiset of goods:

$$N^{\text{TAC8}} = \langle \underbrace{8 \ldots, 8}_{\text{8 flights}}, \underbrace{8, \ldots, 8}_{\text{8 hotels}}, \underbrace{8, \ldots, 8}_{\text{12 events}} \rangle \subseteq N^{\text{TAC}}.$$

A trip corresponds to a package, specifically some $M \subseteq N^{\text{TAC8}}$ that satisfies the feasibility constraints governing TAC travel packages (see Section 2.1).

Let $\mathcal{N}$ denote the set of all submultisets of N: i.e., packages comprised of the goods in N. Throughout this book, the function $v : \mathcal{N} \to \mathbb{R}$ describes the value the agent attributes to each viable package.

A value function v exhibits *free disposal* iff $v(M_1) \leq v(M_2)$ whenever $M_1 \subseteq M_2$. Although we do not assume this condition everywhere, we note that in TAC Travel, free disposal holds for both the agent and its clients. This assumption also holds in most real-world travel markets (e.g., train tickets, car rentals), and applies in many other domains as well. With free disposal, marginal values are guaranteed to be nonnegative.

In TAC, each agent's objective is to compile packages for $m = 8$ individual clients. As such, the agent's value function takes special form. Each client c is characterized by its own value function $v_c : \mathcal{N} \to \mathbb{R}$, and the agent's value for a collection of packages is the sum of its clients' respective values for those packages: given a vector of packages $\vec{X} = (X_1, \ldots, X_m)$,

$$v(\vec{X}) = \sum_{c=1}^{m} v_c(X_c).$$

TAC is an example of the more general situation where an agent is charged with compiling packages devoted to m independent uses. In this instance, the uses correspond to client trips. Given our focus on TAC, throughout this section we refer to clients specifically rather than uses generally, although the concept applies more broadly.

PRICELINES

With the exception of allocation, our bid determination problems refer to *market prices*, which specify the terms at which the agent presumes it can buy or sell the various goods. Typically, these are prices predicted in the projection step of the bid cycle. We represent this information in constructs called *pricelines*.

A *buyer priceline* for good g is a vector $\vec{p}_g \in \mathbb{R}_+^{N_g}$, where the kth component, p_{gk}, stores the *marginal cost* to the agent of acquiring the kth unit of good g. For example, if an agent currently holds four units of a good $\tilde{g}$, and if four additional units of $\tilde{g}$ are available at costs of \$25, \$40, \$65, and \$100, then the corresponding buyer priceline (a vector of length 8) is given by $\vec{p}_{\tilde{g}} = \langle 0, 0, 0, 0, 25, 40, 65, 100 \rangle$. The leading zeros indicate that the four goods the agent holds may be "acquired" at no cost. We assume buyer pricelines are nondecreasing.

A *seller priceline* for good g is a vector $\vec{\pi}_g \in \mathbb{R}_+^{N_g}$. Much like a buyer priceline, the kth component of a seller priceline for g stores the *marginal revenue* that an agent could earn from the kth unit it sells. For example, if the market demands four units of good $\tilde{g}$, which can be sold at prices of \$20, \$15, \$10, and \$5, then the corresponding seller priceline is given by $\vec{\pi}_{\tilde{g}} = \langle 20, 15, 10, 5, 0, 0, 0, 0 \rangle$. Analogously to buyer pricelines, the tail of zero revenues indicates that the market demands only four of those units. We assume seller pricelines are nonincreasing.

If a priceline is constant, we say that prices are *linear*. We refer to the constant value as a *unit price*. With linear prices, the cost of acquiring k units of good g is k times the unit price of good g.

Equipped with this formalism, we now proceed to define our bid determination problems. In our formal problem statements, we list all arguments explicitly (except G, since N subsumes G). In later uses, however, we elide arguments that are clear from context, particularly N and the agent's value function, typically v.

Allocation

Given an agent's holdings, represented as a submultiset $H \subseteq N$ of the goods in the marketplace, the allocation problem is to arrange those holdings into a collection of packages for its clients, maximizing the agent's valuation, that is, the sum of its respective clients' package-values.

DEFINITION 3.2: Allocation$(H, \vec{v})$.

Inputs: a multiset of holdings H;
a vector $\vec{v}$ of m client value functions.
Output: a vector $\vec{X}$ of packages to allocate to clients.

$$\text{ALL}(H, \vec{v}) = \max_{\bigoplus_{c=1}^{m} X_c \subseteq H} \sum_{c=1}^{m} v_c(X_c)$$

In allocation, if the free disposal assumption holds for all client value functions, then without loss of generality, we can assume the constraint is tight: $\bigoplus_{c=1}^{m} X_c = H$. In general, the loose constraint implicitly encodes an assumption of free disposal in the agent's valuation.

The allocation problem is precisely the winner determination problem in multiunit combinatorial auctions. As winner determination in single-unit combinatorial auctions is equivalent to weighted set-packing [Rothkopf et al., 1998], and hence NP-hard, allocation is also NP-hard.

Acquisition

In acquisition, for each good g, we are given an agent's current holdings, the market supply, and the prices of acquiring additional units of g. All of this information is compactly represented in buyer pricelines.

Given a set of buyer pricelines $P = \{\vec{p}_g \mid g \in G\}$, we define costs additively, that is, the *cost* of the goods in multiset $Y \subseteq N$ is given by

$$\begin{aligned} \forall g, \quad \text{Cost}_g(Y, P) &= \sum_{k=1}^{Y_g} p_{gk}, \\ \text{Cost}(Y, P) &= \sum_{g \in G} \text{Cost}_g(Y, P). \end{aligned} \tag{3.2}$$

In acquisition, the agent's goal is to determine what set of goods it should buy to maximize surplus: the value of its resulting optimal allocation less the cost of the goods. An allocation is feasible if it allocates no more than the number of goods the agent buys.

DEFINITION 3.3: Acquisition(N, P, v).

Inputs: a multiset of goods N;
a set of buyer pricelines P;
the agent's value function v.
Output: a package $X \subseteq N$ to allocate;
a multiset of goods $Y \subseteq N$ to buy.

$$\text{ACQ}(N, P, v) = \max_{X \subseteq Y} (v(X) - \text{Cost}(Y, P))$$

Of particular interest is the special case of the acquisition problem where the agent's value is decomposable into a sum of client values, $v = \sum_{c=1}^{m} v_c$. The allocation problem reduces to acquisition with additively decomposable value. In this reduction, we construct pricelines that represent the agent's holdings, and admit no further buying opportunities: all entries are either zero (for holdings) or ∞. Since allocation is NP-hard, it follows that the acquisition problem with additively decomposable value is NP-hard as well.

In contrast, a further specialized case, where prices are linear (i.e., buyer pricelines are constant as far out as the agent would ever demand), avoids the hardness implication. In this case, the acquisition problem decomposes into a set of smaller subproblems, the complexity of each depending on aspects of v_c. That is, it suffices for the agent to acquire an optimal package for each client in turn. Note that the assumption of linear prices precludes representing an agent's own holdings in pricelines.

Completion

In completion, in addition to the inputs to acquisition, we are given the market demand for g, and the revenue that could be achieved by selling each unit of g. All of this information is compactly represented in seller pricelines.

Given a set of seller pricelines $\Pi = \{\vec{\pi}_g \mid g \in G\}$, we define revenue additively, that is, the *revenue* associated with multiset $Z \subseteq N$ is given by

$$\forall g, \quad \text{Revenue}_g(Z, \Pi) = \sum_{k=1}^{Z_g} \pi_{gk}, \tag{3.3}$$

$$\text{Revenue}(Z, \Pi) = \sum_{g \in G} \text{Revenue}_g(Z, \Pi). \tag{3.4}$$

In completion, the agent's goal is to determine what sets of goods it should buy and sell to maximize surplus: the value of its resulting optimal allocation less the cost of the goods, plus any revenue earned from sales. Here, an allocation is feasible if it allocates no more than the number of goods the agent buys less the number the agent sells. Note that completion generalizes acquisition.

DEFINITION 3.4: Completion(N, P, Π, v).

Inputs: a multiset of goods N;
a set of buyer pricelines P;
a set of seller pricelines Π;
the agent's value function v.
Output: a package $X \subseteq N$ to allocate;
a multiset of goods $Y \subseteq N$ to buy;
a multiset of goods $Z \subseteq N$ to sell.

$$\text{COM}(N, P, \Pi, v) = \max_{X \oplus Z \subseteq Y} (v(X) - \text{Cost}(Y, P) + \text{Revenue}(Z, \Pi))$$

Arbitrage

Arbitrage is an opportunity for an agent to simultaneously buy and sell goods and instantaneously profit from any price discrepancies. Given the buyer priceline $\vec{p}_{\tilde{g}} = \langle 1, 50, 100, 5000 \rangle$ and the seller priceline $\vec{\pi}_{\tilde{g}} = \langle 40, 30, 20, 10 \rangle$, for example, an agent can both buy and sell one unit of $\tilde{g}$ and turn a profit of $\$40 - 1 = \$39$ immediately.

In the arbitrage problem, an agent's goal is to determine what set of goods to buy and sell, if any, strictly for profit, not for allocation. Specifically, an agent seeks a set of goods for which it can obtain a level of revenue, as prescribed by the seller pricelines, that exceeds the cost of buying, as prescribed by the buyer pricelines.

DEFINITION 3.5: Arbitrage(N, P, Π).

Inputs: a multiset of goods N;
a set of buyer pricelines P;
a set of seller pricelines Π.
Output: a multiset of goods $Y \subseteq N$ to buy;
a multiset of goods $Z \subseteq N$ to sell.

$$\text{ARB}(N, P, \Pi) = \max_{Z \subseteq Y} (\text{Revenue}(Z, \Pi) - \text{Cost}(Y, P))$$

Given sorted buyer and seller pricelines, in nondecreasing and nonincreasing orders, respectively, a solution to the arbitrage problem is straightforward: simply buy and sell the kth unit of good g iff $\pi_{gk} \geq p_{gk}$. Indeed, because buy (or sell) prices are nonnegative, there is really only one output of the arbitrage problem: the multiset A of arbitrage opportunities where

$$A_g = \max_{k \in \{1, \ldots, N_g\}} k \text{ such that } \pi_{gk} \geq p_{gk}.$$

Hence, the arbitrage problem can be solved in time linear in the size of the pricelines (see Algorithm 1). The complexity of completion derives from the fact that it generalizes allocation, not arbitrage.

Algorithm 1 Arbitrage(G, N, P, Π)

```
1: A = ∅
2: for all g ∈ G do
3:    for k = 1 ... N_g do
4:       if π_gk ≥ p_gk then
5:          increment A_g
6:       end if
7:    end for
8: end for
9: return A
```

Reducing Completion to Acquisition

Recall that completion is a two-sided problem—it addresses both buying and selling decisions—whereas acquisition is one-sided—it addresses only buying. Perhaps surprisingly, the completion problem reduces to the seemingly simpler acquisition problem. Via a reduction, an agent can solve a completion problem by instead solving an acquisition problem, and then mapping an optimal solution to acquisition back into an optimal solution to the original completion problem. Here we present a reduction from completion to acquisition based on the technique implemented in the TAC agent RoxyBot-00 [Greenwald and Boyan, 2005]. This reduction folds the seller pricelines into the buyer pricelines, after accounting for any potential arbitrage (i.e., opportunities to buy a good for less than it could be sold). The intuition is that in completion, an agent cannot simply allocate the goods it buys without weighing into its decisions the opportunity costs of not selling those goods on the open market.

In the reduction, the value of an optimal completion differs from the value of an optimal acquisition by a constant value $C = \text{ARB}(P, \Pi)$. By adding this constant C to the acquisition value, an agent implicitly takes advantage of all arbitrage opportunities, even though the agent cannot explicitly sell goods in acquisition. Since it is assumed that all arbitrage opportunities are exploited, so that the kth unit of good g is bought and "sold" whenever $\pi_{gk} \geq p_{gk}$, the only decision an agent faces in acquisition regarding such goods is to perhaps allocate them to packages, overriding the implicit "sell" decision. Accordingly, the buyer and seller pricelines are *unified* so that the agent incurs cost $\max\{\pi_{gk}, p_{gk}\}$. In effect, the agent pays an opportunity cost π_{gk} to allocate an arbitrage opportunity $g.k$ to a package rather than "sell" it; otherwise, it pays p_{gk} to allocate a non-arbitrage opportunity $g.k$ as usual. Note that the prices of goods for which there exist arbitrage opportunities in completion are irrelevant to decision making in acquisition under this reduction.

Combining the buyer priceline $\vec{p}_g$ and seller priceline $\vec{\pi}_g$ for each good g proceeds in several steps. First, an intermediate priceline $\vec{q}_g$ is formed with $q_{gk} = \max\{\pi_{gk}, p_{gk}\}$. For all arbitrage opportunities, $q_{gk} = \pi_{gk}$; otherwise, $q_{gk} = p_{gk}$. Next, $\vec{q}_g$ is sorted in nondecreasing order. Formally, the reordering of $\vec{q}_g$ is achieved by applying a *permutation* σ, that is, a bijection on $\{1, \ldots, N_g\}$. Finally, we define $\vec{p}'_g$ to be $\vec{q}_g$ permuted according to σ. For notational convenience, we also define $k' = \sigma_g(k)$ so that $g.k'$ refers to the

$\sigma_g(k)$th entry in $\vec{p}_g$.[4] We call the output of this procedure *unified pricelines*, the set of which we denote by P'. Note that these operations can be carried out in polynomial time (see Algorithm 2). Specifically, the time complexity of Unify(G, N, P, Π) (and of this reduction overall) is $O(|G|K \log K)$, where $K = \max_g N_g$.

Algorithm 2 Unify(G, N, P, Π)

for all $g \in G$ **do**
    for $k = 1 \dots N_g$ **do**
        let $q_{gk} = \max\{\pi_{gk}, p_{gk}\}$
    end for
    find a permutation σ that sorts the entries in $\vec{q}_g$ in nondecreasing order $\{$e.g., $\sigma = \{1 \mapsto 2, 2 \mapsto 1\}$ sorts $\langle 20, 10 \rangle$ accordingly$\}$
    for $k = 1 \dots N_g$ **do**
        let $k' = \sigma_g(k)$
        let $p'_{gk'} = q_{gk}$
    end for
end for
return P'

For example, say there are four units of some good $\tilde{g}$ on the market with buyer priceline $\vec{p}_{\tilde{g}} = \langle 0, 1, 10, 30 \rangle$ and seller priceline $\vec{\pi}_{\tilde{g}} = \langle 40, 20, 0, 0 \rangle$. First, the arbitrage opportunities are identified: $\tilde{g}.1$ can be bought for 0 and sold for 40; $\tilde{g}.2$ can be bought for 1 and sold for 20; there are no further arbitrage opportunities. Next, the intermediate priceline $\vec{q}_{\tilde{g}} = \langle 40, 20, 10, 30 \rangle$ is formed, reflecting these arbitrage opportunities. Finally, $\vec{q}_{\tilde{g}}$ is sorted so that $\vec{p'}_{\tilde{g}} = \langle 10, 20, 30, 40 \rangle$. In particular, $\sigma_{\tilde{g}} = \{1 \mapsto 4, 2 \mapsto 2, 3 \mapsto 1, 4 \mapsto 3\}$. We interpret the unified priceline as follows. The agent can allocate $\tilde{g}.3$ and $\tilde{g}.4$ at prices determined by the buyer priceline, specifically $p'_{\tilde{g}1} = q_{\tilde{g}3} = \max\{p_{\tilde{g}3}, \pi_{\tilde{g}3}\} = p_{\tilde{g}3} = 10$; similarly, $p'_{\tilde{g}3} = 30$. But if it chooses to allocate $\tilde{g}.1$ or $\tilde{g}.2$, it must "pay back" the opportunity cost that is automatically added to the objective value in acquisition within the constant C. For $\tilde{g}.1$, the agent charges itself $p'_{\tilde{g}4} = q_{\tilde{g}1} = \max\{p_{\tilde{g}1}, \pi_{\tilde{g}1}\} = \pi_{\tilde{g}1} = 40$, its worth on the open market; similarly, for $\tilde{g}.2$, it charges itself $p'_{\tilde{g}2} = 20$.

After solving the acquisition problem with unified pricelines, an optimal

4. This notation is used to elide explicit reference to σ in theorems and algorithms.

acquisition (X'_*, Y'_*) maps (under h) into an optimal solution to the completion problem as follows. First, $X_* = X'_*$, so that the allocation of goods to packages is identical in completion and acquisition. Second, for all $g.k$ (i.e., for all units of all goods), $g.k$ is bought in completion if it is an arbitrage opportunity *or* bought in acquisition; $g.k$ is sold in completion if it is an arbitrage opportunity *and not* bought in acquisition. Moreover, an optimal completion (X_*, Y_*, Z_*) maps (under i) into an optimal solution to the acquisition problem with unified pricelines as follows. First, $X'_* = X_*$, so that the allocation of goods to packages remains identical in completion and acquisition. Second, $g.k$ is bought in acquisition if it is bought in completion *but not* sold. More precisely, $Y' = Y \setminus Z$.

It is straightforward to define the mapping i: $i(X, Y, Z) = (X, Y \setminus Z)$, for all completions (X, Y, Z). Algorithm 3 can be used to implement the mapping h. To explain the workings of this algorithm, we run through an example. Our example involves only a single good $\tilde{g}$ in the marketplace, of which there exist many copies.

EXAMPLE 3.6: Let us assume a single client whose value function is linear: in particular, let $v_{\tilde{g}}(k) = 10k$. Also, let $\vec{p}_{\tilde{g}} = \langle 1, 2, 3, 6, 8, 10, \infty, \ldots \rangle$ and $\vec{\pi}_{\tilde{g}} = \langle 11, 9, 7, 0, \ldots \rangle$, so that $A_{\tilde{g}} = 3$, since $11 > 1$, $9 > 2$, and $7 > 3$. The Unify algorithm returns $\vec{p}'_{\tilde{g}} = \langle 6, 7, 8, 9, 10, 11, \infty, \ldots \rangle$. (The Unify algorithm also implicitly computes the permutation $\sigma_{\tilde{g}} = \{1 \mapsto 6, 2 \mapsto 4, 3 \mapsto 2, 4 \mapsto 1, 5 \mapsto 3, 6 \mapsto 5\}$.)

In this setup, $Y'_{\tilde{g}} = 5$ in an optimal solution to acquisition. To compute the values of $Y_{\tilde{g}}$ and $Z_{\tilde{g}}$ in the corresponding optimal completion, we invoke Algorithm 3. First, both values are initialized to the value of $A_{\tilde{g}}$. Next, running through the first $Y'_{\tilde{g}}$ entries in $\vec{p}'_{\tilde{g}}$, we find (i) three of these entries correspond to units that were not arbitrage opportunities (the first, third, and fifth, which correspond to $g.4$, $g.5$, and $g.6$), so the value of $Y_{\tilde{g}}$ is incremented by 3; and (ii) two of these entries correspond to units that were arbitrage opportunities (the second and fourth, which correspond to $g.3$ and $g.2$), so the value of $Z_{\tilde{g}}$ is decremented by 2. Ultimately, $Y_{\tilde{g}} = 6$ and $Z_{\tilde{g}} = 1$ in the corresponding optimal completion. Note that $Y'_{\tilde{g}} = (Y \setminus Z)_{\tilde{g}}$.

THEOREM 3.1[GREENWALD, 2005]:

Given a completion problem Completion(P, Π), consider the acquisition problem Acquisition(P') with unified pricelines P'. Algorithm 3 (the mapping

Algorithm 3 $h(X', Y', P', \sigma)$

$X = X'$
$Y = A$
$Z = A$
for all $g \in G$ **do**
  for $k = 1 \ldots Y'_g$ **do**
    if $g.\sigma_g^{-1}(k) \notin A$ **then**
      increment Y_g
    end if
    if $g.\sigma_g^{-1}(k) \in A$ **then**
      decrement Z_g
    end if
  end for
end for
return (X, Y, Z)

h) returns an optimal solution to this completion problem, given an optimal solution to this acquisition problem. Conversely, the mapping i returns an optimal solution to this acquisition problem, given an optimal solution to this completion problem.

Implementing Pricelines Assuming "No Arbitrage"

In TAC, the only type of goods agents may sell (and hence the only potential arbitrage opportunity) is entertainment. Entertainment is exchanged through continuous double auctions (CDAs), which execute transactions whenever compatible bids are received. At any time, the state of a CDA is represented by the highest buy offer (BID) and the lowest sell offer (ASK), with $BID < ASK$. In TAC, therefore, it might appear that there are no arbitrage opportunities.

In fact, there are two ways that arbitrage may present itself in TAC. First, an agent may project an arbitrage opportunity based on predicted price movements. For example, even if the current BID in an entertainment auction is \$20 and the current ASK is \$40, if an agent predicts that a future buy offer will come in at \$60, this is an arbitrage opportunity.

Second, since we encode an agent's holdings as goods that it can acquire at no cost, the ability to sell a held good at positive cost technically qualifies as arbitrage. We refer to this mode of arbitrage as "holdings" arbitrage, in contrast with the "transactional" mode above where the agent makes a profit through a combination of actual buying and selling. The agent has a potential holdings arbitrage opportunity for every saleable good that it holds.

In this section, we describe the operations for constructing and maintaining pricelines, based on the implementation of RoxyBot-00 [Greenwald and Boyan, 2005]. RoxyBot-00's module for determining target holdings takes as input, for each good $g \in G$: a nondecreasing vector of buy prices, a nonincreasing vector of sell prices, and a constant H indicating the agent's holdings. Within this module, first the agent greedily capitalizes on any projected (transactional) arbitrage opportunities, eliminating corresponding buy and sell prices from the relevant price vectors. Second, the agent calls a "completer" to solve the completion problem, assuming no transactional arbitrage, heareafter *no arbitrage*. The completer converts the (possibly truncated) buy and sell price vectors into single unified pricelines, properly handling any holdings arbitrage opportunities. More specifically, the entries in the unified pricelines corresponding to the agent's own holdings are not zeros if those holdings can be sold on the open market, but rather the agent charges itself sell prices for its own holdings. These sell prices represent the *opportunity costs* to the agent of allocating its holdings to its clients rather than selling them. If, however, the agent owns more units of a good than can be sold on the open market, then the corresponding entries for those excess units are zeros, indicating *sunk costs*. In principle, RoxyBot-00 solves completion by reducing it to acquisition as in the reduction theorem (Theorem 3.1), under the no-arbitrage assumption.

CONSTRUCTION

Let $\langle a_1, a_2, \ldots, a_S \rangle$ be the buy prices indicating the marginal costs of acquiring incremental units of a good, up to the total supply $S \geq 0$. By assumption, $a_1 \leq a_2 \leq \cdots \leq a_S$. Let $\langle b_1, b_2, \ldots, b_D \rangle$ be the sell prices indicating marginal revenues that would be realized by selling incremental units of the good, up to the total demand $D \geq 0$. Again, by assumption, $b_D \leq b_{D-1} \leq \cdots \leq b_1$.

Define the *pre-priceline* $\vec{q} = \langle \circ, q_1, \ldots, q_{S+D} \rangle$ by concatenating the buy and sell prices as follows: $\langle b_D, \ldots, b_1, a_1, \ldots, a_S \rangle$, and prepending a pointer $\circ$. A package's cost is computed by popping off prices from the relevant pricelines, starting at these pointers and moving from left to right. Note that $q_1 \leq \cdots \leq q_{S+D}$, by the no-arbitrage assumption.

Finally, define the priceline $\vec{p}$ by shifting the pointer by $|D - H|$ entries, where H is the quantity of the good currently held.

If $D - H < 0$, then the pointer shifts to the left: i.e., $H - D$ zeros are inserted to the left of $\vec{q}$. These leftmost zeros represent the sunk costs of allocating goods that the agent holds but cannot sell on the open market. The next D values, the sell prices $b_D, \ldots, b_1$, indicate the opportunity costs to the agent of allocating its holdings rather than selling them on the open market.

If $D - H > 0$, then the pointer shifts to the right. As above, the values immediately to the right of the pointer, namely $b_H, \ldots, b_1$, indicate the opportunity costs to the agent of allocating its holdings rather than selling them.

Note that H may be negative, representing the short-selling of goods. If $S + H < 0$, then $|S + H|$ infinities are appended to $\vec{q}$. These infinities represent the cost of allocating goods that the agent sold short but cannot buy back on the open market.

Armed with this construction, the completer's task is much simplified. It need not reason about selling goods explicitly. It need only reason about allocating packages to its clients, computing the cost of a package by popping off prices from left to right, starting at the pointer $\circ$, from the unified pricelines.

Examples

We now illustrate some examples of pricelines constructed in this way.

- $S = \infty$, $D = H = 0$, $\vec{q} = \vec{p} = \langle \circ, 315, 315, \ldots \rangle$
This linear priceline illustrates a typical priceline for flights: an infinite supply is predicted to be available, at an expected price of 315 each. The agent currently holds none of this good.
- $S = \infty$, $D = 0$, $H = 2$, $\vec{q} = \langle \circ, 315, 315, \ldots \rangle$, $\vec{p} = \langle \circ, 0, 0, 315, 315, \ldots \rangle$
In this priceline, the agent owns two units of this flight (which cannot be sold back). The amount spent on those flights is treated as a sunk cost: the agent need not consider the costs already incurred when allocating them to clients. Allocating more than two of these flights, however, is expected to incur an additional cost of 315 each.
- $S = 16$, $D = H = 0$, $\vec{q} = \vec{p} = \langle \circ, 105, 155, 205, 255, 305, 355, 405, 455, 505, 555, 605, 655, 705, 755, 805, 855 \rangle$
An agent can use this type of priceline to mitigate risk in hotel auctions. Although the hotel auctions charge a uniform price to all winning bidders, an agent can model its own impact on that price by assuming that each additional room is more expensive than the last. Such a model encourages the agent to diversify its acquisition of hotel rooms, not relying too heavily on any

particular room.

• $S = 2, D = 2, H = 4, \vec{q} = \langle \circ, 25, 65, 75, 115 \rangle, \vec{p} = \langle \circ, 0, 0, 25, 65, 75, 115 \rangle$
This priceline reflects a typical scenario in an entertainment market. The agent currently holds four of this ticket. The priceline indicates that there is market demand for two of its four tickets, the first unit of which can be sold for 65, and a second unit of which can be sold for 25. In addition, there is a supply of two additional tickets on the market, one of which can be purchased at 75 and another at 115. The priceline summarizes all of this information. Now if the completer allocates one or two of these tickets to the agent's clients, it incurs no cost, since its first two tickets were not marketable anyway. If the completer allocates four tickets to clients, it incurs an opportunity cost of 90, which reflects the revenue it could have obtained by selling the tickets. If the completer allocates all six tickets, it incurs the total cost of the priceline, representing the opportunity cost plus the expense of purchasing two additional tickets.

• $S = 2, D = 2, H = -1, \vec{q} = \langle \circ, 25, 65, 75, 115 \rangle, \vec{p} = \langle 25, 65, 75, \circ, 115 \rangle$
This priceline corresponds to a situation similar to the previous one except that the agent has short-sold one unit of this entertainment ticket (i.e., $H = -1$). The cost to the completer of allocating this ticket to one of the agent's clients is the cost of the *second* ticket for sale on the open market, namely 115. It is assumed that the ticket available at the first price of 75 will be purchased automatically to replace that which has been sold short, after which the next ticket on the priceline can be allocated.

Discussion

Since completion generalizes acquisition, which in turn generalizes allocation (assuming decomposable value, $v = \sum_{c=1}^{m} v_c$), it follows that these bid determination problems are all NP-hard, at least for the decomposable value case. Consequently, for bid determination problems of even modest size, including those arising in TAC (see Appendix B), one must generally resort to inexact or incomplete methods such as heuristic search. In TAC-00, for example, RoxyBot used an A^* search algorithm to optimally solve the allocation problem within the alloted four minutes at game end, and beam search to approximately solve the completion problem in the inner loop of its bidding cycle [Greenwald and Boyan, 2005]. ATTac-00 solved acquisition in its inner loop using integer linear programming (ILP),[5] except in instances where runtime exceeded a hard-coded threshold, in which case it reverted to a greedy algorithm [Stone et al., 2001].

In an experimental study, Boyan et al. [2001] compared the performance of A^* search, beam search, and ILP on instances of the allocation problem in TAC-00 using data generated during the final round of TAC-00, and on larger data sets built by merging TAC-00 data sets. The key experimental findings were as follows:

1. For the dimensions of TAC, optimal solutions to allocation can be obtained within reasonable time spans.
2. As the problem size increases, A^* scales poorly. ILP fares better on average, but has very high variance.
3. Beam search scales well, achieving near-optimal solutions with predictable time and space requirements.

Another heuristic that is known to scale is *LP relaxation*, in which the solution to an ILP is approximated by relaxing the integrality constraints. The value of the relaxation is an upper bound on the value of the ILP solution. If it is only the value of an optimal solution that is of interest (for example in calculating marginal values), then the relaxation can provide a useful estimate. If, in addition, the actual solution is of interest, rounding any fractional values in the relaxed solution to integers in an intelligent way can yield a feasible solution to the ILP with decent performance guarantees. The agent ATTac-01, for one, relied heavily on the value of the LP relaxation of the acquisition problem in computing its bids (see Section 5.4).

3.3 Marginal Values and Prices

As alluded to several times already, marginal values are often employed—as a baseline reservation value at least—in calculating bid prices. In this section, we generalize our basic concept of marginal value (Definition 3.1), defined with respect to a fixed collection of goods, to account for buying opportunities. Given the reduction theorem (Theorem 3.1), we need not consider selling opportunities explicitly.

Equipped with a more general notion of marginal value, we present two

5. ILP formulations of the TAC allocation, acquisition, and completion problems are provided in Appendix B.

fundamental theorems that completely characterize the relationship between buyer and seller pricelines—the inputs to the bid determination problems—and marginal values. These theorems are invoked in Chapter 5 to prove that certain bidding heuristics that calculate bids based on marginal values are optimal with respect to given pricelines.

Marginal Values, Revisited

Expanding our concept of marginal value to accommodate further buying opportunities, we redefine it as the difference between the values of two acquisition problems.

Let P be a set of buyer pricelines, representing the buy prices the agent faces. Define $P(g, k)$ to be a set of buyer pricelines identical to P except that $\vec{p}_g$ is replaced by a vector with k zeros and ∞ thereafter: i.e., the agent holds k units of g and there are no further buying opportunities for that good (all other goods can still be bought as usual).

DEFINITION 3.7 MARGINAL VALUE WITH BUYING OPPORTUNITIES:
The marginal value of the kth unit of g given buyer pricelines P is

$$\mu(g.k, P) = \text{ACQ}(P(g, k)) - \text{ACQ}(P(g, k-1)). \tag{3.5}$$

In words, $\mu(g.k, P)$ is the difference between optimal acquisition values in two cases: when the agent holds k units of g, and when it holds $k-1$ units. In both cases the agent has no further buying opportunities for g, but may purchase other goods as desired.

This definition of marginal value with buying opportunities coincides with our earlier definition of marginal value in the special case of a fixed collection of goods. To interpret Definition 3.1 in terms of this new definition, simply choose P to be the set of buyer pricelines that encodes an agent's holdings: all entries are either zero (for holdings) or ∞.

Characterization Theorems

The next theorem, which generalizes Greenwald [2003b], characterizes the relationship between marginal values and buy prices.

THEOREM 3.2 ACQUISITION CHARACTERIZATION: Given buyer pricelines P, let $(X_1, Y_1), \ldots, (X_K, Y_K)$ denote all the optimal solutions to Acquisition(P). If the marginal values of all goods are monotonically nonincreasing, then for all goods $g.k$,

- $\mu(g.k, P) > p_{gk}$ iff $g.k \in \bigcap_{i=1}^{K} Y_i$
- $\mu(g.k, P) = p_{gk}$ iff $g.k \in \bigcup_{i=1}^{K} Y_i$ but $g.k \notin \bigcap_{i=1}^{K} Y_i$
- $\mu(g.k, P) < p_{gk}$ iff $g.k \notin \bigcup_{i=1}^{K} Y_i$

In words, assuming diminishing marginal values, if $g.k$ is contained in an optimal acquisition, then either $g.k$ is contained in all optimal acquisitions, in which case its marginal value is strictly greater than its buy price, or $g.k$ is not contained in any optimal acquisitions, in which case its marginal value is strictly less than its buy price; otherwise ($g.k$ is contained in some but not all optimal acquisitions), its marginal value is exactly equal to its buy price (see Examples 5.7 and 5.8).

The proof of Theorem 3.2 relies on Observation 3.3. To state this observation concisely, we introduce the following notation: Let $G(g, k)$ denote the multiset of goods containing k units of good g. For example, the multiset $\langle 0, 3, 0 \rangle$ containing three units of the second good in an economy of three goods is represented by $G(2, 3)$.

OBSERVATION 3.3:

The following equalities are equivalent. Moreover, the same holds when the equal signs are replaced by (weak or strict) inequalities.

$$\mu(g.k, P) = p_{gk} \tag{3.6}$$

$$\text{ACQ}(P(g, k)) - \text{ACQ}(P(g, k-1)) = p_{gk}$$

$$\text{ACQ}(P(g, k)) - \text{Cost}(G(g, k-1), P) - p_{gk} = \text{ACQ}(P(g, k-1)) - \text{Cost}(G(g, k-1), P)$$

$$\text{ACQ}(P(g, k)) - \text{Cost}(G(g, k), P) = \text{ACQ}(P(g, k-1)) - \text{Cost}(G(g, k-1), P) \tag{3.7}$$

Based on this observation, we interpret the assertion that $\mu(g.j, P) > p_{gj}$ to mean that buying exactly j units of good g is better than buying exactly $j-1$ units. But if $\mu(g.k, P) > p_{gk}$, the assumptions of diminishing marginal values and nondecreasing buyer pricelines imply that $\mu(g.j, P) > p_{gj}$, for all $j = 1, \ldots, k$. Hence, buying exactly k units of good g is better than buying exactly $k-1$ units; buying exactly $k-1$ units of good g is better than buying exactly $k-2$ units; and so on. In sum, buying exactly k units of good g is better than buying fewer than k units, so all optimal acquisitions buy at least k units of good g. In Table 3.2, we sketch the proof of this theorem in three tables: the first interprets Observation 3.3, the second outlines the implications of the monotonicity assumptions, and the third draws the relevant conclusions.

Table 3.2
Proof sketch for acquisition characterization (Theorem 3.2).

$\mu(g.j, P) > p_{gj}$	buying exactly j units of good g is better than buying $j-1$
$\mu(g.j, P) = p_{gj}$	buying exactly j units of good g is equivalent to buying $j-1$
$\mu(g.j, P) < p_{gj}$	buying exactly j units of good g is worse than buying $j-1$

$\mu(g.k, P) > p_{gk}$	$\mu(g.j, P) > p_{gj}$, for all $j = 1, \ldots, k$
$\mu(g.k, P) = p_{gk}$	$\mu(g.j, P) \geq p_{gj}$, for all $j = 1, \ldots, k$
	$\mu(g.j, P) \leq p_{gj}$, for all $j = k, \ldots, N_g$
$\mu(g.k, P) < p_{gk}$	$\mu(g.j, P) < p_{gj}$, for all $j = k, \ldots, N_g$

$\mu(g.k, P) > p_{gk}$	all optimal acquisitions buy k units or more of good g
$\mu(g.k, P) = p_{gk}$	some optimal acquisitions buy k units or more of good g
$\mu(g.k, P) < p_{gk}$	no optimal acquisitions buy k units or more of good g

Table 3.3 summarizes the "acquisition characterization theorem" (Theorem 3.2), which characterizes the relationship between *buy* prices and marginal values. In particular, the marginal value of any unit of any good in any optimal acquisition is at least its buy price.

As a corollary of this theorem and the reduction theorem (Theorem 3.1), we obtain the "completion characterization theorem" (Theorem 3.4), which characterizes the relationship between buy and *sell* prices and marginal values. Table 3.4 summarizes the "completion characterization theorem":

- the marginal value of any nonarbitrage opportunity in any optimal completion is at least its buy price;
- the marginal value of any (non) arbitrage opportunity that the agent does not sell in any optimal completion is at least its (buy) sell price;
- the marginal value of any arbitrage opportunity that the agent sells in any

Table 3.3
Acquisition characterization theorem, summarized.

Acquisition	$g.k \in \bigcup_{i=1}^{K} Y_i$
$g.k \in N$	$\mu(g.k, P) \geq p_{gk}$

Table 3.4
Completion characterization theorem, summarized. The cell labeled "impossible" corresponds to an empty set of goods, since $Z_i \subseteq A$ for all $i = 1, \ldots, K$. For the cell with the question mark, we cannot make any definitive claims about the relationship between marginal values and prices.

Completion	$g.k \in \bigcup_{i=1}^K Y_i$	$g.k \in \bigcup_{i=1}^K Y_i \setminus Z_i$	$g.k \in \bigcup_{i=1}^K Z_i$
$g.k \notin A$	$\mu(g.k', P') \geq p_{gk}$	$\mu(g.k', P') \geq p_{gk}$	impossible
$g.k \in A$	?	$\mu(g.k', P') \geq \pi_{gk}$	$\mu(g.k', P') \leq \pi_{gk}$

optimal completion is at most its sell price.

THEOREM 3.4 COMPLETION CHARACTERIZATION: Given buyer and seller pricelines P and Π, let $(X_1, Y_1, Z_1), \ldots, (X_K, Y_K, Z_K)$ denote all the optimal solutions to Completion(P, Π) and let A denote the set of arbitrage opportunities and let P' denote the set of unified pricelines.

If the marginal values of all goods are monotonically nonincreasing, then for all goods $g \in G$ and for all $k = 1, \ldots, N_g$,

- Case $g.k \notin A$:
  1. $\mu(g.k', P') > p_{gk}$ iff $g.k \in \bigcap_{i=1}^K Y_i \setminus Z_i$ iff $g.k \in \bigcap_{i=1}^K Y_i$
  2. $\mu(g.k', P') = p_{gk}$ iff $g.k \in \bigcup_{i=1}^K Y_i \setminus Z_i$ but $g.k \notin \bigcap_{i=1}^K Y_i \setminus Z_i$ iff $g.k \in \bigcup_{i=1}^K Y_i$ but $g.k \notin \bigcap_{i=1}^K Y_i$
  3. $\mu(g.k', P') < p_{gk}$ iff $g.k \notin \bigcup_{i=1}^K Y_i \setminus Z_i$ iff $g.k \notin \bigcup_{i=1}^K Y_i$
- Case $g.k \in A$:
  1. $\mu(g.k', P') > \pi_{gk}$ iff $g.k \in \bigcap_{i=1}^K Y_i \setminus Z_i$ iff $g.k \notin \bigcup_{i=1}^K Z_i$
  2. $\mu(g.k', P') = \pi_{gk}$ iff $g.k \in \bigcup_{i=1}^K Y_i \setminus Z_i$ but $g.k \notin \bigcap_{i=1}^K Y_i \setminus Z_i$ iff $g.k \in \bigcup_{i=1}^K Z_i$ but $g.k \notin \bigcap_{i=1}^K Z_i$
  3. $\mu(g.k', P') < \pi_{gk}$ iff $g.k \notin \bigcup_{i=1}^K Y_i \setminus Z_i$ iff $g.k \in \bigcap_{i=1}^K Z_i$

Marginal Value Monotonicity

The characterization theorems rely on the assumption of diminishing marginal values. Moreover, multiunit auctions (including the TAC auctions) commonly require that multiunit bids be monotone in prices. That is, the price offered to buy the kth unit must be nonincreasing in k, and similarly sell prices must be nondecreasing. Monotonicity ensures that an auctioneer can set a uniform clearing price such that all buys above the clearing price and all sells below it are winning bids.

A problem with bidding based on marginal values is that marginal values may not be monotone. Thus, marginal-value based bidding heuristics may not generate legal bids in the multiunit case. The following example illustrates how nonmonotonicity can arise as a consequence of complementary preferences.

EXAMPLE 3.8: Several units of two goods, x and y, are up for auction. Consider an agent bidding on behalf of two clients, such that the agent's valuation is the sum of the clients' values.

Suppose the goods are perfect complements for client 1, $v_1(\{x, y\}) = V > 0$, and perfect substitutes for client 2, $v_2(\{x\}) = v_2(\{y\}) = V$. Assume neither client values any other subsets. The agent owns one unit of y.

The marginal value of the first unit of x is zero, but the marginal value of the second unit of x is V (increases the agent's valuation from V to $2V$).

Example 3.8 is artificial, but nonmonotone marginal values arise in many practical settings. For example, whenever an agent has indivisible demand, such as minimum quantity requirements or fixed lot size requirements, we may observe nonmonotone marginal values. Neither of these phenomena arise in TAC, though it is possible to construct examples where valuations for hotel rooms violate monotonicity. In our experience, this is quite rare: instances are encountered in roughly 1 of every 300 TAC games.

Financial markets often accommodate "all-or-none" bids, although these are typically handled in an ad hoc manner [Miller, 2002]. Optimal clearing with nonmonotone bids can be feasible, but raises subtle issues [Schvartzman and Wellman, 2007]. In any case, it is important to remain cognizant of the issue, especially when adopting a marginal value based bidding approach. In TAC, where monotonicity violations are rare, most agents impose a simple check and adjust bids to conform when necessary.

3.4 The Bidding Cycle, Revisited

The bid determination problems defined in this chapter figure in many of the bidding strategies developed elsewhere in this book. By exploiting the common subtask structure, we can compare alternative bidding strategies in terms of how they pose and solve these bid determination problems. By precisely specifying these core optimization problems, we clarify the complexity of common bidding subtasks, and demonstrate the relation of these problems to each other.

In addition, characterizing the relationship between marginal values and prices sets the stage for an analysis of bidding heuristics that incorporate marginal values.

To conclude this chapter, we recall our skeletal view of the generic trading agent bidding cycle, displayed here as Table 3.5 with annotations naming formal subproblems and pointing to detailed discussions elsewhere in this book. We begin these discussions with an analysis of price prediction in Chapter 4.

Table 3.5
Trading agent bidding cycle, with labels naming bid determination subproblems and pointers to chapters elaborating these steps.

While at least one auction remains open, do:
1. Update current prices and holdings for each auction.
2. Predict, or project, future prices and holdings based on a model of the market environment [*price prediction*, Chapter 4].
3. Construct and place bids [*general bidding problems*, Chapter 5], for example employing an optimization process with the following steps:
(a) Determine target holdings: which goods to attempt to buy or sell [*completion problem*].
(b) Decide which target goods to bid on now [e.g., *flight bid timing*; see Section 7.1].
(c) Compute bid prices for these goods [e.g., *marginal values*].
After markets close: transact goods, and allocate holdings to their respective uses [*allocation problem*].

4 Price Prediction

In the generic trading agent bidding cycle presented at the end of the previous chapter (Table 3.5), executing Step 1 ("update prices and holdings") for the TAC environment requires only a routine retrieval of information from the game server. Step 2 is more substantial, calling for the agent to "predict, or project, future prices and holdings based on a model of the market environment". In this chapter we focus on the Step 2 prediction task, examining the particular case of predicting hotel prices in the TAC market game. We first discuss the problem generally, and then present results from an in-depth study of approaches to hotel price prediction employed by agents in the 2002 TAC tournament.

4.1 Predicting TAC Hotel Prices

TAC participants recognized early on the importance of accurately predicting hotel prices for effective overall performance [Stone and Greenwald, 2005]. The prices of hotels are highly variable from game to game, yet a hotel's price is not finalized until its auction closes—some minutes into the game,[1] depending on the random closing order. Complementarity among goods dictates how the outcomes of early auctions can significantly affect the value an agent places on a particular hotel later in the game, and conversely, the prices of hotels revealed later dictate whether an agent had bid wisely early in the game.

Anticipating hotel prices is a key element in several decisions facing a TAC agent, in particular:

1. *Determine target holdings.* Because flight prices tend to increase, agents are incentivized to commit to traveling on particular days early in the game. Yet the choice of which days depends crucially on the hotel prices on the included travel days.
2. *Compute bid prices.* The likelihood of obtaining a good with a given bid depends on the good's clearing price. Moreover, the value of any particular

1. The study reported in this chapter concerns TAC-02 agents, designed for 2001 rules where the first hotel closing is at minute 4. Because agents tend not to submit serious hotel bids until the first closing is imminent, under these rules no useful information is revealed by price quotes until well into the game. The 2004 rules moved this up to minute 1, but it remains the case that prices are formed and revealed to agents only gradually. Except where otherwise specified, in this chapter we assume the TAC-02 context of 2001 rules.

good is a function of the price of others. For example, the value of obtaining a room at Shanties day i is an increasing function of the projected cost of the alternative hotel on that day, Towers day i, and a decreasing function of the projected cost of complementary Shanties hotel rooms on the adjacent days, $i - 1$ and $i + 1$.

Given the importance of price prediction, it is not surprising that TAC researchers have explored a variety of approaches. In TAC-01, we observed the following price-prediction methods, associated in some cases with agents that seemed to exemplify that approach:

1. Just use the current price quote, p_t.
2. Adjust based on historical data. For example, if Δ_t is the average historical difference between clearing price and price at time t, then the predicted clearing price is $p_t + \Delta_t$.
3. Predict by fitting a curve to the price points seen in the current game (polimi_bot).
4. Predict based on closing prices for that hotel in past games (livingagents). 006 combined this approach with extrapolation from current prices.
5. Same as above, but condition on hotel closing time, recognizing that the closing sequence will influence the relative prices (Retsina, which conditioned on current prices as well).
6. Same as above, but condition on full ordering of hotel closings (Tacsman), or which hotels are open or closed at a particular point (RoxyBot, Urlaub01).
7. Learn a mapping from features of the current game (including current prices) to closing prices based on historic data (ATTac).
8. Hand-construct rules based on observations about associations between abstract features (SouthamptonTAC).

The diversity of approaches offers a prime opportunity for an empirical evaluation of alternative techniques. With the refinement of these methods and the introduction of new approaches for TAC-02, the 2002 tournament was ripe for a case study devoted to the price-prediction task.

Although the price-prediction subtask is not completely separable from other components of trading strategy, to a useful extent it can be isolated and evaluated in its own terms. In this chapter, we directly formulate the problem of predicting prices, and introduce natural accuracy measures. As we see below, most agent developers independently chose to define price prediction as a distinct task in their own agent designs.

We divide price prediction into two phases: *initial* and *interim*. Initial refers to the beginning of the game, before any hotel auctions close or the agents receive any quote information. Interim refers to the method employed thereafter. Since the information available for initial prediction (e.g., flight prices, client preferences) is a strict subset of that available for interim (which adds transaction and hotel price data), most agents treat initial prediction as a (simpler) special case.

Initial prediction is relevant to bidding policy for the first hotel closing, and was especially salient for trip choices in 2001–03, as these were typically made early in those games. Interim prediction supports ongoing revision of bids as the hotel auctions start to close. The study presented here focuses on initial prediction, mainly because it is the simpler of the two tasks, involving less potential information. Moreover, agents initially have relatively comparable information sets, thus providing for a cleaner analysis. Interim prediction is also important and interesting, and should be the focus of further work.

4.2 TAC-02 Agents

Detailed records for the TAC-02 tournament are provided in Appendix A, Section A.3. Table A.5 lists the 19 agents who participated in 2002, and scores in the tournament round are compiled in Table A.6. For overviews of most of these agents, see the survey article by Greenwald [2003a].

4.3 Price-Prediction Survey

Shortly after the TAC-02 event, we distributed a survey to all the entrants eliciting descriptions and data documenting their agents' price-prediction methods. Sixteen out of 19 teams responded to the survey, including 14 of 16 semifinalists, and all eight finalists. The result provides a detailed picture of the prediction techniques employed, and enables some comparison of their efficacy with respect to a common experience—the TAC-02 finals and semifinals.

Thirteen out of the 16 respondents reported that their agents did indeed form explicit price predictions for use in their trading strategies. These 13 are listed in Table 4.1, along with some high-level descriptors of their approach to the initial prediction task. In addition, tniTac and zepp responded that price predictions were part of their agent designs, but were not developed sufficiently to be deployed in the tournament. TOMAhack reported an ambitious design (also not actually employed) based on model-free policy learning, which accounts for other agents' bidding behavior without formulating explicit price predictions.

Table 4.1
Agents reporting prediction of hotel prices in TAC-02.

Agent	Approach	Form	Notes
ATTac	machine learning	prob	boosting
cuhk	historical	priceline	moving average
harami	historical	prob	
kavayaH	machine learning	point	neural net
livingagents	historical	point	
PackaTAC	historical	prob	
RoxyBot	historical	prob	histogram
006	historical	priceline	
SouthamptonTAC	historical	point	classification to reference categories
Thalis	historical (?)	point	survey incomplete
umbctac	historical	point	
Walverine	competitive	point	competitive equilibrium
WhiteBear	historical	point	

Forms of Prediction

One important distinction among methods is in the *form* of predictions they produce. For instance, an agent may predict a particular price point, or a probability distribution over possible prices. Point estimates are simpler, whereas distributions in principle enable the agent to better account for price uncertainty in decision making.

Although most agents generate point predictions, there are notable exceptions. As described in Section 6.2, ATTac's boosting algorithm [Stone et al., 2003] expressly learns probability distributions associated with game features. RoxyBot-02 tabulates game price statistics for a direct estimation of deciles for each hotel auction. PackaTAC and harami measure historical variance, combining this with historical averaging to define a parametric distribution for each hotel price. Walverine predicts point prices, but its "hedging" approach for some decisions amounts to forming an effective distribution around them.

Given a prediction in the form of a distribution, agents may make decisions by sampling or through other decision-theoretic techniques. The distribution may also facilitate the interim prediction task, enabling updates based on treating observations such as price quotes as evidence.

However, the first controlled experiment evaluating the distribution feature, in the context of ATTac [Stone et al., 2003], did not find an overall advantage to decision making based on distributions compared to using mean values (using the StraightMU heuristic, introduced in Section 5.4). The discussion of this finding in Section 6.4 offers several possible explanations for the observed performance, including (i) that the implementation employs insufficient samples, and (ii) that ATTac's use of distributions (the AverageMU heuristic, also introduced in Section 5.4) makes the unrealistic assumption that subsequent decisions can be made with knowledge of the actual realized price values. Analogous trials using Walverine, which generates and applies distributions in a different way [Cheng et al., 2005], also found bidding based on means to be superior to the distribution-based bidding the agent actually employed in TAC-02.

This evidence does not preclude the existence of alternative ways of using predicted distributions that actually yield benefits. The study by Greenwald and Boyan [2004] demonstrated an advantage to RoxyBot-02's strategy of evaluating candidate bid sets with respect to distributions (BidEvaluator, described in Section 5.4), compared to its 2000 strategy of bidding based on point estimates. In experiments reported in Chapter 5, AverageMU outperforms StraightMU by a statistically insignificant margin, but six other bidding heuristics (including BidEvaluator) surpassed both AverageMU and StraightMU. RoxyBot-06, whose heuristic came out on top in these experiments, demonstrated particularly effectively use of distributional predictions in TAC-06.

Nevertheless, for agents that predict probability distributions, we take the mean of these distributions as the subject of our analysis. This may discount potential advantages, but based on the discussion above, we suspect that—with the possible exception of RoxyBot—agents did not actually benefit from predicting distributions in TAC-02.[2]

Another variation in form is the prediction of prices as a function of quantity demanded. From the first TAC, entrants recognized that purchasing additional units may cause the price to increase, and introduced the *priceline* construct (defined in Section 3.2) to express estimated prices that varied by unit [Boyan and Greenwald, 2001; Stone and Greenwald, 2005]. Agents 006 and cuhk reported predicting pricelines.[3] In both cases, the agent started with

2. Given progress in TAC agent design, a study of price prediction in more recent tournaments could not make this simplifying assumption.

3. WhiteBear also reported using pricelines for interim prediction [Vetsikas and Selman, 2003],

a baseline point prediction for the first unit of each hotel, and derived the remainder of the priceline according to some rule. For example, 006 predicted the price for the nth unit (i.e., price given it demands n units) to be px^{n-1}, where p is the baseline prediction and x is 1.15 for hotels on day 1 or 4, and 1.25 for hotels on day 2 or 3.

In the succeeding analysis, we evaluate predictions in terms of baseline prices only. As noted below, our accuracy measures applied to pricelines would not reflect their actual value.

Information Employed

The set of information available at the beginning of the game includes all data from past games, the initial vector of flight prices, and the agent's own client preferences. For TAC-02, all agents except Walverine reported using historical information in their predictions. Only ATTac and kavayaH, both learning agents, and Walverine, an agent that computes competitive equilibrium prices, employ flight prices. All agents that construct pricelines effectively take account of own client preferences. Walverine does not construct pricelines but does factor its own client preferences into its equilibrium calculations.

The identities of other agents participating in a game instance are not known during the TAC preliminary (qualifying and seeding) rounds, as agents are drawn randomly into a round-robin style tournament. However, the semifinal and final rounds fix a set of eight agents for a series of games, and so the identity of other agents is effectively observable. ATTac is the only agent to exploit this information.

4.4 Approaches to Price Prediction

Based on survey responses, we divide TAC-02 prediction techniques into three categories.

Historical Averaging

Most agents took a relatively straightforward approach to initial price prediction,[4] estimating the hotel clearing prices according to observed historical av-

but initial predictions were essentially points.

4. Several agents complement this simple initial prediction with a relatively sophisticated approach to interim prediction, using the evidence from price quotes to gradually override the initial estimate. All else equal, straightforwardness is an advantage. As discussed in Section 2.3, simplicity was likely a significant ingredient of livingagents's success in TAC-01 [Fritschi and Dorer,

erages. For example, harami calculates the mean hotel prices for the preceding 200 games, and uses this as its initial prediction. The respective agents classified as adopting the "historical" approach in Table 4.1 differ on what set of games they include in the average, but most used games from the seeding round. Given a data set, agents tend to use the sample mean or distribution itself as the estimate, at least as the baseline.

The majority of averaging agents fixed a pool of prior games, and did not update the averages during the finals. An exception was cuhk, which employed a moving average of the previous ten games in the current round, or from previous rounds at the beginning of a new round.

The designers of umbctac reported employing mean prices as predictions with respect to decisions about trips of two or more days, but median prices (which tended to be lower) for decisions about one-day trips. For the semifinals they based their statistics on the last 100 seeding games. For the finals their data set comprised the 14 games of their semifinal heat. In our analysis below, we attribute predictions to umbctac based on the mean values from these samples.

The approach taken by SouthamptonTAC [He and Jennings, 2003] was unique among TAC agents. The SouthamptonTAC designers partitioned the seeding-round games into three categories: "competitive", "noncompetitive", and "semicompetitive". They then specified a reference price for each type and day of hotel in each game category. As it plays a game, the agent monitors the recent game history, and then chooses a category for that game. In the actual tournament, SouthamptonTAC began the semifinals predicting the semicompetitive reference prices, maintaining this stance until switching to noncompetitive for the last eight games of the finals.

Machine Learning

Two TAC-02 agents employed machine-learning techniques to derive relationships between observable parameters and resulting hotel prices. The premise of this approach is that game-specific features provide potentially predictive information, enabling the agent to anticipate hotel price movements before they are manifest in price quotes themselves. As one would expect, the two learning agents employed more kinds of information than typical TAC-02 agents (see Section 4.3).

ATTac predicts prices using a boosting algorithm for conditional density estimation [Stone et al., 2003]. Development of the technique was expressly

---

2002; Wellman et al., 2003b].

motivated by the TAC price-prediction problem, though the resulting algorithm is quite general. We describe ATTac's method in detail in Chapter 6, as a case study of machine learning in TAC. ATTac learns a predictor for each hotel type and day category. The predictor applied at the beginning of the game maps the following features into a predicted price for that hotel:

- initial flight prices,
- closing time of each hotel room, and
- identity of agents participating in the game.

Since the hotel closing times are unknown at game start, this predictor induces a distribution over price predictions, based on the distribution of hotel closing sequences. This distribution constitutes ATTac's initial price prediction.

kavayaH [Putchala et al., 2002] predicts initial hotel prices using neural networks trained via backpropagation. The agent has a separate network for each hotel. The output of each network is one of a discrete set of prices, where the price set for each hotel (type, day) was specified by kavayaH's designers based on historical prices. The inputs for each network are based on initial flight prices, specifically thresholded differences between flights on adjacent days. For example, the node for Towers hotel day 1 might have a binary input that indicates whether the price difference between inflights on days 1 and 2 is greater than 50. Shanties day 2 might have this input, as well as another based on the difference in flight prices on days 2 and 3. kavayaH's designers selected the most relevant inputs based on experimentation with their agent.

Competitive Equilibrium Analysis

Walverine's overall approach to TAC markets is to presume that they are well approximated by an economy in *perfect competition* [Cheng et al., 2005]. Its method for predicting hotel prices is a direct application of this assumption. Specifically, Walverine calculates the *competitive*, or *Walrasian equilibrium*, of the TAC economy, defined as the set of prices at which all markets would clear, assuming other agents behave as price takers [Katzner, 1989]. Taking into account the exogenously determined flight prices, Walverine finds a set of hotel prices that support such an equilibrium, and returns these values as its prediction for the hotels' final prices.

Let $\vec{p}$ be a vector of hotel prices, consisting of elements $p_{h,i}$ denoting the price of hotel type h on day i. Let $x^j_{h,i}(\vec{p})$ denote agent j's demand for hotel h day i at these prices. If we write the vector of such demands as $\vec{x}^j(\vec{p})$, *aggregate demand* is simply the sum of agent demands, $\vec{x}(\vec{p}) = \sum_j \vec{x}^j(\vec{p})$.

Prices $\vec{p}$ constitute a *competitive equilibrium* if aggregate demand equals aggregate supply for all hotels. Since there are 16 rooms available for each hotel on each day, in competitive equilibrium, $\vec{x}(\vec{p}) = \vec{16}$.

Starting from an initial vector $\vec{p}^0$, Walverine searches for equilibrium prices using the *tâtonnement* protocol, an iterative price adjustment mechanism originally conceived by Walras [Arrow and Hahn, 1971; Walras, 1954]. Given a specification of aggregate demand, tâtonnement iteratively revises the price vector according to the following difference equation:

$$\vec{p}^{t+1} = \vec{p}^t + \alpha^t[\vec{x}(\vec{p}^t) - \vec{16}]. \tag{4.1}$$

The adjustment parameter α^t decays with time. Although equilibrium prices are not guaranteed to exist given the discreteness and complementarities of the TAC environment, we have found that in practice we can find a price vector such that aggregate demand comes quite close to aggregate supply. The tâtonnement procedure typically produces such an approximate equilibrium well within the 300 iterations Walverine devotes to the prediction calculation.

A critical step in competitive equilibrium analysis is determining the aggregate demand function. Walverine estimates $\vec{x}(\vec{p})$ as the sum of (i) its own demand to serve its eight clients, and (ii) the expected demand of the other seven agents (to serve their 56 clients), based on the specified distribution of client preferences. The calculation of expected demand for the other agents is exact, modulo a summarization of entertainment effects, whenever agent demands are separable by client. As noted in Section 3.2, the acquisition problem can be decomposed into client-by-client optimization when prices are linear. The competitive model assumes linear prices; however, since TAC agents may not sell flights and hotels, linearity breaks down in the presence of holdings.[5] Thus the separability condition holds at the beginning of the game (hence, for initial prediction), but is invalidated once agents accumulate holdings. To see why separability fails, consider, for example, that if the agent holds one unit of a particular flight, it must reason about tradeoffs before allocating that unit to an individual client. Overall, although the analytical expression of expected demand is somewhat complicated [Cheng et al., 2005], its derivation is not conceptually or computationally difficult.

Note that the larger component of Walverine's demand estimation is an

5. Recall that pricelines encode holdings as zero-price units. The overall priceline is nonconstant (thus representing nonlinear prices) if it includes zero as well as nonzero prices for units in the relevant demand range.

expectation over the defined distribution of client preferences. Therefore, the prices it derives should properly be viewed as an equilibrium over the expectation, rather than the expected equilibrium prices. The latter might actually be a more appropriate price prediction. However, since expected equilibrium is more computationally expensive than equilibrium of the expectation (and we suspect the difference would be relatively small for 56 i.i.d. clients), Walverine employs the simpler prediction.

4.5 Predictions

As part of the survey, entrants provided their agents' actual predictions in the TAC-02 finals and semifinals, a total of 60 games. In many cases, predictions are constant (i.e., the same for every game), so it is straightforward to evaluate them with respect to the full slate of final and semifinal games. For two of the agents whose initial predictions change every game (ATTac and Walverine), entrants constructed what their agent *would have predicted* for each of these games, whether or not they actually participated. In one case (kavayaH), we have partial data. kavayaH reported its predictions for the 32 final games, and for the semifinal heat in which it participated (H1), except for one game in which its predictor crashed.

We include two versions of ATTac, corresponding to predictors learned from the 2001 and 2002 preliminary rounds. ATTac-01 and ATTac-02, respectively, represent the prediction functions employed in the TAC-01 and TAC-02 finals. In applying the ATTac-01 predictor to the TAC-02 finals, its use of agent identity information was disabled.

The predictions—price vectors—supplied by entrants and employed in our analysis are presented in Table 4.2. Prices are rounded to the nearest integer for display, though our analysis employed whatever precision was provided. Agents who condition on game-specific information (ATTac, kavayaH, and Walverine) produce distinct vectors in each instance, so are not tabulated here.

The first six rows of Table 4.2 (harami through WhiteBear) correspond to constant predictions for their associated agents. As noted above, SouthamptonTAC switched between two prediction vectors: "S" represents the reference prices for its "semicompetitive" environment, and "N" its "noncompetitive" prices. umbctac also switched prediction vectors within the 60 games—in their case introducing for the finals a prediction based on average semifinal (H1) prices.

Table 4.2
Predicted price vectors: Shoreline Shanties, followed by Tampa Towers, each for days 1–4. The first ten rows represent predictions employed by agents in the tournament. The last five represent various benchmarks, discussed below.

Agent	S1	S2	S3	S4	T1	T2	T3	T4
harami	21	58	80	16	47	108	101	64
livingagents	27	118	124	41	73	163	164	105
PackaTAC	21	116	119	38	76	167	164	97
RoxyBot[a]	20	103	103	20	76	152	152	76
006	30	100	100	40	95	160	155	110
WhiteBear	19	102	96	28	75	144	141	81
SouthamptonTAC "S"	50	100	100	50	100	150	150	100
SouthamptonTAC "N"	20	30	30	20	50	80	80	50
umbctac semifinals	20	133	124	45	83	192	158	110
umbctac finals	37	75	87	29	113	141	95	71
Actual Mean	68	85	97	52	121	124	154	109
Actual Median	9	48	38	8	59	105	98	59
Best Euc. Dist	18	73	57	15	71	111	95	69
Best EVPP	28	51	67	0	80	103	100	84
Walverine const	28	76	76	28	73	113	113	73

[a] RoxyBot's prediction is based on statistics from the seeding rounds, expressed as cumulative price distributions for each hotel, discretized into deciles. RoxyBot reportedly based its decisions on samples from this distribution, taking each decile value to occur with probability 0.1. This tends to overestimate prices, however, as the decile values correspond to upper limits of their respective ranges. The prediction vector presented here (and analyzed below) corresponds to an adjusted value, obtained by dropping the top decile and averaging the remaining nine.

The rows labeled "Actual Mean" and "Actual Median", respectively, present the average and median hotel prices in the 60 games of interest. Although clairvoyance is obviously not an admissible approach to prediction, we include them here as a benchmark. The actual central tendencies represent the best that agents taking the historical averaging approach can hope to capture.

The price vectors labeled "Best Euc. Dist", "Best EVPP", and "Walverine const" are discussed in Section 4.6.

4.6 Evaluating Prediction Quality

It remains to assess the efficacy of the various prediction approaches, in terms of the agents' price predictions in the actual TAC-02 final and semifinal games. In order to do so, we require some measure characterizing the accuracy of a prediction $\hat{\vec{p}}$ given the actual prices $\vec{p}$ in a given game.

Euclidean Distance

A natural measure of the closeness of two vectors is their Euclidean distance:

$$d(\hat{\vec{p}}, \vec{p}) \equiv \left[\sum_{(h,i)} (\hat{p}_{h,i} - p_{h,i})^2 \right]^{1/2},$$

where (h, i) indexes the price of hotel $h \in \{\mathrm{S}, \mathrm{T}\}$ on day $i \in \{1, 2, 3, 4\}$. Lower values of d are preferred, and for any $\vec{p}$, $d(\vec{p}, \vec{p}) = 0$.

Calculating d is straightforward, and we have done so for all of the reported predictions for all 60 games. Note that if the price prediction is in the form of a distribution, the Euclidean distance of the mean provides a lower bound on the average distance of the components of this distribution. Thus, according to this measure, our evaluation of distribution predictions in terms of their means provides a bias in their favor.

It is likewise the case that among all constant predictions, the actual mean $\bar{\vec{p}}$ for a set of games minimizes the aggregate *squared* distance for those games. That is, if $\vec{p^j}$ is the actual price vector for game j, $1 \leq j \leq N$,

$$\bar{\vec{p}} \equiv \frac{1}{N} \sum_{j=1}^{N} \vec{p^j} = \arg\min_{\hat{\vec{p}}} \sum_{j=1}^{N} [d(\hat{\vec{p}}, \vec{p^j})]^2.$$

There is no closed form for the prediction minimizing aggregate d, but one can derive it numerically for a given set of games [Bose and Morin, 2002].

Expected Value of Perfect Prediction

Euclidean distance d is a reasonable measure of accuracy in an absolute sense. However, the purpose of prediction is not accuracy for its own sake, but rather to support decisions based on these predictions. Thus, we seek a measure that correlates with performance in TAC. By analogy with standard value-of-information measures [Howard, 1965], we introduce the concept of *value of perfect prediction* (*VPP*).

Suppose an agent could anticipate perfectly the eventual closing price of all hotels. Then, among other things, the agent would be able to purchase all flights immediately with confidence that it had selected optimal trips for all its clients.[6] Since TAC-02 agents committed to trips at the beginning of the game

6. Modulo some residual uncertainty regarding availability of entertainment tickets, which we ignore in this analysis.

anyway, perfect prediction would translate directly to better trip choices.[7] We take this as the primary worth of predictions, and measure the quality of a prediction in terms of how it supports trip choice in comparison with perfect anticipation. The idea is that VPP will be particularly high for agents that otherwise have a poor estimate of prices. If an agent is already predicting well, then the value of obtaining a perfect prediction will be relatively small. This corresponds to the use of standard value-of-information concepts for measuring uncertainty: for an agent with perfect knowledge, the value of additional information is nil.

Specifically, consider a client c with preferences (IAD, IDD, HP). A trip's *surplus* for client c at prices $\vec{p}$, $\sigma_c(r, \vec{p})$ is defined as value minus cost,[8]

$$\sigma_c(r, \vec{p}) \equiv v_c(r) - \text{Cost}(r, \vec{p}),$$

where $\text{Cost}(r, \vec{p})$ is simply the total price of flights and hotel rooms included in trip r. Let

$$r_c^*(\vec{p}) \equiv \arg\max_r \sigma_c(r, \vec{p})$$

denote the trip that maximizes surplus for client c with respect to prices $\vec{p}$. The expression

$$\sigma_c(r_c^*(\hat{\vec{p}}), \vec{p})$$

then represents the surplus of the optimal trip based on prices $\hat{\vec{p}}$, evaluated with respect to prices $\vec{p}$. From this we can define value of perfect prediction:

$$VPP_c(\hat{\vec{p}}, \vec{p}) \equiv \sigma_c(r_c^*(\vec{p}), \vec{p}) - \sigma_c(r_c^*(\hat{\vec{p}}), \vec{p}). \tag{4.2}$$

Note that our *VPP* definition (Equation 4.2) is relative to client preferences, whereas we seek a measure applicable to a pair of price vectors outside the context of a particular client. To this end we define the *expected value of perfect prediction*, *EVPP*, as the expectation of *VPP* with respect to TAC's distribution

---

7. We compiled statistics on the temporal profile of flight purchases for the eight agents in the TAC-02 finals. Four of the agents purchased 16 flights (enough for round trips for all clients) within 45 seconds on average. All eight agents purchased more than half their flights by that time, on average. Vetsikas and Selman [2003] verified experimentally that predicting prices benefits agents who commit to flights early to a greater extent than it does those who delay flight purchases.

8. We overload the Cost function to apply to trips and price vectors, in lieu of the multiset and priceline arguments as defined in Section 3.2.

of client preferences:

$$\begin{aligned} EVPP(\hat{\vec{p}},\vec{p}) &\equiv E_c[VPP_c(\hat{\vec{p}},\vec{p})] \\ &= E_c[\sigma_c(r_c^*(\vec{p}),\vec{p})] - E_c[\sigma_c(r_c^*(\hat{\vec{p}}),\vec{p})]. \end{aligned} \tag{4.3}$$

Note that as for d, lower values of *EVPP* are preferred, and for any $\vec{p}$, $EVPP(\vec{p},\vec{p}) = 0$.

From Equation (4.3) we see that computing *EVPP* reduces to computing $E_c[\sigma_c(r_c^*(\hat{\vec{p}}),\vec{p})]$. We can derive this latter value as follows. For each (*IAD*,*IDD*) pair, determine the best trip for the Shanties hotel and the best trip for Towers, respectively, at prices $\hat{\vec{p}}$ ignoring any contribution from the hotel premium, *HP*. From this we determine the threshold value of *HP* (if any) at which the agent would switch from Shanties to Towers. We then use that boundary to split the calculation of surplus into two cases, with probabilities defined by the underlying distribution of *HP*. Below the threshold (where the agent chooses Shanties) the surplus is independent of *HP*, and above the surplus is linear in *HP*. The calculation procedure is analogous to Walverine's method for deriving expected client demand [Cheng et al., 2005] in its competitive equilibrium computation.

Results

Figure 4.1 plots the 13 agents for whom we have prediction data according to our two quality measures. With one exception (kavayaH), the d and *EVPP* values shown represent averages over the 60 games of TAC-02 finals and semifinals.[9]

The two dashed lines in Figure 4.1 represent best-achievable constant predictions with respect to the two accuracy measures. "Best Euc. Dist" minimizes average Euclidean distance, as indicated by the vertical line. For *EVPP*, we performed hill-climbing search from a few promising candidate vectors to derive a local minimum on that measure, represented by the horizontal line. Both reference vectors are provided in Table 4.2. Note that in principle, only agents that varied their predictions across game instances (ATTac, kavayaH, cuhk, and Walverine, and to a coarser degree, SouthamptonTAC and umbc-tac) have the potential to perform outside the upper-right quadrant.

9. Since kavayaH predicted only 45 games, we normalized its average d and *EVPP* values to account for the relative difficulty of the games it omitted compared to the games it predicted. The normalization multiplied its raw average by the ratio of prediction qualities for these game sets by another representative agent (ATTac-01, which proved most favorable for kavayaH, though other normalizations would have produced qualitatively similar results).

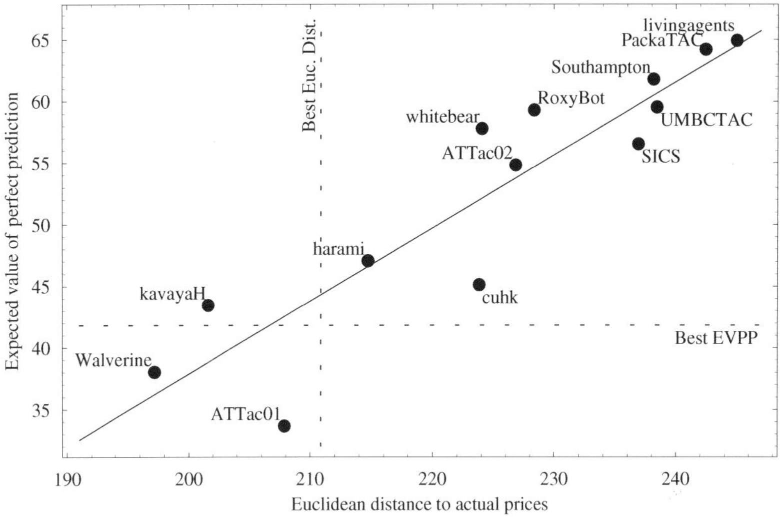

Figure 4.1
Prediction quality for 11 TAC-02 agents. Dashed lines delimit the accuracy achievable with constant predictions: "best Euclidean distance" and "best EVPP" for the two respective measures. The diagonal line is a least-squares fit to the points. Observe that the origin of this graph is at (190,32).

To assess the significance of the accuracy rankings among agents, we performed paired t-tests on all pairs of agents for both of our measures. The differences between Walverine and ATTac-01 do not reach a threshold of statistical significance on either measure. Walverine beats ATTac-01 for d at $p = .16$ while ATTac-01 beats Walverine for *EVPP* at $p = .18$. Walverine significantly ($p \leq .03$) outperforms all other agents on both measures. ATTac-01 significantly ($p \leq .01$) outperforms all other agents for *EVPP*, but for d it is not statistically distinguishable ($p \geq .08$) from kavayaH, harami, or cuhk. For *EVPP*, Walverine and ATTac-01 are the only agents that beat "Best *EVPP*" ($p = .015$ and $p = .048$), and "Best *EVPP*" in turn beats all other agents (all but cuhk significantly). For d, Walverine is the only agent to significantly ($p < .001$) "beat Best Euc. Dist", which in turn beats every other agent but ATTac-01 and kavayaH. No agent but Walverine does significantly better than Actual Mean (not shown), with ATTac-01, kavayaH, and harami statistically indistinguishable.

The large discrepancy in performance between ATTac-01 and ATTac-02 is unexpected, given that their predictors are generated from the same learning algorithm. This might be explainable if the 2002 preliminary rounds were somehow less predictive of the TAC-02 finals than was the case in 2001. The relative success of another learning agent, kavayaH, is evidence against this, however. The more likely hypothesis is that the 2002 agent suffered from a bug emerging from a last-minute change in computing environments.

To directly evaluate a prediction in the form of pricelines, we would need to know an agent's initial demand, so that we could determine the relevant price prediction. We did obtain such information from 006, but found that the accuracy of the priceline prediction according to these measures was far worse than that of the baseline prediction. While pricelines may well be advantageous with respect to the decisions the agents based on them, our impression is that they do not improve nominal accuracy as measured by Euclidean distance and *EVPP*. Since *EVPP* is based inherently on linear prices (i.e., the cost function presumes linearity), it may not provide a proper evaluation of priceline predictions.

The Influence of Flight Prices

Observe that the three best price predictors—ATTac-01, Walverine, and kavayaH—are precisely those agents that take flight prices into account. Initial flight prices potentially affect hotel prices through their influence on agents' early trip choices. In theory, lower flight prices should increase the tendency of agents to travel on those days, all else equal, thus increasing the prices of hotels on the corresponding days of stay. Walverine's approach is designed to capture this relationship in terms of the equilibrium between flight and hotel prices. ATTac and kavayaH attempt to induce the associations from game data. kavayaH's designers, in particular, explored neural network models based on their hypotheses about which flights were likely to affect which hotel prices [Putchala et al., 2002].

To isolate and quantify the effect of flight prices, we investigated the contribution of different factors employed by Walverine in its predictions. We defined three additional versions of Walverine's prediction model, each of which ignores some information that Walverine takes into account:

- Walv-no-cdata ignores its own client knowledge, effectively treating own demand as based on the same underlying client preference distribution assumed for the other agents.
- Walv-constF ignores the initial flight prices, assuming that they are set at the mean of the initial flight distribution (i.e., 325) in every game instance.

• Walverine const ignores its own client knowledge *and* takes flight prices at their mean rather than actual values. The result is a constant prediction vector, presented in Table 4.2.

Figure 4.2 plots the prediction qualities of these agents. Ignoring client knowledge degraded prediction quality only slightly, increasing *EVPP* from 38.0 to 38.6. Neglecting initial flight prices, however, significantly hurt predictions, increasing *EVPP* to 47.9. Ignoring both, Walverine const incurred an average *EVPP* of 49.1.

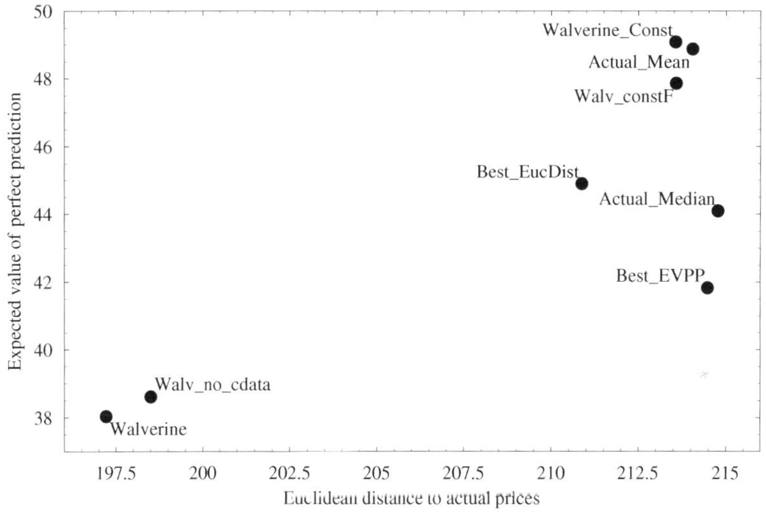

Figure 4.2
Prediction quality for Walverine variants and various central tendency benchmarks. Note that the axes span a much narrower range than the plot of Figure 4.1.

The results confirm the predictive value of flight prices. On the *EVPP* measure, Walverine does not gain a significant advantage from considering its own client data, but cannot beat "Best *EVPP*" without considering initial flight prices. For d, client data do make a significant ($p = .03$) difference when also considering flight data. Flight data significantly ($p < .001$) affect Walverine's prediction quality for the d metric, regardless of client data.

Relating Accuracy to Performance

As indicated by the scatterplot of Figure 4.1, our two accuracy measures are highly correlated ($\rho = .908$). Given that *EVPP* is value-based, this does suggest that accuracy improves performance. However, *EVPP* is a highly idealized proxy for actual game scores, and so does not definitively establish the relation between prediction accuracy and overall TAC performance.

Such a relation was also observed in an analysis of ATTac-01, reported in Section 6.4. Employing yet another measure of prediction quality to evaluate four variants of ATTac-01, we find a monotonic relation between average score and average predictive accuracy.

In an effort to more directly connect our accuracy measures to the bottom line, we regressed the actual TAC-02 game scores against the accuracy measures for all reported predictions—one data point per agent per game. We controlled for favorability of random client preferences, employing the same summary statistics used to construct the "client preference adjustment" (see Section 8.3) in our analysis of the TAC-01 tournament [Wellman et al., 2003b]. In two separate regressions, we found highly significant coefficients ($p < 10^{-10}$) for both d and *EVPP*. Predictive accuracy explained score variance quite poorly ($R^2 \leq 0.12$), however, as might be expected given all the other unmodeled variation across agents.

To reduce the variation, we undertook a series of controlled trials involving variants of Walverine [Cheng et al., 2005]. Each trial comprised a set of games with a fixed configuration of agents. The agents were constant within trials, but varied across, as they were conducted weeks or months apart while Walverine was undergoing modifications. For each trial, we regressed the actual score of the first agent on *EVPP*, controlling as above for favorability of random client preferences. We considered only one agent per game, since the data points for the other agents would be dependent given their common game instance. The results of our linear regression are summarized in Table 4.3.

Table 4.3
Regression of score on *EVPP* in three trials.

Trial	N	Mean *EVPP*	*EVPP* Coeff	R^2
1	200	70.4	–8.89	0.57
2	151	32.2	–11.59	0.26
3	110	59.5	–10.26	0.65

The *EVPP* coefficient was highly significant in all cases ($p < 10^{-5}$).

Note that since *EVPP* is measured per client in the same units as scores, a direct translation would equate reducing *EVPP* by one with an increase of eight score points. Our regressions yielded coefficients ranging from –8.89 to –11.59, which we take as a rough confirmation of the expected relationship. If anything, the results indicate that *EVPP* understates the value of prediction—which we might expect since it addresses only initial trip choice. Interestingly, the regression model seems to provide a better fit (as measured by R^2) for the trials involving worse price predictors (as measured by mean *EVPP*). This suggests that as prediction is optimized, other unmodeled factors may have relatively greater incremental influence on score.

It should be noted that the games in these trials are not representative of TAC tournament games. Since the agents are all versions of Walverine, they tend to make trip choices on the same basis.

4.7 Discussion

There are several limitations of this study, which must qualify any conclusions drawn about the efficacy of prediction methods evaluated here. First, we have focused exclusively on initial price prediction, whereas many agents placed greater emphasis on the interim prediction task.

Second, in many cases we have represented agents' predictions by an abstraction of the actual object produced by their prediction modules. In particular, we reduce probability distributions to their means, and consider only the first unit of a priceline prediction. More generally, we do not account for the very different ways that agents *apply* the predictions they generate. The *EVPP* measure itself was inspired by thinking in terms of how one agent, Walverine, uses its predictions. Perhaps measures tailored to the processes of other agents would (justifiably) show their predictions in a more favorable light.

Third, it should be recognized that despite the desirability of isolating focused components of an agent for analysis, complete separation is not possible in principle. Prediction evaluation is relative not only to how the agent uses its prediction but also to how it handles other tradeoffs (e.g., when it commits to flights), and ultimately to its entire strategy, in all its complexity. Studies such as this must strive to balance the benefits of decomposition with appreciation for the interconnections and synergies among elements of a sophisticated agent's behavior.

With these caveats, we draw several conclusions about price prediction in

TAC from this exercise. First, the results clearly demonstrate that instance-specific information can provide significant leverage over pure background history. Three agents use instance-specific information to perform better on at least one measure than any constant prediction. In particular, the initial flight prices provide substantial predictive value. The relation of flight and hotel prices can be induced and verified empirically, as seen through the success of the machine-learning agents. The predictive value flows from the influence of flight prices on demand for hotels, as indicated by the success of competitive equilibrium analysis in capturing this relationship.

We find it striking that a purely analytical approach, without any empirical tuning, could achieve accuracy comparable to the best available machine-learning method. Surely, many would have been skeptical that straight competitive equilibrium analysis could prove so successful, given the manifest unreality of its assumptions as applied to TAC. Our findings do not show that competitive equilibrium analysis is the best possible model for price formation in TAC, but it does demonstrate that deriving the shape of a market from an idealized economic theory can be surprisingly effective.

There are several advantages to predicting prices based on an economic model, most obviously the ability to perform with minimal or no empirical data. Even when historical information is available, it can be misleading to rely on it in a nonstationary environment. A tournament setup like TAC naturally violates stationarity, as the agent pool evolves over time, through selection as well as individual learning and development. Of course, dealing with time variance, particularly in multiagent environments, is an active area of current research, and ultimately the best methods will combine elements of model-based and data-based reasoning.

5 Bidding with Price Predictions

Once it has generated price predictions, using methods from the preceding chapter or other techniques, a trading agent proceeds to the decisive step of its bidding cycle: "construct and place bids". In this chapter, we investigate the bidding decision in depth. Our study addresses a general class of bidding problems characterized by two key features:

1. The agent must bid in separate markets simultaneously for interdependent goods.
2. The agent's information about the markets is wholly encapsulated in its price predictions.

We elaborate on the technical assumptions and motivations underlying our analysis in the next section.

Given price predictions, the bidding problem can be cast as optimization: compute a set of bids maximizing the agent's expected surplus with respect to the distribution of possible outcomes in each market. Because finding an optimal solution to the bidding problem is not generally tractable, our study centers around a series of candidate algorithms that construct bids based on approximations or simplifications. These *bidding heuristics* take various approaches to identifying the set of goods to bid on and calculating bid prices, employing as building blocks many of the bid determination subproblems and associated computations presented in Chapter 3.

We begin by analyzing a simple special case: bidding when market prices are known with certainty. Although the assumption of known prices may be unrealistic, exploring this case helps us understand the limitations of some intuitive heuristics, and suggests an alternative family of heuristics, guaranteed to be optimal for this case. These ideas provide a starting point for tackling the bidding problem under uncertainty: predict point price estimates, then bid as if those estimates were known prices. After working through a series of examples that reveals the limitations of bidding based on point price estimates, we introduce heuristics that employ distributional price predictions. Further examples elucidate the operation of these heuristics, and their respective advantages and limitations. Ultimately, we introduce a distribution-based bidding heuristic that produces optimal bids in the limit, as more computation becomes available.

We conclude the chapter by testing our entire suite of bidding heuristics within a simplified version of TAC designed to isolate their effects.

5.1 Auction Framework

In its most general form, bidding in markets can be viewed as a *game of incomplete information*, where each agent has private information about its own situation and beliefs about the private information of others. In such games, agents' bidding strategies are functions of their private information, and in game-theoretic equilibrium represent optimal responses to the other agents' strategies. This is the framework adopted by *auction theory*, as pioneered by Vickrey [1961] and developed by many economists in recent decades.

Auction theory has been applied successfully to characterize equilibrium behavior in relatively simple market environments, generally involving a single good or good type [Krishna, 2002]. For situations involving multiple interdependent goods, the theory extends to *combinatorial auctions* [Cramton et al., 2006], where agents bid directly on bundles and allocations are determined by a single mechanism operating over the entire scope of the market.

As argued in Chapter 3, however, the hallmark of the TAC game is multiple interdependent goods exchanged through separate markets. Such environments are generally too complex for standard auction-theoretic analysis. The dynamic operation of markets over time, characterized by incremental revelation of price information, compounds the analytical complexity.

Simplifying Assumptions

In our analysis of the problem of bidding in auctions for interdependent goods, we address a somewhat narrower question and adopt some simplifying assumptions. Rather than tackle the game-theoretic problem of characterizing strategic equilibria, we focus on a single agent's problem of optimizing its own bidding behavior, assuming the other agents' strategies are fixed. In other words, we treat the bidding problem as primarily *decision-theoretic* rather than game-theoretic.[1] In keeping with our basic agent architecture, we further assume that the environment can be modeled in terms of the agent's predictions about prices it will face in the market. These prices serve to summarize the relevant information hidden in other agents' bidding strategies.

We introduce the term *pseudo-auction* for a market mechanism defined by these two assumptions—fixed other-agent behaviors and market information encapsulated by prices. Our bidding problems, defined with respect to

---

1. In Chapter 8, we describe how game-theoretic analysis can be brought back in to evaluate bidding strategy within an overall experimental methodology.

pseudo-auctions, differ technically from bidding in the standard full-blown auction-theoretic setting. Nonetheless, we often abbreviate pseudo-auctions as *auctions*, taking as understood the underlying assumptions of our analysis.

Like many treatments of the bidding problem in the literature (as well as elsewhere in this book), in our experiments with bidding heuristics we employ a linear pricing model, where the unit price for a good is independent of the quantity the agent chooses to buy or sell. This is akin to treating the agent as a *price taker*, ignoring the effect of its own bids on the market. Price taking is warranted under *perfect competition*—where the market has a sufficient number of participants to render negligible the effect of any individual agent. Although the TAC market comprises a mere eight agents, we observed in Chapter 4 that a model based on perfect competition predicts hotel prices quite accurately. Thus, adopting a price-taking model can provide a reasonable approximation for TAC (at least for hotels) and is a useful starting point for a broad class of market environments. Nonetheless, when the agent has a sound basis for modeling the effect of its own bids on the market, it should certainly do so, for example, by predicting nonlinear prices. In our general definitions of the bidding problem we allow nonlinear pricelines, and all of the bidding heuristics presented in this chapter can exploit nonlinear price predictions when available.

Finally, we focus our attention on *one-shot auctions*, where the agent submits its bid and then observes the final outcome, with no chance to revise its bid or bid again based on new information. Although dynamic bidding is an important component of TAC markets and many other mechanisms of interest, a thorough understanding of the one-shot case is an essential prerequisite for tackling the more complex problem.

Bids and Prices

We employ the notation for goods, packages, and pricelines introduced in Chapter 3. The agent submits a bid β expressing offers to buy or sell various units of the goods in the marketplace. We divide β into two components $\langle \vec{b}, \vec{a} \rangle$ where for each good g the bid consists of a *buy offer*, $\vec{b}_g = \langle b_{g1}, \ldots, b_{gN_g} \rangle$, and a *sell offer*, $\vec{a}_g = \langle a_{g1}, \ldots, a_{gN_g} \rangle$. Recall that N_g denotes the number of units of good g in the marketplace. The bid price $b_{gk} \in \mathbb{R}_+$ (resp. $a_{gk} \in \mathbb{R}_+$) represents an offer to buy (sell) the kth unit of good g at that price.

By definition, the agent cannot buy (sell) the kth unit unless it also buys (sells) units $1, \ldots, k-1$. To accommodate this fact, we require that buy offers be nonincreasing in k, and sell offers nondecreasing. In addition, an agent may not offer to sell a good for less than the price at which it is willing to buy that good: that is, $b_{g1} < a_{g1}$. Otherwise, it would simultaneously buy and sell good g. We refer to these two restrictions as *bid monotonicity* constraints.

We encode auction prices using pricelines. The buyer priceline $\vec{p}_g$ (seller priceline $\vec{\pi}_g$) for good $g \in G$ specifies the effective buy (sell) price for each unit of g. As in Chapter 3, we assume that pricelines are monotone: buyer pricelines nondecreasing, and seller pricelines nonincreasing.

A strength of the priceline representation is its flexibility in modeling the prices faced by a bidding agent. Pricelines with constant unit price reflect a linear pricing model. Pricelines with variable unit price can be interpreted in two ways: (i) reflecting a nonuniform auction clearing price, or (ii) modeling the agent's effect on an actual uniform price. In either case, the effective per-unit price to the agent varies with its demand. For example, if the market supply consists of two units of good g, the priceline $\vec{p}_g = \langle 10, 20\rangle$ means that if the agent buys one unit of g, it pays a total of 10 (10 per unit); but if the agent buys two units, it pays a total of 30 (15 per unit).

Auction Rules

As in a true auction, the outcome of a pseudo-auction dictates the quantity the agent will exchange, and at what prices, conditional on its bid. We refer to the former question as *winner determination*; the latter issue is resolved by the *payment rule*.

Definition 5.1 Pseudo-Auction Winner Determination Rule: Given buyer and seller pricelines P and Π, and bid $\beta = \langle \vec{b}, \vec{a}\rangle$, the agent buys the multiset of goods $\mathrm{Buy}(\beta, P)$ and sells the multiset of goods $\mathrm{Sell}(\beta, \Pi)$, where

$$\mathrm{Buy}_g(\beta, P) = \max_{k \in \{1,\ldots,N_g\}} k \text{ such that } b_{gk} \geq p_{gk}$$

and

$$\mathrm{Sell}_g(\beta, \Pi) = \max_{k \in \{1,\ldots,N_g\}} k \text{ such that } a_{gk} \leq \pi_{gk}.$$

Note that the monotonicity restrictions on bids and pricelines ensure that the agent's offer is better than or equal to the price for every unit it exchanges, and that the agent does not simultaneously buy and sell any good.

There are at least two alternative payment rules an agent may face. In a *first-price pseudo-auction*, the agent pays its bid price (for buy offers, or receives its bid price for sell offers) for each unit it wins. In a *second-price pseudo-auction*, the agent pays (or receives) the prevailing prices, as specified by the buyer and seller pricelines. Our terminology derives by analogy from the standard first- and second-price sealed bid auctions [Krishna, 2002; Vickrey, 1961]. In these mechanisms, the high bidder for a single item pays its bid (the first price), or the highest losing bid (the second price), respectively. The salient property is that in first-price pseudo-auctions, the price is set by the bid of the winner, whereas in second-price pseudo-auctions an agent's bid price determines whether it wins but not the price it pays.

In this chapter, we focus on the second-price model. Our basic problem definitions presume second-price auctions, and our bidding heuristics are designed for this case. As in true auctions, adopting the second-price model in pseudo-auctions simplifies the problem for the bidder, and as we argue next, provides a reasonable approximation to the situation faced by TAC agents.

Modeling TAC Auctions

Before proceeding with our analysis, it is instructive to relate our abstract auction model to the particular auctions of the TAC game. In doing so, we see that the second-price model corresponds at least approximately to each of the TAC auction types.

In TAC entertainment auctions, agents submit bids (i.e., buy and sell offers) of the form specified above. If we interpret an agent's buyer and seller pricelines as the current order book (not including the agent's own bid), then the agent's immediate winnings are as determined by the winner determination rule (Definition 5.1), and payments are according to the second-price rule (i.e., the order-book prices prevail).

In TAC hotel auctions, only buy bids are allowed. Assuming a static order book, an accurate buyer priceline would indicate that the agent can win k units of a good if it pays—for *all* k units—a price just above the $(17 - k)$th existing (other-agent) offer. The actual price it pays will be that of the 16th highest unit offer (including its own offer). Since the agent's own bid may affect the price,[2] this situation lies between the first- and second-price definitions stated above.

In TAC flight auctions, agents may buy any number of units at the price posted by the seller. The situation at any given time is modeled exactly by the

2. It can do so in two ways. First, the agent may submit the 16th highest unit offer, in which case it sets the price. Second, when it bids for multiple units, the number it wins determines the price-setting unit, thus affecting the price for all winning units. Note that this second effect would be present even if the auction cleared at the 17th highest price.

second-price pseudo-auction abstraction, with linear prices.

Another important characteristic of the TAC auctions not modeled here is that they are extended in time. Flights are available throughout the game, entertainment trading occurs continuously, and the hotel auctions run iteratively, allowing agents to increase their bids during each round for any open hotels. Our model of one-shot auctions does not capture these opportunities. However, we experimentally evaluate the bidding strategies presented here in the richer TAC context. Many qualitative features of the bidding strategies that emerge in our analysis of the one-shot setting also manifest themselves in the iterative context. Moreover, some strategies prove more robust and adaptable to dynamic features of the TAC environment. Detailed discussion of bidding strategies expressly addressing timing and bid updating, and accounting for other market-specific details of TAC auctions, is deferred to Chapter 7.

5.2 Optimal Bidding with Known Prices

We start our analysis of the bidding problem by considering the very special case where prices are known with certainty. Within our generic trading agent architecture, this boils down to an assumption that the agent is *clairvoyant*—it models prices in the form of point estimates (as opposed to distributions; see Section 4.3), and each price prediction is accurate. Understanding how to bid in this idealized case will prove useful for developing methods to address the more realistic problem of bidding under uncertainty.

We focus on the case of *simultaneous* auctions. Simultaneity constrains an agent to place bids on all goods at once. An alternative is *sequential auctions*, where the agent bids on each auction in turn, learning the outcome for each before generating its bid for the next. In the case of known prices, the issue of simultaneous vs. sequential auctions is moot (the agent can determine in advance the outcome of its chosen bid with certainty anyway, so there is no advantage to waiting for the serial resolution of auctions), but this distinction manifests itself when prices are unknown [Greenwald and Boyan, 2004].

DEFINITION 5.2 DETERMINISTIC BIDDING PROBLEM: Given buyer and seller pricelines P and Π, the *deterministic bidding problem*, or the *bidding problem with known prices*, is to identify a surplus-maximizing bid:

$$\max_{\beta=\langle\vec{b},\vec{a}\rangle, X\oplus Z\subseteq Y} v(X) - \text{Cost}(Y, P) + \text{Revenue}(Z, \Pi),$$

where $Y = \text{Buy}(\vec{b}, P)$ and $Z = \text{Sell}(\vec{a}, \Pi)$.

Since prices are fully specified in the deterministic bidding problem, the key decision an agent faces is which goods to buy and sell. But the problem of deciding which goods to exchange is precisely the *completion problem* (Definition 3.4). Indeed, the bidding problem with known prices reduces to completion. Because completion specifies the same optimization task posed in the deterministic bidding problem, converting an optimal solution to the former into corresponding bids yields an optimal solution to the latter.

THEOREM 5.1 OPTIMAL BIDDING WITH KNOWN PRICES: The following procedure solves the deterministic bidding problem.

1. Select an optimal completion (X^*, Y^*, Z^*).
2. Bid to buy:
   - $b^*_{gk} \geq p_{gk}$, for all $k = 1, \ldots, Y^*_g$
   - $b^*_{gk} < p_{gk}$, for all $k = Y^*_g + 1, \ldots, N_g$
   - $b^*_{g,k-1} \geq b^*_{gk}$, for all $k = 1, \ldots, N_g$, taking $b^*_{g0} = \infty$
   (i.e., ensure that buy offers are monotonically nonincreasing in k)
3. Bid to sell:
   - $a^*_{gk} \leq \pi_{gk}$, for all $k = 1, \ldots, Z^*_g$
   - $a^*_{gk} > \pi_{gk}$, for all $k = Z^*_g + 1, \ldots, N_g$
   - $a^*_{g,k-1} \leq a^*_{gk}$, for all $k = 1, \ldots, N_g$, taking $a^*_{g0} = 0$
   (i.e., ensure that sell offers are monotonically nondecreasing in k)

Given a solution to the completion problem, an agent optimizes its outcome by bidding an amount greater than or equal to the specified price on precisely those units of each good it wishes to buy, and an amount less than or equal to the specified price on precisely those units of each good it wishes to sell, subject to the monotonicity requirements for buy and sell offers. The bids generated by the above procedure satisfy these requirements and are designed to buy and sell exactly the goods in Y^* and Z^* mandated by completion. In the buy case, we have $b^*_{gk} \geq p_{gY^*_g}$ iff $k \leq Y^*_g$; thus the agent buys Y^*_g units. In the sell case, we have $a^*_{gk} \leq \pi_{gZ^*_g}$ iff $k \leq Z^*_g$; thus the agent sells Z^*_g units.

5.3 Bidding with Point Price Predictions

The preceding section established an optimal bidding strategy in the deterministic bidding problem, that is, assuming known prices. The strategy consists of solving a completion problem, and then submitting winning bids for the goods in the target set. If prices are truly known, and solving the optimization problem is computationally feasible, then there is no reason for an agent to bid otherwise. However, there are several reasons one might wish to consider *bidding heuristics*—strategies for bidding based on particular problem features, which may or may not be optimal, including:

1. The agent may not have the computational resources necessary to solve the completion problem exactly. (Recall that completion in TAC is NP-hard.)

2. It might be desirable for modularity to decompose the bidding problem into decisions for each individual market even though an optimal solution entails the global consideration of bids on all goods.

3. Auctions are a means of *price discovery*; their clearing prices are not usually known in advance. In case prices are unknown, a heuristic may outperform a strategy that is optimized for the known-price case.

We consider this last reason to be the most significant, and devote the next section to methods that deal explicitly with uncertain price predictions. First, however, we explore the more *implicit* approach, where price predictions take the form of point estimates, even though the actual prices are not perfectly predictable. Methods that construct bids as if these point estimates are known prices can be viewed as heuristic approaches to the more general problem.

Simple Bidding Heuristics

We commence the study of heuristic bidding strategies by investigating two classic and intuitive heuristics: bidding based on (i) independent and (ii) marginal values. We illustrate the performance of these heuristics through a series of numeric examples of the deterministic bidding problem in the simple camera-and-flash scenario, originally introduced to illustrate some of the complexities of bidding in interdependent markets in Chapter 3. In all examples in this chapter, we focus on the special case in which the agent is bidding to buy only; there are no selling opportunities.

Independent Values

Perhaps the most straightforward bidding heuristic is to bid independent values: the values of goods in isolation. However, using this heuristic, an agent can fail to win goods it wishes it had won, when goods are complements, and succeed at winning goods it wishes it had not won, when goods are substitutes.

DEFINITION 5.3 INDEPENDENT VALUE: The *(independent) value* of a multiset of goods $M \subseteq N$ is precisely the value $v(M)$ the agent attributes to that multiset. In particular, the independent value of $g.1$, the first unit of good g, is $v(e_g)$, where e_g denotes the unit vector with exactly one 1 in the gth component.

EXAMPLE 5.4: Suppose an agent values a camera and flash together at 500, but values either good alone at 1. Also, suppose these two goods are sold separately in two simultaneous auctions, and the clearing prices are 200 for the camera and 100 for the flash. If the agent were to bid only its independent values ($v(1,0) = v(0,1) = 1$), it would lose both goods, obtaining surplus of 0 rather than $500 - 200 - 100 = 200$. This outcome is suboptimal: the agent fails to win goods it wishes it had won.

EXAMPLE 5.5: Now suppose an agent values a Canon AE-1 at 300 and a Canon A-1 at 200, but values both cameras together at only 400. Also, suppose these two goods are sold separately in two simultaneous auctions, and the clearing prices are 275 for the AE-1 and 175 for the A-1. If the agent were to bid its independent values, it would win both goods, obtaining surplus $400 - 450 = -50$. This outcome is also suboptimal: the agent wins goods it wishes it had not won.

Marginal Values

A natural alternative to bidding based on independent values is to employ marginal values. However, even with the marginal-value bidding heuristic, an agent can succeed at winning goods it wishes it had not won, when goods are substitutes, although it never fails to win goods (even complements) it wishes it had won (Theorem 3.4, completion characterization).

Recall Definition 3.7, which defines the marginal value of a unit of a good with respect to a set of pricelines, P. In our examples below, we compute the marginal value of a single unit of good g assuming no other holdings of good

g, in which case marginal value is given by:

$$\mu(g.1, P) = \text{ACQ}(P(g,1)) - \text{ACQ}(P(g,0)).$$

Here the acquisition problem is solved under the assumption of holding one or zero units, respectively, of good g. In other words, the marginal value is simply the increase in value associated with owning the unit of good g (i.e., buying it for free), assuming normal buying opportunities for the other goods.

EXAMPLE 5.6: Consider once again the setup of Example 5.4. Given both the camera and flash together, the agent's value is 500; but either one of these components without the other is valued at only 1. If the prices of the camera and flash are 200 and 100, respectively, then bidding marginal values, $400 - 0 = 400$ on the camera and $300 - 0 = 300$ on the flash, the agent wins both goods, as desired.

EXAMPLE 5.7: Consider once again the setup of Example 5.5, where an agent values a Canon AE-1 at 300 and a Canon A-1 at 200, and both cameras together at 400. If the clearing prices of the two cameras are 275 and 175, respectively, then bidding marginal values, $300 - 25 = 275$ on the first camera and $200 - 25 = 175$ on the second, the agent wins both goods. As in Example 5.5, this is not an optimal outcome: the agent wins goods it wishes it had not won.

Example 5.6 shows that, for complementary goods, the marginal-value bidding heuristic can be effective, in spite of the classic exposure problem, in which an agent bids more than its independent value for a good. In Example 5.7, which concerns substitutable goods, the marginal value bidding heuristic suffers from another form of exposure, as it bids more in total for goods that comprise a package than its combined value for that package. Indeed, in the presence of substitutes, this latter form of exposure can cause the marginal-value bidding heuristic to perform arbitrarily badly, even when prices are known, as we see in the next example.

EXAMPLE 5.8: Consider a set of $n > 1$ goods that are up for auction simultaneously. Assume that an agent attributes the value 2 to one or more of these goods and that the price of each good is 1. The marginal value heuristic bids $2 - 1 = 1$ for every good. In the worst case, the agent wins them all, and obtains nonpositive surplus $2 - n$. In contrast, bidding 1 on exactly one good obtains positive surplus $2 - 1 = 1$.

In this section, we described two simple bidding heuristics, and gave examples of how these heuristics perform when bidding on complements and substitutes. We found that both the independent and marginal value bidding heuristics are suboptimal on what is arguably the simplest of all bidding problems: bidding with known prices. Nonetheless, the intuitive appeal of bidding marginal values remains. In the next section, we identify the circumstances in which marginal value bidding itself *is* optimal, and we suitably modify the classic marginal value bidding heuristic to extend these circumstances. Then, we look at examples of how these heuristics perform when prices are unknown (i.e., point price estimates are not necessarily accurate).

Optimal Bidding Heuristics

In this section, we introduce a family of bidding heuristics inspired by the implementation of RoxyBot-00. Using the completion characterization theorem (Theorem 3.4), we argue that the heuristics in this family are instances of the class of optimal bidding heuristics derived in the optimal bidding theorem for the known price case (Theorem 5.1).

In the interest of clarity, we present pseudocode for all the heuristics discussed in this section, and indeed in this chapter. We start by describing the general workings of our heuristic algorithms.

Heuristic Algorithms

In addition to the goods in question, each heuristic takes as input buyer and seller pricelines, P and Π, representing predicted prices for each unit of each good. As output, they return a bid β, consisting of buy and sell offers, $\vec{b}_g$ and $\vec{a}_g$, for each good g. Before submitting these bids to the auctions, however, the agent must adjust them to take holdings into account and to satisfy the auctions' bidding rules.

Although the agent's holdings are reflected in input pricelines, the output bid is constructed from the perspective that the agent needs to buy its holdings (albeit at a predicted price of zero). The first adjustment, therefore, is to remove the buy offers corresponding to units held. Let H_g denote the agent's current holdings of good g. We shift $\vec{b}_g$ by H_g units, taking $b_{gk} \Leftarrow b_{g,k+H_g}$, for $k = 1, \ldots, N_g - H_g$, and we append to this truncated vector H_g zeros.

Next, we consider the auction rules, in particular the bid monotonicity constraints. The buy offer $\vec{b}_g$ (adjusted for holdings) must be nonincreasing, and the sell offer $\vec{a}_g$ nondecreasing. If either constraint is violated, the offer must be adjusted to meet the requirements. There are several reasonable ways to accomplish this, for instance by *flattening* an offer, proceeding left to right, decreasing (or for sell offers, increasing) each price as necessary. For example, to flatten the buy offer $\langle 100, 90, 100\rangle$, we decrease the offer on the third unit, resulting in $\langle 100, 90, 90\rangle$.

Given individually monotone $\vec{b}_g$ and $\vec{a}_g$ for good g, we still need to ensure that $b_{g1} < a_{g1}$. This constraint may be violated if there exist arbitrage opportunities. To rectify such a violation, here are two approaches:

1. Adjust either the buy or sell offer (or both). For instance, we could reassign $a_{g1} \Leftarrow b_{g1} + 1$, then apply flattening to make the overall bid monotone. Given $\vec{b}_g = \langle 100, 90, 90\rangle$ and $\vec{a}_g = \langle 70, 80, 110\rangle$, for example, the buy offer would be unchanged and the sell offer revised to $\langle 101, 101, 110\rangle$.
2. Submit the bid in phases. For example, the agent could submit the buy component now, and the sell component at some future time after the bid containing the buy component clears. For situations of transactional arbitrage (see Section 3.2), this approach is a natural choice, since typically the arbitrage opportunity is based on projections of future price movements, and at most one half of the buy/sell pair can be executed at any given time anyway.

Finally, the agent may need to implement further adjustments to address subtleties arising from specific auction rules. An example method used by Walverine to adjust its hotel bids to deal with the beat-the-quote rule is described in Section 7.2.

STRAIGHTMV

StraightMV (Algorithm 4) is an implementation of the marginal value bidding heuristic. Given an instance of the bidding problem with known prices, let A denote the set of all arbitrage opportunities, that is, the output of the subroutine Arbitrage(G, N, P, Π). A reasonable agent would never fail to buy any goods in A (since it expects to be able to sell them for more than it buys them for), nor would it ever attempt to sell any goods not in A (since it expects it would have to buy them for more than it could sell them for).[3] By the second-price assumption, bidding any value greater than or equal to the buy price on all goods

3. Recall that all owned items with a positive predicted sale price constitute holdings arbitrage (see Section 3.2), thus lie within A and should be considered as selling opportunities.

in A ensures they are bought, and bidding any value greater than or equal to the sell price on all goods not in A ensures they are not are sold. In the interest of satisfying bid monotonicity as nearly as possible, the straight marginal-value bidding heuristic places buy offers at sell prices on all arbitrage opportunities and sell offers at buy prices on all nonarbitrage opportunities. More interestingly (and what gives the heuristic its name), StraightMV places sell offers at marginal value on arbitrage opportunities and buy offers at marginal value on nonarbitrage opportunities. In generating these bids, StraightMV calculates $|N|$ marginal values; hence, it solves $2|N|$ completion problems.

Algorithm 4 StraightMV(G, N, P, Π)

$P' \Leftarrow \text{Unify}(G, N, P, \Pi)$
$A \Leftarrow \text{Arbitrage}(G, N, P, \Pi)$
for all $g \in G$ **do**
  for $k = 1$ to A_g **do**
    $b_{gk} \Leftarrow \pi_{gk}$
    $a_{gk} \Leftarrow \mu(g.k', P')$
  end for
  for $k = A_g + 1$ to N_g **do**
    $b_{gk} \Leftarrow \mu(g.k', P')$
    $a_{gk} \Leftarrow p_{gk}$
  end for
end for
return β

The StraightMV heuristic does not solve the bidding problem with known prices optimally in general (recall Examples 5.7 and 5.8), but does *whenever the optimal completion is unique* and marginal values are diminishing,[4] the latter of which we assume throughout the rest of this chapter. Optimality of StraightMV follows from the results on completion characterization (Theorem 3.4) and optimal bidding in the known-price case (Theorem 5.1). In particular, letting (X^*, Y^*, Z^*) denote the (unique) optimal completion,

- if $g.k \notin A$, then $\mu(g.k', P') > p_{gk}$ iff $g.k \in Y^*$;
- if $g.k \in A$, then $\mu(g.k', P') < \pi_{gk}$ iff $g.k \in Z^*$.

4. Note that the assumption of diminishing marginal values applies to the goods $g.k'$; formally, $\mu(g.\sigma_g(k)) \geq \mu(g.\sigma_g(k+1))$ for all $k = 1, \ldots, N_g - 1$.

Hence, by bidding marginal values, an agent places winning buy offers on precisely those nonarbitrage opportunities in Y^* and winning sell offers on precisely those arbitrage opportunities in Z^*. Augmenting these offers with buy offers at sell prices, for arbitrage opportunities, and sell offers at buy prices, for nonarbitrage opportunities, ensures optimality.

TargetBidder

It was established above that bidding straight marginal values is optimal in the bidding problem with known prices whenever the optimal completion is unique. It is a simple matter to adjust the StraightMV bidding strategy to ensure optimality without this assumption: first solve for an optimal completion (X^*, Y^*, Z^*), and then bid marginal values to sell the goods in Z^* and buy the goods in $Y^* \setminus Z^*$ ensuring that all sold goods are also bought and no allocated[5] goods are also sold. This idea was implemented in the TAC agent RoxyBot in 2000 [Greenwald and Boyan, 2005].

Generalizing RoxyBot-00's heuristic, we define a family of bidding heuristics called TargetBidder (see Algorithm 5), parameterized by a function h. Like RoxyBot, the TargetBidder heuristics first solve for an optimal completion. The function h governs what prices they bid on the goods in this completion. There are many possibilities; recall from Theorem 5.1 that the set of optimal bids is generally not unique. We consider three instances of TargetBidder, namely TargetPrice, which bids predicted prices, TargetMV, which bids marginal values like RoxyBot-00, and TargetMV*, a slight variant of TargetMV.

Let (X^*, Y^*, Z^*) denote TargetBidder's choice of an optimal completion given pricelines P and Π. Heuristics in this family construct buy offers at sell prices for the goods in Z^* (to ensure they are bought) and sell offers at buy prices for the goods in $Y^* \setminus Z^*$ (to ensure they are not sold). In addition, they place optimal sell offers on the goods in Z^* and optimal buy offers on the goods in $Y^* \setminus Z^*$, as we now explain.

TargetPrice bids p_{gk} to buy the goods in $Y^* \setminus Z^*$ and π_{gk} to sell the goods in Z^*:

$$h(g.k, P, \Pi) = \begin{cases} p_{gk} & \text{if } g.k \in Y^* \setminus Z^* \\ \pi_{gk} & \text{if } g.k \in Z^* \end{cases}$$

Not only does this heuristic solve the (second-price) deterministic bidding

5. Recall that $X \oplus Z \subseteq Y$. Moreover, $X \oplus Z \subseteq Y$ implies $X \subseteq Y \setminus Z$. Hence, $X^* \subseteq Y^* \setminus Z^*$ represents the goods to be allocated.

Algorithm 5 TargetBidder(G, N, P, Π, h)

$(X^*, Y^*, Z^*) \Leftarrow \text{Completion}(P, \Pi)$
for all $g \in G$ **do**
  for $k = 1$ to Z_g^* **do**
    $b_{gk} \Leftarrow \pi_{gk}$
    $a_{gk} \Leftarrow h(g.k, P, \Pi)$
  end for
  for $k = Z_g^* + 1$ to Y_g^* **do**
    $b_{gk} \Leftarrow h(g.k, P, \Pi)$
    $a_{gk} \Leftarrow p_{gk}$
  end for
  for $k = Y_g^* + 1$ to N_g **do**
    $b_{gk} \Leftarrow 0$ {don't buy $g.k$}
    $a_{gk} \Leftarrow \infty$ {don't sell $g.k$}
  end for
end for
return β

problem optimally, it also solves the deterministic *first-price* bidding problem optimally. In first-price auctions with known prices it is suboptimal to place a buy offer above a good's buy price or a sell offer below a good's sell price.

TargetMV bids marginal values to buy the goods in $Y^* \setminus Z^*$ and to sell the goods in Z^*. These marginal values are computed based on unified pricelines. Specifically, $h(g.k, P, \Pi) = \mu(g.k', P')$.

To argue that TargetMV bids optimally in the (second-price) deterministic bidding problem, it suffices to show that these marginal values are at least the buy prices of goods in $Y^* \setminus Z^*$ and at most the sell prices of goods in Z^*:

- $\mu(g.k', P') \geq p_{gk}$, for all $g.k \in Y^* \setminus Z^*$
- $\mu(g.k', P') \leq \pi_{gk}$, for all $g.k \in Z^*$

so that TargetMV successfully buys all the goods it intends to allocate and successfully sells all the goods it intends to sell. By Theorem 3.4,

1. if $g.k \in Y^* \setminus A$, then $\mu(g.k', P') \geq p_{gk}$;
2. if $g.k \in A \setminus Z^*$, then $\mu(g.k', P') \geq \pi_{gk}$; and
3. if $g.k \in Z^*$, then $\mu(g.k', P') \leq \pi_{gk}$.

Hence, by bidding the appropriate marginal values, TargetMV successfully buys all the nonarbitrage opportunities in $Y^* \setminus Z^*$ (Claim 1) and successfully sells all the goods in Z^* (Claim 3). It remains to argue that $\mu(g.k', P') \geq p_{gk}$ for all arbitrage opportunities in $Y^* \setminus Z^*$. But this follows immediately, since $\pi_{gk} \geq p_{gk}$ for all arbitrage opportunities and $\mu(g.k', P') \geq \pi_{gk}$ for all arbitrage opportunities in $Y^* \setminus Z^*$ (Claim 2). Therefore, by the optimal bidding theorem in the known-price case (Theorem 5.1), TargetMV is an optimal bidding heuristic for the deterministic bidding problem.

TargetMV* is similar to TargetMV, except instead of bidding $\mu(g.k', P')$ on the relevant goods, it bids $\mu(g.k', P'^*)$, where $p'^*_{gk} = p_{gk}$ for all $g.k \in Y^* \setminus Z^*$ and $p'^*_{gk} = \infty$ for all $g.k \notin Y^* \setminus Z^*$. In effect, TargetMV* calculates marginal values under the assumption that available goods are restricted to those allocated in the optimal completion. Marginal values of those goods increase, since the value of the optimal acquisition with each remains the same (as the good is *in* the completion), and the value of the optimal acquisition without each can only decrease (as buying opportunities are restricted). Similar reasoning applies to goods the agent seeks to sell. Consequently, TargetMV* places higher buy offers and lower sell offers than TargetMV, from which it follows (by the above argument) that TargetMV* is also optimal.

TargetPrice solves only one completion problem. In the worst case (when $Y^* = N$), both versions of TargetMV calculate $|N|$ marginal values, solving $2|N| + 1$ completion problems in total. In practice (e.g., in TAC games), the optimal completion typically involves a small fraction of all goods in the market, and thus TargetMV and TargetMV* calculate far fewer marginal values than StraightMV.

An Example

Methods that construct bids as if prices are known, or perfectly predictable, can be viewed as heuristic approaches to the problem of bidding under uncertainty (formally specified below in Definition 5.10) in which price predictions are likely to be imperfect. We now consider the performance of the four bidding algorithms defined in this section—StraightMV and the three versions of TargetBidder—in an example in which price predictions are not necessarily correct.

Example 5.9: A TAC travel agent is deciding what to bid on hotels for a client for whom it has already purchased flights. The client's value for travel packages including the Towers and Shanties hotels, respectively, are 1055 and 1000. Flights alone are worthless to the client.

Suppose the agent predicts the clearing price of the Towers to be 80, whereas in reality the price is uniformly distributed in the range $[70, 90]$. Similarly, suppose its prediction for Shanties is 30 and the actual price is $U[20, 40]$. The price distributions for the two hotels are independent.

Given its predictions, the marginal value of the Towers is $1055 - (1000 - 30) = 85$, while the marginal value of the Shanties is $1000 - (1055 - 80) = 25$. StraightMV bids precisely these marginal values: 85 and 25, respectively.

The values of the travel packages with the Towers and Shanties are $1055 - 80 = 975$ and $1000 - 30 = 970$, respectively. Hence, the travel package with the Towers is the unique optimal acquisition. TargetPrice bids the predicted price (80) on Towers and nothing on Shanties. TargetMV bids its marginal value (85) on Towers and nothing on Shanties. TargetMV* assumes that Shanties is not available. Under this assumption, the marginal value of Towers is $1055 - 0 = 1055$. This is the only bid TargetMV* submits.

In Table 5.1, we report the expected scores of StraightMV's, TargetPrice's, TargetMV's, and TargetMV*'s respective bids. It can be shown that TargetMV* is optimal. Interestingly, StraightMV outperforms TargetMV. Although TargetMV bids optimally when prices are known, when prices are unknown it can be advantageous to bid on goods in more than one optimal completion, and even on goods in no optimal completion. StraightMV hedges its bets in this example, improving its chance of getting a feasible trip at the risk of obtaining both hotels, thus paying for one it cannot use. Managing such tradeoffs through hedging is a generally accepted component of good trading practice.

In summary, StraightMV performs optimally in the known-price case, when there is a unique solution to completion. But when there are multiple optimal completions, StraightMV can win too many substitutes. In contrast, the TargetBidder heuristics, which simply pick one solution when many exist, cannot bid on too many substitutes. They always perform optimally when prices are known. Although it was shown in Chapter 4 that trading agents can be designed to predict prices fairly accurately, it is unreasonable to assume that they are clairvoyant, that is, capable of perfectly predicting unknown future prices.

Table 5.1
Evaluating bids by StraightMV and TargetBidder heuristics on Example 5.9.

StraightMV's Expected Score: Bid $(85, 25)$

Winnings	Probability	Utility	Cost	Score	Expected Score
Both hotels	$\left(\frac{3}{4}\right)\left(\frac{1}{4}\right)$	1055	100	955	$179\frac{1}{16}$
Towers only	$\left(\frac{3}{4}\right)\left(\frac{3}{4}\right)$	1055	$77\frac{1}{2}$	$977\frac{1}{2}$	$549\frac{27}{32}$
Shanties only	$\left(\frac{1}{4}\right)\left(\frac{1}{4}\right)$	1000	$22\frac{1}{2}$	$977\frac{1}{2}$	$61\frac{3}{32}$
No hotels	$\left(\frac{1}{4}\right)\left(\frac{3}{4}\right)$	0	0	0	0
Total	1				790

TargetPrice's Expected Score: Bid $(80, 0)$

Winnings	Probability	Utility	Cost	Score	Expected Score
Both hotels	$\left(\frac{1}{2}\right)(0)$	–	–	–	0
Towers only	$\left(\frac{1}{2}\right)(1)$	1055	75	980	490
Shanties only	$\left(\frac{1}{2}\right)(0)$	–	–	–	0
No hotels	$\left(\frac{1}{2}\right)(1)$	0	0	0	0
Total	1				490

TargetMV's Expected Score: Bid $(85, 0)$

Winnings	Probability	Utility	Cost	Score	Expected Score
Both hotels	$\left(\frac{3}{4}\right)(0)$	–	–	–	0
Towers only	$\left(\frac{3}{4}\right)(1)$	1055	$77\frac{1}{2}$	$977\frac{1}{2}$	$733\frac{1}{8}$
Shanties only	$\left(\frac{1}{4}\right)(0)$	–	–	–	0
No hotels	$\left(\frac{1}{4}\right)(1)$	0	0	0	0
Total	1				$733\frac{1}{8}$

TargetMV*'s Expected Score: Bid $(1055, 0)$

Winnings	Probability	Utility	Cost	Score	Expected Score
Both hotels	$(1)(0)$	–	–	–	0
Towers only	$(1)(1)$	1055	80	975	975
Shanties only	$(0)(0)$	–	–	–	0
No hotels	$(0)(1)$	0	0	0	0
Total	1				975

5.4 Bidding with Distributional Price Predictions

As is evident from Example 5.9, heuristics that are optimal given known prices may not be ideal in the more realistic situation of price uncertainty. In this section, we formalize the problem of bidding in simultaneous auctions given a probabilistic model of the auctions' clearing prices. This problem statement generalizes the formal statement of the deterministic bidding problem (Definition 5.2), where we assume prices are known with certainty.

DEFINITION 5.10 STOCHASTIC BIDDING PROBLEM: Given a joint probability distribution f over buyer and seller pricelines P and Π, the *stochastic bidding problem*, or the *bidding problem under uncertainty*, is to identify a surplus-maximizing bid:

$$E_{(P,\Pi)\sim f}\left[\max_{\beta=\langle\vec{b},\vec{a}\rangle, X\oplus Z\subseteq Y} v(X) - \text{Cost}(Y,P) + \text{Revenue}(Z,\Pi)\right],$$

where $Y = \text{Buy}(\vec{b}, P)$ and $Z = \text{Sell}(\vec{a}, \Pi)$.

Bidding under uncertainty is a stochastic optimization problem in which the objective is to maximize expected surplus (allocation value minus procurement costs plus sales revenue) with respect to a given distribution of prices.

To solve an instance of the bidding problem in closed form generally requires that we make assumptions about the distribution f over the auctions' clearing prices. In this section, we develop heuristic solutions to the bidding problem that do not rely on any distributional assumptions. On the contrary, our heuristics, which are based on Monte Carlo simulation, can be applied to any distribution f for which a black box is available from which an agent can draw samples. Adopting terminology from the stochastic optimization literature, we call each such sample from the distribution f a *scenario*.

Throughout this section, we assume the agent can sample S scenarios $(P,\Pi)_1, \ldots, (P,\Pi)_S \sim f$, each representing the realization of a buyer and a seller priceline. Our goal is to evaluate a suite of bidding heuristics geared toward solving the bidding problem under uncertainty. We partition this suite into two classes: (i) those which collapse the available distributional information (i.e., the sample set of scenarios) into a point estimate—an *average scenario*; and (ii) those which exploit all available distributional information. We discuss the "collapsing" heuristics first and the "exploiting" heuristics second.

Bidding Heuristics That Collapse Available Distributional Information

The *expected value method* [Birge and Louveaux, 1997] is a standard way of approximating the solution to a stochastic optimization problem. First, the given distribution is collapsed into a point estimate (e.g., the mean); then, a solution to the corresponding deterministic optimization problem is output as an approximate solution to the original stochastic optimization problem. We can apply this idea directly to the problem of bidding under uncertainty.

DEFINITION 5.11: Given a distribution f over buyer and seller pricelines, with expected values $\bar{P}$ and $\bar{\Pi}$, respectively,

$$\text{EVM}(f) = \max_{\beta=\langle\vec{b},\vec{a}\rangle, X\oplus Z\subseteq Y} v(X) - \text{Cost}(Y,\bar{P}) + \text{Revenue}(Z,\bar{\Pi}),$$

where $Y = \text{Buy}(\vec{b},\bar{P})$ and $Z = \text{Sell}(\vec{a},\bar{\Pi})$.

Note that EVM(f) is an instance of the deterministic bidding problem (Definition 5.2), with pricelines corresponding to the mean point estimates. Theorem 5.1, therefore, gives rise to a class of bidding heuristics that solves this approximation of the stochastic bidding problem optimally.

In practice, without full knowledge of the distribution f, we cannot implement the expected value method; in particular, we cannot compute $\bar{P}$ or $\bar{\Pi}$ so we cannot solve EVM(f) exactly. We can, however, solve a further approximation of this problem in which the expected buyer and seller pricelines $\bar{P}$ and $\bar{\Pi}$ are replaced by an average scenario $(\hat{P},\hat{\Pi})$ (i.e., average buyer and seller pricelines), with components as follows:

$$\hat{P} = \frac{1}{S}\sum_{i=1}^{S} P_i, \qquad \hat{\Pi} = \frac{1}{S}\sum_{i=1}^{S} \Pi_i.$$

The approximate problem is also an instance of the deterministic bidding problem. Moreover, as $S \to \infty$, $\hat{P} \to \bar{P}$ and $\hat{\Pi} \to \bar{\Pi}$ so that Theorem 5.1 gives rise to a class of bidding heuristics that solves EVM(f) optimally. Indeed, TargetMU (see Algorithm 6) and TargetMU* (analogous to TargetMU, but calling TargetMV* instead of TargetMV) are examples of such bidding heuristics.

Algorithm 6 TargetMU(G, N, f, S)

1: sample S scenarios $(P,\Pi)_1,\ldots,(P,\Pi)_S \sim f$
2: compute average scenario $\hat{P}$ and $\hat{\Pi}$
3: $\beta \Leftarrow$ TargetMV$(G, N, \hat{P}, \hat{\Pi})$
4: **return** β

The "U" in TargetMU (and TargetMU*) stands for "utility", and is meant to indicate that the marginal value is computed with respect to an expectation over price distributions. In general we make no technical distinction between a value and utility function, and tend to use these terms somewhat interchangeably. As a usage convention, however, we employ "utility" more extensively when dealing with expectations given an explicit distribution.

By applying the idea underlying the expected value method, it is possible to implement any heuristic that solves the deterministic bidding problem in the stochastic setting: first collapse the distribution (or the available distributional information) into a point price estimate; then apply the deterministic bidding heuristic of choice. Thus, we can define a "U" heuristic counterpart to any of the "V" heuristics. In particular, applying this idea to StraightMV yields the StraightMU bidding heuristic (see Algorithm 7).

Algorithm 7 StraightMU(G, N, f, S)

1: sample S scenarios $(P, \Pi)_1, \ldots, (P, \Pi)_S \sim f$
2: compute average scenario $\hat{P}$ and $\hat{\Pi}$
3: $\beta \Leftarrow$ StraightMV$(G, N, \hat{P}, \hat{\Pi})$
4: **return** β

Bidding Heuristics That Exploit Available Distributional Information

The heuristics discussed in the last section collapse the distributional information contained in the sample set of scenarios down to a point estimate, thereby operating on approximations of the expected buyer and seller pricelines. In this section, we discuss heuristics that more fully exploit any available distributional information. These heuristics seek bids that are effective across multiple scenarios, not in just the average scenario.

First, we add to our test suite of heuristics the average marginal utility bidding heuristic, which characterizes the bidding module of ATTac-01 [Stone et al., 2003], described further in Section 6.3.

Average Marginal Utility

The AverageMU bidding heuristic (Algorithm 8) bids the *average* marginal utility of each unit of each good in each auction. Like StraightMU, AverageMU first samples a set of S scenarios. Next, it computes the marginal value of each unit of each good in each scenario. Then, it averages those marginal values to construct its bids. AverageMU performs $|N|S$ marginal value calculations; hence, it solves $2|N|S$ acquisition problems.

Mathematically, for all goods $g.k$,

$$\begin{aligned}\text{StraightMU}(g.k) &= \mu(g.k', \hat{P}'(g,k)) \\ &= \mu\left(g.k', \sum_{i=1}^{S} P_i'(g,k)\right),\end{aligned}$$

whereas

$$\text{AverageMU}(g.k) = \frac{1}{S}\sum_{i=1}^{S} \mu(g.k', P_i'(g,k)).$$

Algorithm 8 AverageMU(G, N, f, S)

1: $\beta \Leftarrow 0$
2: **for all** $i = 1$ to S **do**
3: $\quad\beta \Leftarrow \beta + \frac{1}{S}\text{StraightMU}(G, N, f, 1)$
4: **end for**
5: **return** β

The next two examples demonstrate that the relative performance of AverageMU and StraightMU depends on the problem instance.

EXAMPLE 5.12: A (TAC) travel agent is deciding whether to reserve the Towers or Shanties hotel for a client for whom it can purchase in and out flights for 700. The hotel clearing prices can be described by two equally likely scenarios: $(1000, 1000)$ and $(100, 100)$. In these scenarios, the first entry corresponds to the Towers hotel, and the second entry to the Shanties. The client's utility for travel packages including the Towers and Shanties, respectively, are 950 and 850. Flights alone are worthless to the client.

We derive the heuristics' respective bids and scores in Table 5.2. AverageMU bids $(225, 75)$, the average of the marginal utilities of the goods in the two scenarios. StraightMU bids $(250, 150)$, the marginal utilities of the goods in the average scenario $(550, 550)$. AverageMU's bids yield an expected score of 75, while StraightMU's yield 25.

EXAMPLE 5.13: Consider once again the setup in Example 5.12. Assume, however, that the hotel clearing prices can be described by two equally likely

Table 5.2
Calculations for Example 5.12. AverageMU's bids are $(225, 75)$, the average of the marginal utilities of the goods in the two scenarios. StraightMU's bids are $(250, 150)$, the marginal utilities of the goods in the average scenario $(550, 550)$. AverageMU outscores StraightMU, 75 to 25.

Scenario	Prices	μ(Towers)	μ(Shanties)
1	$(1000, 1000)$	$250 - 0 = 250$	$150 - 0 = 150$
2	$(100, 100)$	$250 - 50 = 200$	$150 - 150 = 0$
Average	$(550, 550)$	$250 - 0 = 250$	$150 - 0 = 150$

Scenario	AverageMU			StraightMU		
Prices	Winnings	Utility	Cost	Winnings	Utility	Cost
$(1000, 1000)$	no hotels	0	0	no hotels	0	0
$(100, 100)$	Towers	250	100	both hotels	250	200
Average		125	50		125	100

scenarios: $(200, 200)$ and $(100, 0)$. AverageMU's bid is $(175, 50)$, the average of the marginal utilities of the goods in the two scenarios. StraightMU's bid is $(200, 50)$, the marginal utilities of the goods in the average scenario $(150, 100)$. (See Table 5.3.) In this instance, StraightMU outscores AverageMU, 100 to 75.

Table 5.3
Calculations for Example 5.13. AverageMU's bid $(175, 50)$ yields an expected score of 75, and StraightMU's bid $(200, 50)$ yields an expected score of 100.

Scenario	Prices	μ(Towers)	μ(Shanties)
1	$(200, 200)$	$250 - 0 = 250$	$150 - 50 = 100$
2	$(100, 0)$	$250 - 150 = 100$	$150 - 150 = 0$
Average	$(150, 100)$	$250 - 50 = 200$	$150 - 100 = 50$

	AverageMU			StraightMU		
Scenario	Winnings	Utility	Cost	Winnings	Utility	Cost
$(200, 200)$	no hotels	0	0	Towers	250	200
$(100, 0)$	both hotels	250	100	both hotels	250	100
Average		125	50		250	150

AverageMU is an extended version of StraightMU, designed to more fully exploit any available distributional information. RoxyBot-02 [Greenwald and Boyan, 2004] was also an extended version of RoxyBot-00, designed to exploit distributional information.[6] In practice, it is an empirical question (i.e., domain-dependent) which of AverageMU or StraightMU is superior. In contrast, RoxyBot-02's bidding heuristic provably dominates RoxyBot-00's bidding heuristic, assuming the average scenario is indeed a valid sample from the distribution. Next, we present an abstract version of RoxyBot-02's bidding heuristic, which we refer to as BidEvaluator.

Bid Evaluation Heuristics

The BidEvaluator heuristic (see Algorithm 9) evaluates K candidate bids on a fixed set of E sample scenarios, by (i) determining the winnings of each bid, then (ii) solving the allocation problem, given those winnings. The candidate that earns the highest average allocation value is selected.

Algorithm 9 BidEvaluator(G, N, f, E, K)

bestval $\Leftarrow -\infty$
sample E scenarios $(P, \Pi)_1 \ldots, (P, \Pi)_E$ from f
for all k = 1 to K **do**
  $\langle \vec{b}, \vec{a} \rangle \Leftarrow$ TargetMU$(G, N, f, 1)$ {candidate bid}
  currval $\Leftarrow 0$
  for i = 1 to E **do**
    $Y = \text{Buy}(\vec{b}, P_i)$
    $Z = \text{Sell}(\vec{a}, \Pi_i)$
    sval = $\max_{X \oplus Z \subseteq Y} (v(X) - \text{Cost}(Y, P_i) + \text{Revenue}(Z, \Pi_i))$
    currval $\Leftarrow$ currval + $\frac{1}{E}$ sval
  end for{evaluate bid}
  if currval $>$ bestval **then**
    bestval $\Leftarrow$ currval
    bestsol $\Leftarrow \langle \vec{b}, \vec{a} \rangle$
  end if
end for
return bestsol

6. RoxyBot-01 was also an extension of RoxyBot-00 designed to exploit distributional information. The former computed an approximate solution to the "stochastic completion problem", before bidding average marginal utilities.

BidEvaluator generates candidate bids (see step 4) using the TargetMU heuristic, which samples a single scenario, solves for an optimal completion in that scenario, and then constructs a bid by computing the marginal utilities of all goods in this optimal completion.

BidEvaluator is an expensive heuristic. It calculates up to $|N|$ marginal utilities and solves one completion and E allocation problems K times, for a total of $(2|N| + 1 + E)K$ optimization problems in the worst case.

BidEvaluator* is identical to BidEvaluator, except that its candidate bids in step 4 are generated by calling TargetMU* instead of TargetMU. In practice, StraightMU is too expensive to appear in this inner loop, but it would certainly be possible for BidEvaluator to employ other bidding heuristics for candidate generation.

BidEvaluator and BidEvaluator* estimate the expected scores of various bids by evaluating candidates in sample scenarios. Returning to the setup of Example 5.9, we recall that TargetMV*, which bids 1055 on the Towers and 0 on the Shanties, is in fact optimal in this example. Consequently, BidEvaluator* is optimal in the limit as $E, K \to \infty$, since the scenario $(80, 30)$, for example, generates the optimal bidding policy $(1055, 0)$. Moreover, although TargetMV's bidding policy is *not* optimal, BidEvaluator is also optimal in this example in the limit as $E, K \to \infty$, since the scenario $(80, 35)$, for example, generates the optimal bidding policy $(90, 0)$.

Let us explain why adducing a single scenario justifying the optimal bid is sufficient to establish optimality of the BidEvaluator heuristics. As K goes to infinity, the heuristic will eventually consider the scenario, and therefore generate the optimal bid as a candidate. As E goes to infinity, the heuristic will evaluate its candidate bids correctly, and the optimal bid will necessarily come out best among these candidates.

Although BidEvaluator is optimal in the limit in Example 5.9, in our next example, BidEvaluator is not optimal. In fact, none of the bidding heuristics introduced to this point bid optimally in this example, even in the limit.

EXAMPLE 5.14: Imagine a TAC agent that owns an inflight on day 1 and an outflight on day 3, and is looking to reserve the Shanties on days 1 and 2 to complete a travel package of value 1000 for a client. (Suppose the Towers auctions for days 1 and 2 have closed already.)

There are two possible scenarios: with probability 0.5, the auctions will clear at prices 100 and 600, respectively; and with probability 0.5, the auctions will clear at prices 500 and 600, respectively. We abbreviate these scenarios

$(100, 600)$ and $(500, 600)$. The average scenario is $(300, 600)$.

The optimal solutions to this bidding problem involve bidding 500 or more for the hotel on the first day and 600 or more for the hotel on the second day. The expected value of each optimal solution is 100. The (suboptimal) bids placed by all bidding heuristics introduced thus far are shown in Table 5.4.

Table 5.4
Bids placed by all bidding heuristics in Example 5.14. BidEvaluator(SMU) is BidEvaluator with candidate bids generated by StraightMU.

Heuristic	Bids	Expected Value
TargetMU	$(400, 700)$	-150
TargetMU*	$(400, 700)$	-150
StraightMU	$(400, 700)$	-150
AverageMU	$(400, 700)$	-150
BidEvaluator(SMU)	$(400, 500)$	-50
BidEvaluator	$(0, 0)$	0
BidEvaluator*	$(0, 0)$	0
Optimal	$(500, 600)$	100

All of the bidding heuristics discussed in this section are marginal-value based, and none of them are optimal in Example 5.14. This observation led the designers of RoxyBot-06 [Lee et al., 2007] to explore an alternative bidding heuristic that would potentially find superior bids, namely sample average approximation (SAA).

Sample Average Approximation

Like the expected value method, *sample average approximation* is a standard way of approximating the solution to a stochastic optimization problem. The idea is simple: (i) generate a set of sample scenarios, and (ii) solve an approximation of the problem that incorporates only the sample scenarios. Applying the SAA heuristic (see Algorithm 10) involves solving the following approximation of the bidding problem.

Definition 5.15 Sample Average Approximation: Given a set of S

scenarios $(P, \Pi)_1, \ldots, (P, \Pi)_S \sim f$,

$$\mathsf{SAA}((P, \Pi)_1, \ldots, (P, \Pi)_S) =$$

$$\max_{\beta = \langle \vec{b}, \vec{a} \rangle} \sum_{i=1}^{S} \left[\max_{X \oplus Z \subseteq Y} v(X) - \text{Cost}(Y_i, P_i) + \text{Revenue}(Z_i, \Pi_i) \right], \quad (5.1)$$

where, $Y_i = \text{Buy}(\vec{b}, P_i)$ and $Z_i = \text{Sell}(\vec{a}, \Pi_i)$, for all $i = 1, \ldots, S$.

The sample average approximation of the TAC bidding problem implemented in RoxyBot-06 is presented in Appendix B.

Algorithm 10 $\mathsf{SAA}(G, N, f, S)$

1: sample S scenarios $(P, \Pi)_1, \ldots, (P, \Pi)_S \sim f$
2: $\beta \Leftarrow \mathsf{SAA}((P, \Pi)_1, \ldots, (P, \Pi)_S)$
3: **return** β

The problem of bidding under uncertainty can be viewed as a two-stage stochastic program with integer recourse [Birge and Louveaux, 1997]. In the first stage, bids are selected; in the second stage, the allocation problem is solved given the first-stage bids. The objective in a stochastic program is to assign values to the first-stage variables (the bids) that maximize the sum of the first-stage objectives (there are none in the bidding problem) and the expected value of the ensuing objective in the second stage. It is in the second stage that the bidder has *recourse*, and since allocation is an integer linear programming problem, the bidding problem is one with integer recourse. Using the theory of large deviations, Ahmed and Shapiro [2002] establish the following result: the probability that an optimal solution to the sample average approximation of a stochastic program with integer recourse is an optimal solution to the original stochastic optimization problem approaches 1 exponentially fast as $S \to \infty$.

Given time and space constraints, however, it is not always possible to sample sufficiently many scenarios to make any reasonable guarantees about the quality of a solution to the sample average approximation. Hence, the designers of RoxyBot-06 [Lee et al., 2007] proposed a modified SAA heuristic, in which SAA is fed some tailor-made "important" scenarios, and applied this idea to the bidding problem.

The bids that SAA places are prices that appear in one of its scenarios. There is no reason for SAA to bid higher on any good than its highest sampled price, because bidding the highest price is enough to win the good in all scenarios. (Similarly, there is also no reason for SAA to bid lower on any good than its lowest sampled price; instead, it suffices to bid zero.) Hence, SAA cannot win a good if the prices of that good in all of its scenarios are lower than the clearing price. How likely is this possibility?

Each draw from the distribution has an equal chance of being the highest-priced, assuming there are no ties. The probability that all of the sampled scenario prices are lower than the clearing price is $1/(S+1)$, where S is the number of scenarios. In particular, the probability that an SAA agent with 49 scenarios bidding in TAC has a chance to win all eight hotels (i.e., the probability that the price in at least one of its scenarios is higher than the clearing price) is only $\left(1 - \frac{1}{49+1}\right)^8 = 0.98^8 \approx 0.85$.

To remedy this situation, the designers of RoxyBot-06 implemented a variant of SAA. The SAA* heuristic (see Algorithm 11) is a close cousin of SAA, the only difference arising in their respective scenario sets. Whereas SAA samples S scenarios, SAA* samples only $S - |N|$ scenarios. SAA* creates an additional $|N|$ scenarios as follows: for each unit $k \in \{1, \ldots, N_g\}$ of each good $g \in G$, it sets the price of the kth unit of good g to the upper limit of its range of possible prices and, after conditioning on this price setting, it sets the prices of the other goods to their mean values.

Algorithm 11 SAA*(G, N, f, S)

Require: $S \geq |N|$
1: hard-code $|N|$ scenarios $(P, \Pi)_1, \ldots, (P, \Pi)_{|N|}$
2: sample $S - |N|$ scenarios $(P, \Pi)_{|N|+1}, \ldots, (P, \Pi)_S \sim f$
3: $\beta \Leftarrow$ SAA$((P, \Pi)_1, \ldots, (P, \Pi)_S)$
4: **return** β

This concludes the discussion of candidate bidding heuristics for simultaneous auctions. We have detailed algorithms based on a variety of ideas, many involving the use of marginal values. Straight marginal-value bidding can be suboptimal even when prices are known (i.e., when there are multiple optimal completions), and for the more general problem of bidding under uncertainty, none of our proposed marginal-value based bidding heuristics are optimal. The bid evaluation heuristic uses a Monte Carlo method to select among candidate bids, and thus offers the potential to improve quality with computation. However, this heuristic is still not optimal for any particular choice of bid generator, short of one that generates candidates exhaustively in a systematic way. In contrast, the sample average approximation method, which can be viewed as a form of bid evaluation, does approximate optimal bidding in our abstract model.

5.5 Experiments in TAC Travel Auctions

The analytical results and simple example cases in this chapter illustrate some of the possible behaviors of a variety of bidding heuristics, under perfect and imperfect price prediction. To evaluate the performance of these heuristics in a richer market game context, we embedded these heuristics in TAC agents and played them in numerous experimental games. As in most environments of interest, perfect price prediction is not possible in TAC, though agents do have substantial basis to generate informed projections (see Chapter 4).

There are three additional features of our experimental environment that distinguish it from the models employed above:

- Our analysis assumed a second-price model, where the winning bid does not determine price. TAC hotels clear at the 16th highest price, so one of the winning bids actually does determine price. Moreover, since agents may demand multiple units, winning bids on additional units impact the price paid for all units.
- Each of our examples depended on an exogenous price distribution, whereas in the actual TAC domain prices are determined endogenously by the agents' bids. Thus, the performance of a bidding strategy will depend on the other strategies included in the experimental trials.
- Our abstract models are based on one-shot auctions, whereas TAC flights and entertainment tickets are available continuously at time-varying prices, and hotel auctions close one at a time, providing opportunities for agents to revise their bids on other hotels.

Our experimental focus here is on hotel bidding. To simplify the game and reduce variance, we modified the TAC game server to eliminate entertainment trading. The agents employ heuristics from our test suite to construct their bids for hotel auctions. Regarding flights, agents also constructed their bid values as the heuristics dictated, but the marginal-value based agents did not bid on a flight unless that flight's price was near its expected minimum. (The computation of expected minimum future prices is explained in Section 7.1.) The SAA agents explicitly deliberate about the timing of flight purchases, and place bids accordingly (for implementation details, see Appendix B).

Bidding with Point Price Predictions

We conducted three experiments. In the first two, agents employed bidding heuristics that depend on point price predictions. In both these experiments, the agents used Walverine's competitive equilibrium analysis approach to predict hotel prices in the form of point estimates, running tâtonnement for 5000 iterations with α fixed at $\frac{1}{48}$ (see Section 4.4). Flight prices were also predicted in the form of point estimates. For each flight, the agents took as their predicted price the expected minimum future price of that flight.

In our first set of experimental games (1200 of them), we pitted two copies of each of our four heuristics against one another—StraightMV, TargetMV, TargetMV*, and TargetPrice. The agents' average scores, trip values, and costs in these games are listed in Table 5.5. In addition, 95% confidence intervals (for scores only) are plotted in Figure 5.1 (left). These intervals were computed based on 1200 independent observations; scores were averaged across agent type in each game to account for any game dependencies.

Table 5.5
Four-agent experiment: Average scores, trip values, and costs for each bidding heuristic.

Rank	Agent	Score	Trip Value	Cost
1	TargetMV*	2848	8329	5481
2	TargetMV	2842	8278	5436
3	StraightMV	2644	8321	5677
4	TargetPrice	2372	7932	5560

Scorewise, TargetMV* ever so slightly outperforms TargetMV, which outperforms StraightMV, which outperforms TargetPrice. These latter differences are statistically significant (see Figure 5.1). It is interesting to note that StraightMV obtains a higher trip value on average than TargetMV (~ 40), but it does so at a substantially higher cost (~ 240). These differences are also statistically significant (not shown), and arise because StraightMV bids on all goods, not only the goods in a single optimal completion. Finally, TargetPrice is unsuccessful because it places too many losing bids, foregoing too many es-

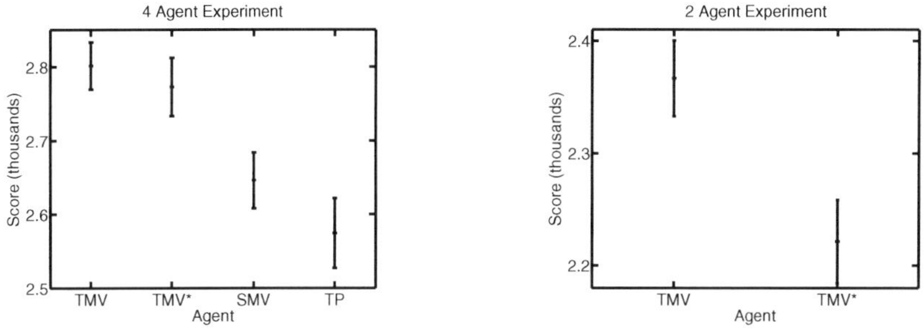

Figure 5.1
Four- and two-agent experiments: scores, with 95% confidence intervals.

sential hotels. It makes up for its losses by buying excess flights, driving up not only flight costs but travel penalties as well, since its ultimate allocation of trips to clients is not entirely satisfactory.

In our second set of experimental games (2400 of them, providing 2400 independent observations as above), we pitted four copies of TargetMV and TargetMV* against one another. The average scores, trip values, and costs in these games are depicted in Table 5.6. The differences between trip values and costs in this experiment are both statistically significant (not shown). Figure 5.1 (right) depicts 95% confidence intervals for scores only.

Table 5.6
Two-agent experiment: Average scores, trip values, and costs for each bidding heuristic.

Rank	Agent	Score	Trip Value	Cost
1	TargetMV	2367	8140	5773
2	TargetMV*	2236	8295	6059

This time, TargetMV outperforms TargetMV*. This outcome can be explained as follows. Embedded in both TargetMV and TargetMV* are optimal bidding heuristics for the deterministic (second-price) bidding problem. TAC hotel bidding is not a second-price auction, however; it is a kth-price k-unit auction. As such, an agent's own bid for a good can determine the price of that good. Thus, the bidders have an incentive to shade their bids downward. But TargetMV* in effect shades its bids *upward*! In so doing, it wins more goods than TargetMV so that it obtains a higher trip value (by 155), but this increase is achieved at an even higher cost (286 more).

This two-agent experiment serves to highlight the distinction between the idealized deterministic bidding problem, and the actual TAC environment. Both TargetMV and TargetMV* are optimal bidding heuristics in the former, but TargetMV is empirically superior in the latter.

Bidding with Distributional Price Predictions

In our third set of experimental games, we embedded in TAC agents each of the bidding heuristics we developed for the bidding problem under uncertainty. The agents in these experiments predicted hotel prices in the form of distributions, represented by sets of sample scenarios. To generate a scenario, the agents (i) sampled a random set of client preferences for each of the other agents, conditioned on its own preferences, and (ii) simulated a simultaneous ascending auction where clients acted as "straightforward" bidders (for a description of both this auction mechanism and this bidding strategy, see Section 7.2). This method of price prediction is similar to the competitive equilibrium analysis approach employed by Walverine. Flight prices were predicted as point estimates using the same technique as in the previous two experiments.

Parameter Settings The parameter settings of the heuristics in the third experiments are shown in Table 5.7.[7] The goal in choosing these parameter settings was to (more or less) equalize total runtimes, listed in the rightmost column of the table. Presumably, all the heuristics (but most notably, AverageMU, the variants of BidEvaluator, and the SAA heuristics) could benefit from higher settings of their parameters.

The heuristics that bid only on the goods in an optimal completion are optimized to bid ∞ on all flights in that optimal completion; they do not bother to calculate the marginal values of their desired flights. This helps explain why the bid construction phase within TargetMU and TargetMU* is so fast. StraightMU is also optimized to stop computing marginal values of additional units of each good once its marginal value hits zero.

Results The agents' average scores, trip values, and costs averaged over 1200 games are shown in Table 5.8, with 95% confidence intervals plotted in Figure 5.2. Scorewise, SAA*, the bidding heuristic that characterizes the TAC-06 winner, RoxyBot-06, is the superior heuristic in this experiment. Only the pure SAA heuristic comes close, with its 95% confidence interval overlapping

7. The heuristics in the first two experiments are not parameterized.

Table 5.7
Parameter settings. E is the number of evaluations, S is the number of scenarios, and K is the number of candidate bids. Breaking down an agent's work into two key steps—price prediction and optimization—the column labeled SG lists the scenario generation (i.e., price prediction) times; the column labeled BC lists the bid construction (i.e., optimization) times. The final column indicates total runtimes. All experiments were run on AMD Athlon(tm) 64 bit 3800+ dual core processors with 2M of RAM. All times are reported in seconds, averaged over 1000 games. The machines were not dedicated, which explains why generating 50 scenarios could take anywhere from 8.7 to 9.4 seconds, on average.

Agent	E	S	K	# of Optimizations	SG	BC	Total
TMU	–	50	–	$2\|N\|+1$	9.4	1.0	10.4
TMU*	–	50	–	$2\|N\|+1$	9.0	1.1	10.1
BE	15	–	25	$(2\|N\|+1+K)E$	7.0	5.3	12.3
BE*	15	–	25	$(2\|N\|+1+K)E$	7.0	4.7	11.7
AMU	–	15	–	$2\|N\|S$	2.3	10.2	12.5
SMU	–	50	–	$2\|N\|$	8.7	1.5	10.2
SAA	–	50	–	N/A	8.8	1.7	10.5
SAA*	–	50	–	N/A	9.0	1.6	10.6

that of SAA* as well as the middle cluster of intervals. That middle cluster contains the TargetBidder heuristics that bid based on marginal values, and the heuristics that evaluate candidate bids generated by these TargetBidder heuristics. The bottom cluster contains the marginal-value based heuristics that do not restrict their bidding attention to goods in one optimal completion.[8]

Table 5.8
Eight-agent experiment: Average scores, trip values, and costs for each bidding heuristic.

Rank	Agent	Score	Trip Value	Cost
1	SAA*	2707	8268	5561
2	SAA	2678	8257	5579
3	BE	2632	8250	5618
4	BE*	2627	8401	5774
5	TMU*	2622	8399	5777
6	TMU	2620	8307	5687
7	AMU	2521	8308	5787
8	SMU	2511	8336	5825

8. Greenwald and Boyan [2004] previously reported that (i) BidEvaluator* outperforms TargetMU* and (ii) StraightMU outperforms AverageMU. Both of these results were deemed statistically significant. There are a number of differences between those experiments and these, most notably the method of price prediction and the agent makeup in each game. In those experiments, prices were sampled from empirical distributions built from past games and four agents encoding each heuristic played in each game. As discussed in Chapter 8, strategic interactions can make a substantial difference in the assessment of trading agent strategies. The results reported here, in which the differences in scores between the two agents in these two pairs are statistically insignificant, should not be interpreted as contradicting past results.

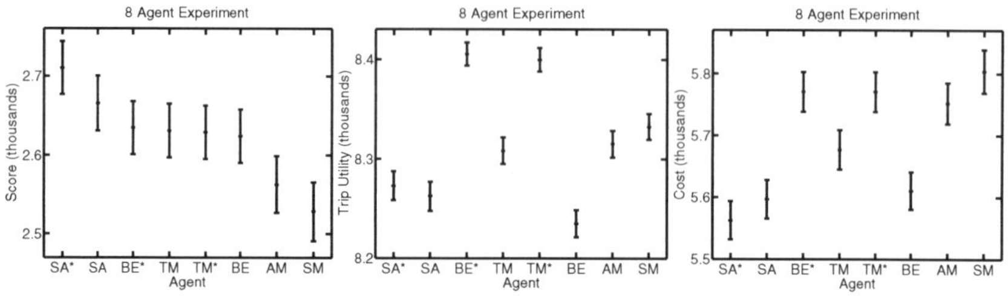

Figure 5.2
Eight-agent experiment: Scores, trip values, and costs with 95% confidence intervals.

Further insight into strategy performance can be obtained by analyzing agent behavior in detail using the statistics presented in Table 5.9. The SAA heuristics—those in the top cluster—are most successful because, working from a global perspective, they minimize costs on both flights and hotels. Indeed, their total costs are lowest among all the heuristics. The savings these heuristics achieve by avoiding costly goods in both markets outweigh the high travel penalties they suffer, and the resulting low trip values.

On hotels in particular, the SAA heuristics place lower bids than all the other heuristics, but they bid on many rooms, thereby hedging their bets. By bidding low prices on many hotels, they maintain flexibility in the event that some hotels turn out to be expensive. Ultimately, the average price they pay per hotel is less than the average across any other cluster, although their total cost is not, since they win many extra hotels. Indeed, their cost of unused hotels is fairly large—exceeded only by those heuristics in the bottom cluster.

The following additional observations can be extracted from the data presented in Table 5.9:

- StraightMU and AverageMU bid fairly low prices on a large quantity of hotels, but not as effectively as the SAA heuristics.
- Although they purchase fewer hotels than the aforementioned heuristics, which hedge their bets, the "star" heuristics incur the largest hotel expenses.
- BidEvaluator puts together short packages for its clients, incurring the lowest hotel cost, but the highest trip penalty, of all.

Although the BidEvaluator heuristics evaluate candidate bids in much the same way as the SAA heuristics, the former are handicapped, as evidenced by BidEvaluator's tendency to buy short packages. None of the heuristics besides the SAAs ever consider postponing their flight decisions until some of the

Table 5.9
Detailed breakdown of performance data in the eight-agent experiments. Boldface indicates large values relative to those of the other agents; italics, small. Note that TargetMU lies in the middle of the pack on all metrics, balancing tradeoffs fairly well. This observation may help explain why the designers of RoxyBot-00 struggled for six years to build an agent that could outperform TargetMU before hitting on their winning approach (see Section 2.3).

	SAA*	SAA	BE*	TMU	TMU*	BE	AMU	SMU
Avg hotel bid	*126*	*95*	636	200	635	207	122	147
# of hotel bids	**74**	**76**	61	63	62	58	**93**	**84**
# of hotels won	15	15	14	13	14	12	17	16
Unused hotel cost	59	51	2	24	2	22	**107**	**118**
Avg hotel cost	60	59	75	69	76	67	56	64
Total hotel cost	970	946	**1057**	955	**1076**	*870*	1003	1056
Hotel bonus	632	626	626	598	621	625	618	634
# of flights won	16.00	16.11	16.00	16.01	16.00	16.01	16.06	16.06
Avg flight cost	286	288	294	294	293	296	295	295
Total flight cost	4591	4650	4713	4721	4693	4740	4748	4747
Travel penalty	358	363	221	289	222	**390**	302	302
Avg trip length	1.60	1.59	1.74	1.66	1.75	*1.51*	1.65	1.64
Avg trip value	8272	8262	8405	8308	8399	8234	8315	8332
Avg cost	5562	5596	5770	5677	5770	5610	5752	5804
Avg score	2710	2665	2634	2631	2628	2623	2562	2528

uncertainty underlying hotel bidding is resolved. Moreover, their hotel bidding does not take advantage of the fact that their flight purchases are not committed until the price reaches its expected minimum. Only the SAA heuristics are designed to explicitly reason about postponing flight decisions.

Thus, the SAA heuristics' apparent superiority in these experiments is likely due to both hotel bidding and flight timing. The reason for incorporating flight timing optimization in SAA is that such an extension is conceptually straightforward within this approach (again, for implementation details, see Appendix B), whereas it is not immediately obvious how to augment any of the other heuristics in a principled way to undertake such reasoning. Additional experimentation may be able to separate these factors, by including versions of the SAA heuristics without the added power of flight timing.

5.6 Discussion

The problem of bidding in interdependent markets given price predictions is fundamental to trading agent design, as reflected in our basic architecture (Table 3.5). In this chapter, we presented an extensive investigation, starting with formal specification of the problem, with and without uncertainty, in a simultaneous-auction framework motivated by TAC-like markets. The backbone of our study was the development of a series of bidding heuristics, each motivated by limitations of the previous. Starting from the simple heuristic of bidding based on marginal value with respect to point price predictions, we progressed to a family of heuristics provably optimal given known prices, to heuristics that make explicit use of price predictions in the form of probability distributions. This latter class can be divided into heuristics that collapse distributions into point prediction values (thereby leaning on the available heuristics for the point-prediction case), and those that exploit distributional information using techniques from stochastic programming. One of these, based on sample average approximation, provably converges to an optimal solution to the stochastic bidding problem.

In practice, the choice of heuristic depends on the availability of computational resources and accurate price predictions. Since our analytical framework included many simplifying assumptions not present in most markets of interest, empirical evaluation—with limited computation and imperfect price prediction models—was necessary. We conducted experiments comparing our test suite of heuristics in the TAC domain: two setups focused on heuristics that use point price prediction, and one compared the heuristics that employ distributional predictions. The results confirm theoretical expectations. Among the heuristics that use point predictions, those that focus bidding on a target set (rather than bidding on everything) come out strongest. Among those employing probabilistic predictions, those that exploit distributional information are generally superior, though the comparisons are not always significant. The winner experimentally was the sample average approximation-based heuristic implemented in RoxyBot-06, the top-scoring agent in TAC-06.

This study culminated in a heuristic that is theoretically justified and empirically successful in both experimentation and tournament competition. The space of heuristics is far from exhausted, however, and we have little basis for gauging the room for improvement. Current state of the art may be close to optimal in stylized models, but is likely much farther off in markets of interest. Another important direction for further study is the influence of strategic interactions. The experimental trials presented here considered only a few strategy configurations, and relative performance may be sensitive to the agent makeup in ways not yet discovered. Finally, extending the model from one-shot simultaneous auctions to a model that includes sequentiality would likely lead to new heuristic ideas, and yet more effective autonomous bidding in a broader class of interdependent market environments.

6 Machine Learning and Adaptivity

When developing a trading agent, it is important to keep in mind that there is not likely to be a bidding strategy that is optimal in all contexts. Rather, an agent's performance is necessarily a function of the overall environment that is created by the other traders. This feature of trading domains—that action effects can depend on the actions of other agents—is a defining property of *multiagent systems*.

The development of ATTac, one of the top-performing agents in three of the first four TAC events, was motivated by the challenge of automatically learning from, and adapting to, aspects of the economy that may be difficult to predict a priori. In particular, as explored in Chapters 4 and 5, the future prices in the hotel markets are particularly crucial for TAC decision making, and (Walverine's competitive equilibrium approach notwithstanding) potentially quite dependent on the bidding strategies of the other agents.

In this chapter, we demonstrate successful adaptive behaviors in two versions of ATTac. The first section presents ATTac-00's adaptive approach to hotel bidding, designed to deal with the potentially skyrocketing prices of TAC-00. The remainder of the chapter provides an in-depth treatment of ATTac-01's machine-learning approach to hotel price prediction. The agent used learned probability distributions over future closing prices within its average marginal utility bidding strategy for TAC hotel bidding.

6.1 Adaptivity for Last-Moment Bidding

In a TAC game instance, the only information available to the agents are price quotes—an agent's individual bids are not observed by others. After each game, transaction-by-transaction data are available, but the lack of within-game information precludes competitors from building detailed models of opponent strategies to assist in decision making. Nonetheless, ATTac-00 adapted its behavior in three different ways:

1. *Adaptable timing of bidding modes:* the agent adapted how long before the end of the game its final bids would be placed, based on network latencies observed during the game,

2. *Adaptable strategy for bid determination:* in solving the acquisition problem in its inner loop, ATTac-00 relied on an integer linear programming (ILP)

solver, but reverted to a greedy solver in cases where the ILP solver failed to complete in a timely manner, and

3. *Adaptable hotel bidding:* the agent predicted the prices of hotels based on their closing prices in recent games.

In this section, we focus on the third, most relevant, aspect of ATTac-00's adaptivity. Details of the other two aspects are provided by Stone et al. [2001].

ATTac-00's Adaptive Hotel-Bidding Strategy

Hotel bidding in TAC-00 was particularly challenging due to the extreme volatility of prices near the end of the game. As described in the TAC-00 portion of Section 2.3, several TAC-00 agents bid their marginal values for each desired hotel room (often in excess of 1000) right before the end of the game. But this strategy was not widely adopted until near the end of the competition. During the preliminary rounds, few agents bid their marginal values, and those that did (including Aster and RoxyBot), generally dominated their competitors (see the preliminary round scores in Appendix A, Table A.2). Such agents were *high bidders*, always winning the hotels on which they bid, but paying far less than their bids. Having observed a successful strategy during the preliminary rounds, other agents, including ATTac-00, adopted this high bidding strategy during the actual competition. The result: many negative scores. Prices skyrocketed in the last moments of the game when suddenly 16 high bids arrived for popular hotels.

Since agent strategies were being updated until the start of the finals, there was no way to identify a priori whether hotel prices would actually skyrocket during the tournament. Should hotel prices eventually become very high, an agent would either end up paying too high a price for the hotel rooms or else fail to procure travel packages for some of its clients. Indeed, the good hotel (called "Grand" in TAC-00) on days 2 and 3 turned out to be the most contentious during the finals, with prices escalating wildly at times. The bad hotel on the same days was also fairly contentious.

To account for this uncertainty, ATTac-00 employed an adaptive strategy. It divided the eight hotel rooms into four equivalence classes, exploiting symmetries in the game (hotel rooms on days 1 and 4 should be in equal demand as should rooms on days 2 and 3), assigned baseline estimates to the expected prices of these hotel types, and then adjusted these estimates based on the observed prices during the tournament. Specifically, if the average price for a hotel type over all of the past games in the finals was greater than the baseline estimate, the agent used the empirical average as its predicted price for the current game. Along with the agent's current holdings, these price predictions were input to ATTac-00's acquisition solver.[1]

One additional method for predicting whether hotel prices would skyrocket in a given game is to notice who the participants were and whether or not they tended to be high bidders in past games (see Figure 6.1). Although such information was not available via the server's API, a game's participants were always published beforehand on the TAC web page. By automatically downloading this information from the web (a practice whose legality was questioned, but ultimately allowed by the GameMaster for TAC-00), and matching against a precompiled database of which agents were high bidders in the recent past, ATTac-00 used the predicted hotel prices (rather than current prices) only in games with three or more high bidders involved: in games with fewer high bidders, the prices of hotel rooms almost never skyrocketed.[2] As it turned out, all but one of ATTac's games in the semifinals, and all games in the finals, involved several high bidders, thus triggering the use of predicted hotel prices.

Note that because ATTac-00's models of which agents are high bidders were precompiled, this aspect of the strategy was not adaptive. Hence, it could have failed had many new agents become high bidders during the finals. But in practice, most agents revealed their tendencies toward high-bidding during the week prior to the finals.

Other TAC-00 agents also had to cope with the problem of escalating hotel prices. Recall from Section 3.2 that RoxyBot-00 manipulated the hotel pricelines in a nonlinear fashion to reflect the expected increase in cost of buying multiple units of the same hotel. In contrast, ATTac-00's strategy assumed linear prices for all open hotels.[3] Though ATTac-00's means of adaptation in its hotel-bidding strategy was straightforward, ATTac was the only TAC-00 agent to condition its strategy during the finals on the observed hotel prices during the finals themselves.

Controlled empirical testing (detailed below) indicates that ATTac-00's bidding strategy is effective in situations in which hotel prices do indeed escalate, while it does not lead to significantly degraded performance when

1. ATTac-00 did not pose the full-blown completion problem, but rather considered the selling of goods in a separate module; see Section 7.3.

2. The only way for the price to escalate was if high bidders bid for a combined total of 16 rooms in the same hotel. With just two high bidders, that could happen only if all of their clients were to stay in the same hotel on the same night, an unlikely scenario given the TAC parameters.

3. ATTac-01's hotel-bidding strategy, described in Section 6.3, incorporates nonlinear pricelines.

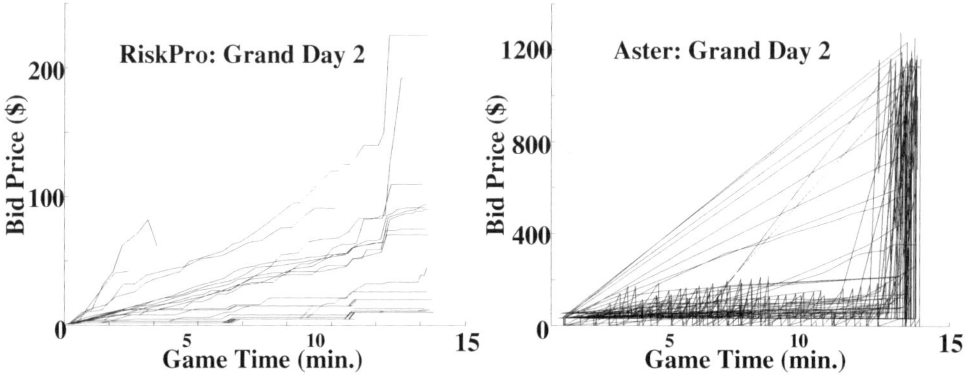

Figure 6.1
Graphs of two different agents' bidding patterns over many games. Each line represents one game's worth of bidding in a single auction. Left: RiskPro never bids over 250 in the games plotted. Right: Aster, a high bidder, consistently bids over 1000 for rooms.

they do not. First, we describe the acquisition solver employed by ATTac-00 to compute Y^*. The same acquisition solver is also used extensively by ATTac-01, whose learning-based strategy is the topic of Section 6.3.

ATTac's Acquisition Solver

As defined in Chapter 3, a core subproblem for TAC agents is the acquisition problem: finding a set of goods to purchase, Y^*, so as to assemble a most profitable allocation of goods to clients, X^*, given a set of pricelines P encoding a set of holdings and prices for all goods. A complete treatment of the acquisition problem appears in Chapter 3. This section serves as a brief recap of the issues as they are addressed by the ATTac agents presented in this chapter.

ATTac solves acquisition, rather than completion. Whenever deciding what goods to bid on to *buy* it assumes that it will not sell any of its current sellable holdings (i.e., its entertainment tickets). In a separate calculation (see Section 7.3), it determines and places sell bids for each of its currently owned entertainment tickets. But until they are actually sold, the buyer pricelines assign them zero cost. Note that this assumption is in contrast to the unified pricelines used by RoxyBot-00 as presented in Section 3.2.

As pointed out in Section 3.2, though the general acquisition problem is NP-hard, it can be solved tractably in TAC via ILP. RoxyBot's ILP solution appears in Appendix B. ATTac's is documented in Stone et al. [2001]. The solution to the ILP is a value-maximizing allocation of owned resources to clients (X^*) along with a list of resources to purchase (Y^*). Using the linear programming package LPsolve, ATTac is usually able to find the globally optimal solution in under 0.01 seconds on a 650 MHz Pentium II. However, since ILP is an NP-complete problem, some inputs can lead to a great deal of search over the integrality constraints (the constraints that specify that only whole units of goods can be purchased and allocated), and therefore significantly longer solution times. When only ACQ($\cdot$) is needed (as opposed to X^* and Y^*), the upper bound produced by LPsolve prior to the search over the integrality constraints, known as the *LP relaxation*, can be used as an estimate. The LP relaxation can always be generated very quickly.

As discussed in Section 3.2, this method is not by any means the only possible means of solving the acquisition problem. Indeed, ATTac-00 used a randomized greedy strategy as a fallback for the cases in which the linear program took too long to solve [Stone et al., 2001]. ATTac-01 (Section 6.3) instead relied extensively on the LP relaxation.

Controlled Testing of Adaptive Bidding

In order to evaluate ATTac-00's adaptive hotel-bidding strategy in a controlled manner, we ran several game instances with ATTac-00 playing against two variants of itself[4]:

1. HighBidder always solved the acquisition problem, taking as input the current hotel prices (as opposed to using baseline estimates and averages of past prices) for all open hotels.
2. LowBidder also solved the acquisition problem using current hotel prices, but limited its bids for hotel rooms to at most $ASK + 50$ (as opposed to the full marginal value, which can exceed 1000).

At the extremes, with ATTac-00 and seven HighBidders playing, at least one hotel price skyrockets in every game since all agents bid very high for the hotel rooms. On the other hand, with ATTac-00 and seven LowBidders playing, hotel prices never skyrocket since all agents but ATTac-00 bid close to the price quote. Our goal was to measure whether ATTac-00 could perform

4. An additional sensible variant would be an agent that takes as input to the acquisition problem the maximum of each hotel's current price and its baseline estimate. However, because the baseline estimates only arose in the creation of the adaptive agent, we used HighBidder and LowBidder as representative nonadaptive strategies.

well in both extreme scenarios as well as various intermediate ones. Table 6.1 summarizes our results.

Table 6.1
The difference between ATTac's score and the score of each of the other seven agents averaged over all games in a controlled experiment.

#high	agent 2	agent 3	agent 4	agent 5	agent 6	agent 7	agent 8
7 (14)	←	9526	———	———	———	——→	
6 (87)	←	10679	———	———	——→		1389
5 (84)	←	10310	———	——→		←	2650
4 (48)	←	10005	——→		←——	———	4015
3 (21)	←	5067	→		←——	———	3639
2 (282)	←	*209*		←——	———	———	2710

Each row of Table 6.1 corresponds to a different number of high-bidding agents in the game; for example, the row labeled with #high $= 4$ corresponds to ATTac-00 playing with four copies of variant 1 (HighBidder) and three copies of variant 2 (LowBidder). In the first column, we also show in parentheses the number of games played for the results in each row.

Each column labeled agent i shows the difference between ATTac's score and the score of agent i averaged over all games. Results for identical agents are averaged to obtain a single average score difference for each type of agent in each row. Scores above the stair-step line are for HighBidder (variant 1) and scores below the line are for LowBidder (variant 2). In all experiments, these differences are positive, showing that ATTac-00 outscored all other agents on average. Statistical significance was computed from paired t-tests; all results are significant at the 0.001 level except for the one marked in italics. As mentioned above, if the number of HighBidders is greater than or equal to three, we expect the price for contentious hotels to rise, and in all such scenarios ATTac-00 significantly outperforms all the other agents. The large score differences appearing in the top rows of Table 6.1 are due to the fact that the other agents get large, negative scores since they buy many expensive hotel rooms. In general, ATTac's average raw score (not shown in the table) decreased with increasing numbers of HighBidders, as hotel prices tended to skyrocket more often, affecting all agents adversely.

In these experiments, ATTac-00 always uses its adaptive hotel price predictions, even when there are fewer than three HighBidders. In the last row, when the number of HighBidders is two, very little bidding up of hotel prices is expected and in this case, we do not get statistical significance relative to the two HighBidders (agent 2 and agent 3), since their strategies are nearly identical to ATTac's in this case. We do get high statistical significance relative to LowBidder, however. Thus, ATTac's adaptivity to hotel prices seems to help when hotel prices do skyrocket and does not seem to prevent ATTac-00 from winning on average when they do not.

The results of Table 6.1 provide strong evidence for ATTac's ability to adapt robustly to varying numbers of competing agents that bid up hotel prices near the end of the game. Note that ATTac-00 is *not* designed to perform well against itself. If eight copies of ATTac-00 play against each other repeatedly, they will all favor the same hotel rooms and thus consistently *all* get large negative scores. In the case that it is known that all other agents will play the ATTac-00 strategy, an agent is better off placing no bids and accepting a score of zero, than bidding like ATTac-00.

This exercise also provides a stark illustration of the multiagent nature of TAC. The quality of a given strategy depends on the other strategies in the environment, and so in general we must consider combinations of strategies in evaluating an agent's performance. For example, the combination of all agents playing ATTac-00 is *unstable* (as are all LowBidder or all HighBidder), in that at least one agent would be better off changing strategies. We explore the issue of stable strategy combinations in TAC in Chapter 8 using game-theoretic analysis.

6.2 Learning Distributions for Hotel Price Prediction

When the rules changed in 2001 to eliminate the possibility of last-moment bidding for hotels, the straightforward adaptivity described above was no longer necessary. In its place, a much richer bidding problem was introduced in which a randomly chosen hotel auction closes each minute, thus necessitating periodic bids in all open hotel auctions. Nonetheless, hotel price prediction remains a critical prerequisite for bid construction.

This section details ATTac-01's learning-based approach to hotel price prediction. In order to predict hotel prices as accurately as possible, ATTac uses a machine-learning technique that examines the hotel prices actually paid in previous games to predict *distributions* over future prices in the current game [Stone et al., 2003]. Section 6.3 then shows how the resulting predictions can be embedded in a complete hotel-bidding strategy.

Representing predictions as distributions is useful because of the inherent uncertainty regarding hotel prices: they depend on many unknown factors, such as the time at which the hotel auction will close, who the other agents are, what kind of clients have been assigned to each agent, etc. Thus, predicting the closing price of a hotel auction *exactly* is hopeless. Instead, ATTac regards each hotel closing price as a random variable that can be estimated, conditional on the current state of knowledge (i.e., number of minutes remaining in the game, ASK price of each hotel, flight prices, etc.). An agent might then attempt to predict this variable's conditional expected value. However, ATTac's bidding strategy, which is a variant of AverageMU, requires that the agent predict not point estimates, but rather the *entire* conditional distribution so that it can *sample* hotel prices as in Section 5.4.

The Learning Problem

A *supervised learning* problem takes as input a set of labeled training examples, with each example represented as a set of feature values and a corresponding target label. The output is a function that maps the features to the labels, ideally covering the training examples accurately, as well as generalizing to unseen examples drawn from the same distribution as the training set.

To set up hotel price prediction in TAC as a learning problem, we gathered a set of training examples from previously played games. We defined a set of features for describing each example that together are meant to comprise a snapshot of all the relevant information available at the time each prediction is made. All of our features are real-valued; a couple of the features can also take on a special value $\perp$ indicating "value unknown".

We used the following basic features:

- The number of minutes remaining in the game.
- The price of each hotel room—specifically, the current ASK price for rooms that have not closed or the actual selling price for rooms that have closed.
- The closing time of each hotel room.
- The prices of each of the flights.

To this basic list, we added a number of redundant variations, which we thought might help the learning algorithm by aggregating information into potentially useful individual features:

- The closing price of hotel rooms that have closed (or $\perp$ if the room has not yet closed).

• The ASK price of hotel rooms that have not closed (or $\perp$ if the room has already closed).

• The closing time of each hotel room minus the closing time of the room whose price we are trying to predict.

• The number of minutes from the current time until each hotel room closes.

The TAC-01 rules explicitly prohibited agents from downloading information from the TAC web pages to identify one's opponents during the play of a game. Hence, ATTac-01 did not know who its opponents were during the seeding rounds in 2001, although this information was available at the end of each game and used during training. In the semifinals and finals, the agents in each heat remained constant; hence, ATTac was aware of the identities of its competitors. In preparation for the semifinals and finals, the following features were added to ATTac's learner:

• The number of agents playing (ordinarily eight, but sometimes fewer, for instance if one or more agents crashed).

• A bit for each player indicating whether or not that agent participated in this game.

We trained specialized predictors for predicting the price of each type of hotel room. One predictor was specialized for predicting only the price of the Towers day 1, another for predicting the Shanties day 2, etc. This would seem to require eight separate predictors. However, similarly to ATTac-00, ATTac-01 exploits the game's natural symmetry about its middle in the sense that we can create an equivalent game by exchanging the hotel rooms on days 1 and 2 with those on days 4 and 3 (respectively), and by exchanging the inbound flights on days 1, 2, 3, and 4 with the outbound flights on days 5, 4, 3, and 2 (respectively). That is, for every game used for training, we create a second artificial game that is identical except that whatever happened on day 1 in the original game happened on day 4 in the artificial game, etc. Thus, with appropriate transformations, the outer days (1 and 4) can be treated equivalently, and likewise for the inner days (2 and 3), reducing the number of specialized predictors by half.

We also created specialized predictors for predicting in the first minute after flight prices had been quoted but prior to receiving any hotel price information. Thus, a total of eight specialized predictors were built (for each combination of Towers vs. Shanties hotel, inner vs. outer day, and first minute vs. not first minute).[5]

We trained our predictors to predict not the actual closing price of each room per se, but rather how much the price would increase: the difference between the closing price and the current ASK price. We thought that this might be an easier quantity to predict, and, because our predictor never outputs a negative number when trained on nonnegative data, this approach also ensures that we never predict a closing price below the current ASK.

From each of the previously played games, we were able to extract many examples. Specifically, for each minute of the game and for each room that had not yet closed, we extracted the values of all of the features described above at that moment in the game, plus the actual closing price of the room (which we are trying to predict). The closing price is the label for that training example in the supervised learning problem.

Note that during training, there is no problem extracting the closing times of all of the rooms. During the actual play of a game, we do not know the closing times of rooms that have not yet closed. However, we do know the exact probability distribution for closing times of all of the rooms that have not yet closed. Therefore, to sample a vector of hotel prices, we can first sample according to this distribution over closing times, and then use our predictor to sample hotel prices conditioned on these sampled closing times.

The Learning Algorithm

Having described the learning problem, we are now ready to present details of ATTac's learning algorithm.[6] Briefly, we solved this learning problem by first reducing to a multiclass, multilabel classification problem (or alternatively a multiple logistic regression problem), and then applying boosting techniques developed by Schapire and Singer [1999, 2000] combined with a modification of boosting algorithms for logistic regression proposed by Collins et al. [2002]. The result is a new machine-learning algorithm for solving conditional density estimation problems, described in detail in the remainder of this section. Table 6.2 shows pseudocode for the algorithm.

Abstractly, we are given pairs $(x_1, y_1), \ldots, (x_m, y_m)$ where each x_i belongs to a space X and each y_i is in $\mathbb{R}$. In our case, the x_i are the auction-specific feature vectors described above; for some n, $X \subseteq (\mathbb{R} \cup \{\perp\})^n$. Each target quantity y_i is the difference between closing price and current price.

5. The predictors evaluated in Chapter 4 were the first-minute combinations.

6. This section, adapted from [Stone et al., 2003], was written in large part by Robert Schapire.

Table 6.2
The boosting-based algorithm for conditional density estimation.

Input: $(x_1, y_1), \ldots, (x_m, y_m)$ where $x_i \in X$, $y_i \in \mathbb{R}$
positive integers k and T

Compute breakpoints: $b_0 < b_1 < \cdots < b_{k+1}$ where

- $b_0 = \min_i y_i$
- $b_{k+1} = \max_i y_i$
- $b_1, \ldots, b_k$ chosen to minimize $\sum_{j=0}^{k} q_j \ln q_j$ where $q_0, \ldots, q_k$ are fractions of the y_i in $[b_0, b_1), [b_1, b_2), \ldots, [b_k, b_{k+1}]$ (using dynamic programing)

Boosting:

- for $t = 1, \ldots T$:

  –compute weights $W_t(i, j) = \dfrac{1}{1 + e^{s_j(y_i) f_t(x_i, j)}}$
  where $s_j(y)$ is as in Eq. (6.2)
  –use W_t to obtain base function $h_t : X \times \{1, \ldots, k\} \to \mathbb{R}$ minimizing
  $\sum_{i=1}^{m} \sum_{j=1}^{k} W_t(i, j) e^{-s_j(y_i) h_t(x_i, j)}$ over all decision rules h_t considered. The decision rules can take any form. In our work, we use "decision stumps," or simple thresholds on one of the features.

Output sampling rule:

- let $f = \sum_{t=1}^{T} h_t$
- let $f' = (\overline{f} + \underline{f})/2$ where

$$\begin{aligned} \overline{f}(x, j) &= \max\{f(x, j') : j \le j' \le k\} \\ \underline{f}(x, j) &= \min\{f(x, j') : 1 \le j' \le j\} \end{aligned}$$

- to sample, given $x \in X$

  –let $p_j = \dfrac{1}{1 + e^{-f'(x, j)}}$
  –let $p_0 = 1, p_{k+1} = 0$
  –choose $j \in \{0, \ldots, k\}$ randomly with probability $p_j - p_{j+1}$
  –choose y uniformly at random from $[b_j, b_{j+1}]$
  –output y

Given a new x, our goal is to estimate the conditional distribution of y given x.

We proceed with the working assumption that all training and test examples (x, y) are i.i.d. (i.e, drawn independently from identical distributions).

Although this assumption is false in our case (for example because the agents, including ours, are changing over time), it seems like a reasonable approximation that greatly reduces the difficulty of the learning task.

Our first step is to reduce the estimation problem to a classification problem by breaking the range of the y_i into bins:

$$[b_0, b_1), [b_1, b_2), \ldots, [b_k, b_{k+1}]$$

for some breakpoints $b_0 < b_1 < \cdots < b_k \leq b_{k+1}$ where for our problem, we chose $k = 50$.[7] The endpoints b_0 and b_{k+1} are chosen to be the smallest and largest y_i values observed during training. We choose the remaining breakpoints $b_1, \ldots, b_k$ so that roughly an equal number of training labels y_i fall into each bin. (More technically, breakpoints are chosen so that the entropy of the distribution of bin frequencies is maximized.)

For each of the breakpoints b_j ($j = 1, \ldots, k$), the learning algorithm attempts to estimate the probability that a new y (given x) will be at least b_j. Given such estimates p_j for each b_j, we can then estimate the probability that y is in the bin $[b_j, b_{j+1})$ by $p_{j+1} - p_j$ (and we can then use a constant density within each bin). We thus have reduced the problem to one of estimating multiple conditional Bernoulli variables corresponding to the event $y \geq b_j$, and for this, we use a logistic regression algorithm based on boosting techniques as described by Collins et al. [2002].

Our learning algorithm constructs a real-valued function $f : X \times \{1, \ldots, k\} \to \mathbb{R}$ with the interpretation that

$$\frac{1}{1 + \exp(-f(x, j))} \tag{6.1}$$

is our estimate of the probability that $y \geq b_j$, given x. The negative log likelihood of the conditional Bernoulli variable corresponding to y_i being above or below b_j is then

$$\ln\left(1 + e^{-s_j(y_i) f(x_i, j)}\right),$$

where

$$s_j(y) = \begin{cases} +1 & \text{if } y \geq b_j \\ -1 & \text{if } y < b_j. \end{cases} \tag{6.2}$$

We attempt to minimize this quantity for all training examples (x_i, y_i) and

7. We did not experiment with varying k, but expect that the algorithm's performance is not sensitive to k, assuming sufficiently large values.

all breakpoints b_j. Specifically, we try to find a function f minimizing

$$\sum_{i=1}^{m}\sum_{j=1}^{k} \ln\left(1 + e^{-s_j(y_i)f(x_i,j)}\right).$$

We use a boosting-like algorithm described by Collins et al. [2002] for minimizing objective functions of exactly this form. Specifically, we build the function f in rounds. On each round t, we add a new base function $h_t : X \times \{1, \ldots, k\} \to \mathbb{R}$. Let

$$f_t = \sum_{t'=1}^{t-1} h_{t'}$$

be the accumulating sum. Following Collins et al. [2002], to construct each h_t, we first let

$$W_t(i,j) = \frac{1}{1 + e^{s_j(y_i)f_t(x_i,j)}}$$

be a set of weights on example-breakpoint pairs. We then choose h_t to minimize

$$\sum_{i=1}^{m}\sum_{j=1}^{k} W_t(i,j)e^{-s_j(y_i)h_t(x_i,j)} \tag{6.3}$$

over some space of "simple" base functions h_t. For this work, we considered all "decision stumps" h of the form

$$h(x,j) = \begin{cases} A_j & \text{if } \phi(x) \geq \theta \\ B_j & \text{if } \phi(x) < \theta \\ C_j & \text{if } \phi(x) = \perp, \end{cases}$$

where $\phi(\cdot)$ is one of the features described above, and θ, A_j, B_j, and C_j are all real numbers. In other words, such an h simply compares one feature ϕ to a threshold θ and returns a vector of numbers $h(x,\cdot)$ that depends only on whether $\phi(x)$ is unknown ($\perp$), or above or below θ. Schapire and Singer [2000] show how to efficiently search for the best such h over all possible choices of ϕ, θ, A_j, B_j, and C_j. (We also employed their technique for "smoothing" A_j, B_j, and C_j.)

When computed by this sort of iterative procedure, Collins et al. [2002] prove the asymptotic convergence of f_t to the minimum of the objective function in Equation (6.3) over all linear combinations of the base functions. For this problem, we fixed the number of rounds to $T = 300$. Let $f = f_{T+1}$

be the final predictor.

As noted above, given a new feature vector x, we compute p_j as in Equation (6.1) to be our estimate for the probability that $y \geq b_j$, and we let $p_0 = 1$ and $p_{k+1} = 0$. For this to make sense, we need $p_1 \geq p_2 \geq \cdots \geq p_k$, or equivalently, $f(x, 1) \geq f(x, 2) \geq \cdots \geq f(x, k)$, a condition that may not hold for the learned function f. To force this condition, we replace f by a reasonable (albeit heuristic) approximation f' that is nonincreasing in j, namely, $f' = (\overline{f} + \underline{f})/2$ where $\overline{f}$ (respectively, $\underline{f}$) is the pointwise minimum (respectively, maximum) of all nonincreasing functions g that everywhere upper-bound f (respectively, lower-bound f).

With this modified function f', we can compute modified probabilities p_j. To sample a single point according to the estimated distribution on $\mathbb{R}$ associated with f', we choose bin $[b_j, b_{j+1})$ with probability $p_j - p_{j+1}$, and then select a point from this bin uniformly at random. Expected utility according to this distribution is easily computed as

$$\sum_{j=0}^{k} (p_j - p_{j+1}) \left(\frac{b_{j+1} + b_j}{2} \right).$$

6.3 ATTac-01

We now present the details of ATTac's hotel-bidding algorithm which takes advantage of the learned price predictions described in Section 6.2. This section serves also as the main overview of the ATTac-01 agent, one of the top performers in TAC-01 and TAC-03. In some regards, this presentation would be most appropriately placed in Chapter 7, where specialized TAC bidding strategies are described. However, an understanding of the overall ATTac-01 strategy and its hotel strategy in particular is necessary to understand the learning experiments presented in this chapter. Discussions of ATTac's flight-bidding and entertainment-bidding components are reserved for Sections 7.1 and 7.3, respectively. Our discussion of hotel bidding proceeds top-down.

Overview

Table 6.3 depicts a high-level overview of ATTac-01. The italicized portions are described in the remainder of this section or in Chapter 7. The acquisition solver described in Section 6.1 is a subroutine called throughout the algorithm.

Table 6.3
ATTac's high-level algorithm. The italicized portions are described in the remainder of this section, or elsewhere in the book as indicated in parentheses.

When the first flight price quotes are issued:

- Compute a target set of goods Y^* by solving the acquisition problem given current holdings and *expected prices* (i.e., using expectations over the learned distributions)
- Buy the flights in Y^* for which *expected cost of postponing commitment* exceeds the *expected benefit of postponing commitment* (Section 7.1)

Starting one minute before each hotel close:

- Compute a target set of goods Y^* by solving the acquisition problem given current holdings and *expected prices* (i.e., using expectations over the learned distributions)
- Buy the flights in Y^* for which *expected cost of postponing commitment* exceeds *expected benefit of postponing commitment* (30 seconds) (Section 7.1)
- Bid *hotel room average marginal utilities* given holdings (including any new flights) and *expected hotel purchases* (30 seconds)

Last minute: Buy remaining flights as required by Y^*

In parallel (continuously): Buy/sell entertainment tickets based on their *average utilities* (Section 7.3)

Cost of Additional Rooms

ATTac's hotel price predictor generates linear price predictions, that is, a single estimate of the price of each hotel independent of its own bidding behavior. Such estimates might be accurate in cases where the agent's demands are modest relative to the overall market (for example, in a large economy where perfect competition prevails). In TAC, however, each hotel auction involves only eight agents competing for 16 mutually desirable hotel rooms. Therefore, even a single agent demanding more than a few rooms can have an appreciable effect on prices. This effect should be taken into account when constructing bids.

One approach, taken by RoxyBot-00 (Section 3.2), is to build nonlinear pricelines, thereby modeling the agent's effect on uniform prices. ATTac-01 implements this idea based on the simplifying assumption that the nth highest bid in a hotel auction is roughly proportional to c^{-n} (over the appropriate range of n) for some $c \geq 1$. It takes as a baseline the situation where the agent buys two rooms—its average share given that there are 16 rooms and eight agents. In this baseline bid set, it assumes that its predicted hotel price p is the 16th highest unit bid (counting ATTac's two units plus 14 others). Beyond two, successfully bidding on another unit moves the price-setting offer to the 15th highest from the baseline set, then the 14th, and so on, thus raising the price for all rooms by a factor of c: one or two rooms each cost p, but three each cost pc, four each cost pc^2, five each cost pc^3, etc. Thus, in total, one room costs p, two rooms cost $2p$, four cost $4pc^2$, five cost $5pc^3$, etc.

The constant c was calculated from the data of several hundred games during the TAC-01 seeding round. In each hotel auction, the ratio of the 14th and 18th highest bids (reflecting the most relevant range of n) was taken as an estimate of c^4, and the (geometric) mean of the resulting estimates was taken to obtain $c = 1.35$.

When using this method, three heuristics are applied to improve stability and to avoid pathological behavior. First, prices below 1 are replaced by 1 in estimating c. Second, $c = 1$ is used for purchasing fewer than two hotel rooms. Third, hotel rooms are divided into early-closing and late-closing (and cheap and expensive) ones, and the c values from the corresponding subsets of auctions of the seeding rounds are used in each case.

ATTac compiles the resulting price estimates into buyer pricelines which it feeds to its acquisition solver. Assigning higher costs to larger purchase volumes tends to spread out ATTac's demand across different hotel auctions.

Hotel Average Marginal Utilities

Using the hotel price prediction module described above coupled with a model of its own effect on the economy, ATTac-01 is equipped to determine its bids for hotel rooms. ATTac-01 employs a version of the AverageMU bidding heuristic (Algorithm 8 defined in Section 5.4), sampling from its learned distributions.

As noted above, by the TAC-01 rules, it is advisable to periodically submit bids in all open hotel auctions, because a random one closes each minute. Thus every minute, for each hotel auction that is still open, ATTac-01 computes a bid under the assumption that that auction will close next. If the auction does not close next, then it will have a chance to revise its bids. Using the full minute between closing times for computation (or 30 seconds if there are flights to consider as well), ATTac-01 divides the available time among the different open hotel auctions and generates as many price samples as possible for each hotel. Hotel auctions are considered one at a time, with bids for previously considered hotels treated as commitments.[8] With the idea that commitments to inexpensive hotels are less constraining than commitments to expensive

8. This aspect of ATTac's strategy is a departure from the standard AverageMU heuristic, which computes all bids in parallel.

ones, and based on informal experimentation, they are considered in order of increasing expected price. In the end, ATTac-01 bids the average marginal utility for each of the rooms. The evidence in Section 5.5 notwithstanding, AverageMU turned out to be a reasonably effective bidding heuristic for ATTac as it used it to finish at the top of the standings in TAC-01 and TAC-03. The algorithm is described precisely and with explanation in Table 6.4.

Table 6.4
ATTac's algorithm for generating hotel bids.

For each hotel h (in order of increasing expected price), repeat until time bound:

1. Generate a random closing order for all open hotels.
2. Conditioned on this order, sample hotel closing prices from predicted price distributions.
3. Encode the agent's current and projected holdings, the sampled hotel prices, and the current flight and entertainment prices in pricelines P. To compute projected holdings, assume outstanding bids above sampled prices are winning bids, since they cannot be withdrawn.
4. for $i = 0, \ldots, n$
   - Compute $U_i = \text{ACQ}(P(h, i))$
     - –Recall from Chapter 3 (prior to Definition 3.7) that $P(h, i)$ denotes a set of buyer pricelines identical to P except that $\vec{p}_h$ is replaced by a vector with i zeros and ∞ thereafter: i.e., the agent holds i units of h and there are no further buying opportunities for that good.
     - –Estimate $\text{ACQ}(P(h, i))$ using an LP relaxation.
     - –Note that $U_0 \leq U_1 \leq \cdots \leq U_n$: the utilities are monotonically nondecreasing given free disposal: owning additional hotel rooms cannot make an agent worse off.
5. The (average marginal) utility of the ith unit of each hotel is the mean of $U_i - U_{i-1}$ over all the samples.
6. Note further that we expect $U_1 - U_0 \geq U_2 - U_1 \geq \cdots \geq U_n - U_{n-1}$: the utility differences are *usually* monotonically nonincreasing because, as discussed in Section 3.3, monotonicity violations are caused by complementarity, and additional units of the same hotel are unlikely to be complements. Though counterexamples do exist, nonmonotonicity in TAC is rare.
7. For all units i such that the marginal utility $(U_i - U_{i-1})$ is at least the current price, bid this marginal utility on the ith unit. As long as the monotonicity condition noted in Step 6 holds, the desired number of units will be purchased regardless of the eventual closing price.

One additional complication regarding hotel auctions is that bids are not fully retractable. According to the beat-the-quote rule, any replacement bid must offer at least $ASK + 1$ for all units the standing bid was winning at ASK. This rule leads to the challenge of predicting an agent's holdings referred to in Section 3.1. If the current bid includes offers at ASK for units that ATTac-01 no longer wants, it may be advantageous to refrain from changing the bid in the hopes that another agent will outbid it.[9] That is, the current bid may have a higher expected value than the best possible new bid. To address this issue, ATTac-01 samples from the learned price distributions to estimate the values of the current and proposed bids, and only submits the proposed bid if its estimated value is higher. For each price sample, the value of a bid is determined by solving the allocation problem given the set of goods that would be acquired by that bid at those prices, as is done by BidEvaluator (Algorithm 9).

6.4 ATTac-01 Results

This section presents empirical results deferredstrating the effectiveness of the ATTac-01 strategy. Though a full specification of ATTac's flight and entertainment strategies are deferred until Chapter 7, the experiments are presented here because they are designed to test the hotel price prediction and bidding strategies presented in this chapter.

Competition Results

First, we summarize ATTac's performance in the TAC-01, TAC-02, and TAC-03 tournaments.[10] These summaries of its performance provide evidence of the strategy's overall effectiveness, but, due to the small number of games in the competitions, are anecdotal rather than scientifically conclusive. In the next section, we present controlled experiments that provide more conclusive evidence of the proficiency of the decision-theoretic and machine-learning approaches embedded within ATTac-01.

TAC-01

Of the 19 teams that entered the qualifying round, ATTac-01 was one of eight agents to make it to the TAC-01 finals, consisting of 24 games among the same eight agents. As summarized in Section 2.3 with further details in Appendix A, Section A.2, the final game came down to a close contest between ATTac-01 and livingagents, with livingagents coming out on top.

Nonetheless, as ATTac's developers are quick to point out, postgame anal-

9. For further explanation of this point, including an example, see the discussion of beat-the-quote in the case study of Walverine's hotel bidding (Section 7.2).

10. ATTac-00, presented in Section 6.1, did not use learned hotel price predictions. ATTac has not participated in the competitions since TAC-03.

ysis indicated that livingagents had more favorable client preferences in the finals. Based on the preference adjustment detailed in Section 8.3, ATTac-01 had the highest handicapped score. The final scores, as well as the handicapped scores, are shown in Appendix A, Table A.4.

TAC-02

A year after the TAC-01 competition, ATTac-01 was reentered in the TAC-02 competition using the models trained at the end of TAC-01. Specifically, the price predictors were left unchanged throughout (no learning). ATTac-01 was the top-scoring agent in the seeding round, as shown in Appendix A, Table A.6.

On the one hand, it is striking that ATTac-01 was able to finish so strongly in a field of agents that had presumably improved over the course of the year. On the other hand, most agents were being tuned, for better and for worse, while ATTac-01 was consistent throughout. In particular, we are told that SouthamptonTAC experimented with its approach during the later days of the round, perhaps causing it to fall out of the lead (by weighted score) in the end. During the 14-game semifinal heat, ATTac-01, which was now restored with its learning capability and retrained over the data from the 2002 seeding round, finished sixth out of eight, thereby failing to reach the finals.

There are a number of possible reasons for this sudden failure. One relatively mundane, but also most likely, explanation is that the agent had to change computational environments between the seeding rounds and the finals, and there may have been a bug or computational resource constraint introduced. Another possibility is that due to the small number of games in the semifinals, ATTac-01 simply got unlucky with respect to clients and the interaction of opponent strategies. It might also have been plausible that the training data from the 2002 qualifying and seeding round data were less representative of the 2002 finals than the training data from 2001; and/or that the competing agents improved significantly over the seeding round while ATTac-01 remained unchanged. However, as described in Section 4.6, the TAC-02 price prediction study suggests the bug hypothesis is most plausible. Another agent (kavayaH) succeeded at learning based on the 2002 data. Meanwhile, according to one of the two accuracy measures used in that study, the ATTac-01 predictor from 2001 outperforms all other predictors from 2002, including the (presumably buggy) ATTac-02 predictor, on the data from the 2002 semifinals and finals; according to the other accuracy measure and over this same 2002 data set, it finishes second only to Walverine.

TAC-03

TAC-03 provided still further evidence that there was a bug in the ATTac-02 learning module. In that competition, ATTac-01 was entered exactly as it ran in TAC-01, specifically with the same trained hotel prediction models. Despite not having been improved for two years, ATTac achieved the top score in the competition. Complete scores are shown in Appendix A, Table A.8.

Controlled Experiments

ATTac's success in the TAC-01 and TAC-03 competitions demonstrates its effectiveness as a complete system. However, since competing agents differ along multiple dimensions, we cannot readily isolate successful strategy components based on the outcome of a competition. In this section, we report controlled experiments specifically designed to test the efficacy of ATTac's machine-learning approach to price prediction.

Varying the Predictor

In our first set of experiments, we attempted to determine how the quality of ATTac's hotel price predictions affects its performance. To this end, we devised seven price prediction schemes, varying considerably in sophistication and inspired by approaches taken by other TAC competitors, and incorporated these schemes into our agent. We then played these seven agents against one another repeatedly, with regular retraining as described below. These experiments can be seen as a variant of the general bidding experiments presented in Section 5.5. Specifically, the experiments provide another data point relating the performance of StraightMU and AverageMU.

Following are the seven hotel prediction schemes that we used, in decreasing order of sophistication:

- ATTac-01$_s$: This is the "full-strength" agent based on boosting that was used during the tournament. (The s denotes sampling.) In the terminology of Chapter 5, it is a variant of AverageMU.
- Cond'lMean$_s$: This agent samples prices from the empirical distribution of prices from previously played games, conditioned only on the closing time of the hotel room (a subset of the features used by ATTac-01$_s$). In other words, it collects all historical hotel prices and breaks them down by the time at which the hotel closed (as well as room type, as usual). The price predictor then simply samples from the collection of prices corresponding to the given

closing time. This strategy is also a variant of AverageMU.

- SimpleMean$_s$: This agent samples prices from the empirical distribution of prices from previously played games, without regard to the closing time of the hotel room (but still broken down by room type). It uses a subset of the features used by Cond'lMean$_s$. Again, it is a variant of AverageMU.
- ATTac-01$_E$, Cond'lMean$_E$, SimpleMean$_E$: These agents predict in the same way as their corresponding predictors above, but instead of returning a random sample from the estimated distribution of hotel prices, they deterministically return the expected value of the distribution. (The E denotes expected value.) These agents are all instances of StraightMU.
- CurrentBid: This agent uses a very simple predictor that always predicts that the hotel room will close at its current price. This is the same predictor as the one used by the strategy known as straightforward bidding (SB: see Section 7.2), though its ultimate use within ATTac is quite different from its use in SB.

In every case, whenever the price predictor returns a price that is below the current price, it is replaced with the current price (since prices cannot decrease).

We also included in our experiments an eighth agent EarlyBidder, inspired by the livingagents agent [Fritschi and Dorer, 2002]. EarlyBidder used SimpleMean$_E$ to predict closing prices, determined a target set of goods to acquire, and then placed bids for those goods at sufficiently high prices to ensure that they would be purchased (1001 for all hotel rooms, just as livingagents did in TAC-01) right after the first flight quotes (Section 2.3). It then never revised these bids.

Each of these agents requires training, based on data from previously played games. However, in designing experiments, we are faced with a "chicken and egg" problem: to run the agents, we need to first train the agents using data from games in which they were involved, but to get this kind of data, we need to first run the agents. To get around this problem, we ran the agents in phases. In Phase I, which consisted of 126 games, we used training data from the seeding, semifinals, and finals rounds of TAC-01. In Phase II, lasting 157 games, we retrained the agents once every six hours using all of the data from the seeding, semifinals, and finals rounds as well as all of the games played in Phase II. Finally, in Phase III, lasting 622 games, we continued to retrain the agents once every six hours, but now using only data from games played during Phases I and II, and not including data from the seeding, semifinals and

Table 6.5
The average relative scores ($\pm$ standard deviation) for eight agents in the three phases of our controlled experiment in which the hotel price prediction algorithm was varied. The relative score of an agent is its score minus the average score of all agents in that game. The agent's rank within each phase is shown in parentheses.

Agent	*Relative Score*		
	Phase I	*Phase II*	*Phase III*
ATTac-01$_E$	105.2 ± 49.5 (2)	131.6 ± 47.7 (2)	166.2 ± 20.8 (1)
ATTac-01$_s$	27.8 ± 42.1 (3)	86.1 ± 44.7 (3)	122.3 ± 19.4 (2)
EarlyBidder	140.3 ± 38.6 (1)	152.8 ± 43.4 (1)	117.0 ± 18.0 (3)
SimpleMean$_E$	-28.8 ± 45.1 (5)	-53.9 ± 40.1 (5)	-11.5 ± 21.7 (4)
SimpleMean$_s$	-72.0 ± 47.5 (7)	-71.6 ± 42.8 (6)	-44.1 ± 18.2 (5)
Cond'lMean$_E$	8.6 ± 41.2 (4)	3.5 ± 37.5 (4)	-60.1 ± 19.7 (6)
Cond'lMean$_s$	-147.5 ± 35.6 (8)	-91.4 ± 41.9 (7)	-91.1 ± 17.6 (7)
CurrentBid	-33.7 ± 52.4 (6)	-157.1 ± 54.8 (8)	-198.8 ± 26.0 (8)

finals rounds.

Table 6.5 shows how the agents performed in each of these phases. Much of what we observe in this table is consistent with our expectations. The more sophisticated boosting-based agents (ATTac-01$_s$ and ATTac-01$_E$) clearly outperformed the agents based on simpler prediction schemes. Moreover, with continued training, these agents improved markedly relative to EarlyBidder, whose performance improved from Phase I to Phase II, but then degraded. We also see the performance of the simplest agent, CurrentBid, which does not employ any kind of training, significantly decline relative to the other data-driven agents.

On the other hand, some phenomena in this table surprised us. Most surprising was the failure of bidding based on learned distributions to outperform bidding based on point summaries of these distributions.[11] The ATTac strategy relies heavily on sampling from the predicted distributions of hotel prices.Yet these results indicate that using an estimate of a hotel's expected price is preferable to using the sampled distribution directly. We speculate that this may be because an insufficient number of samples are being used (due to computational limitations) so that the numbers derived from these samples have too high a variance. Another possibility is that the method of using samples consistently overestimates expected utility because it assumes the agent can behave with perfect knowledge for each individual sample—a property of

11. In contrast, AverageMU comes out on top of StraightMU in the experiments reported in Section 5.5, albeit by an insignificant margin. This difference in experimental outcomes again emphasizes that the method of price prediction, and perhaps even more so the configuration of agent strategies, is a key factor in determining which bidding heuristics yield better results.

ATTac's approximation scheme. The experiments of Section 5.5 suggest that alternative ways of using distributional information can prove advantageous. Finally, as ATTac-01 uses sampling at several different points (computing hotel expected values, deciding when to buy flights, pricing entertainment tickets, etc.), it is possible that sampling is beneficial for some decisions while detrimental for others. For example, when directly comparing versions of ATTac with sampling used at only subsets of the decision points, the data suggest that sampling for the hotel decisions is most beneficial, while sampling for the flights and entertainment tickets is neutral at best, and possibly detrimental. This outcome is not entirely surprising given that the distributional bidding approach is motivated primarily by the task of bidding for hotels.

We were also surprised that Cond'lMean$_s$ and Cond'lMean$_E$ eventually performed worse than SimpleMean$_s$ and SimpleMean$_E$. One possible explanation for this outcome is that the simpler model predicts just as well as the more sophisticated model, perhaps because closing time is not a very informative feature, or because the current price is more informative. Other things being equal, the simpler model has the advantage that its statistics are based on all of the price data, regardless of closing time, whereas the conditional model makes each prediction based on only an eighth of the data (since there are eight possible closing times, each equally likely).

In addition to agent performance, it is possible to measure the inaccuracy of the eventual predictions, at least for the nonsampling agents, as done in Section 4.6. For these agents, we measured the root mean-squared error of the predictions made in Phase III. These were: 56.0 for ATTac-01$_E$, 66.6 for SimpleMean$_E$, 69.8 for CurrentBid, and 71.3 for Cond'lMean$_E$. Thus, we see that the lower the error of the predictions (according to this measure), the higher the score (correlation $R = -0.88$).

ATTAC-01 VS. EARLYBIDDER

In a sense, the two agents that finished at the top of the standings in TAC-01 represented opposite ends of a spectrum. Agent livingagents uses a simple open-loop strategy, committing to a set of desired goods right at the beginning of the game, while ATTac-01 uses a closed-loop, adaptive strategy.

The open-loop strategy relies on the other agents to stabilize the economy and create consistent final prices. In particular, if all eight agents are open-loop and place very high bids for the goods they want, prices will skyrocket, evaporating any potential profit (see Section 6.1). Thus, a set of open-loop agents would tend to get negative scores—the open-loop strategy is a parasite, in a manner of speaking.

Table 6.6 shows the results of running 27 games with seven copies of the open-loop EarlyBidder and one of ATTac-01. The price predictors are all from Phase I in the preceding experiments. EarlyBidder's high-bidding strategy backfires, as it ends up overpaying significantly for its goods. As our experiments above indicate, ATTac-01 may have performed even better were it allowed to train on the games of the ongoing experiment as well.

Table 6.6
Results of running ATTac-01 against seven copies of EarlyBidder over the course of 27 games. EarlyBidder achieves high trip value, but overpays significantly, resulting in low scores.

Agent	Score	Trip Value
ATTac-01	2431 ± 464	8909 ± 264
EarlyBidder(7)	-4880 ± 337	9870 ± 34

EarlyBidder has the advantage of buying a minimal set of goods. That is, it never buys more than it can use. On the other hand, it is susceptible to unexpected prices in that it can get stuck paying high prices for the hotel rooms it decides to buy.

Notice in Table 6.6 that the average value of the EarlyBidder's clients is significantly greater than that of ATTac-01's clients. Thus, the fact that ATTac-01 earns a higher score is accounted for entirely by the cost of the goods. EarlyBidder tends to pay exorbitant prices, while ATTac-01 tends to steer clear of the more expensive hotels. ATTac-01's clients' value suffers, but the cost savings are well worth it.

Compared to the open-loop strategy, ATTac's strategy is relatively stable against itself. Its main drawback is that as it changes its decision about what goods it wants and as it may also buy goods to hedge against possible price changes, it can end up getting stuck paying for some goods that are ultimately useless to any of its clients. Of course at bidding time, the hope is that the benefits of owning extra goods in order to obtain a higher utility would outweigh the dangers of buying too much. But hedging too aggressively in this way can lead to significant waste.

Table 6.7 shows the results of seven copies of ATTac-01 playing against each other and one copy of the EarlyBidder. Again, training is from the seeding round and finals of TAC-01: the agents do not adapt during the experiment. Included in this experiment are three variants of ATTac-01, each with a different value of the *flight-lookahead* parameter. This parameter is explained further in Section 7.1, but in brief, higher values bias the agent toward committing sooner to flight purchases. There were three copies each of the agents with *flight-lookahead* set to 2 and 3 (ATTac(2) and ATTac(3), respectively), and one ATTac-01 agent with *flight-lookahead* set to 4 (ATTac(4)).

Table 6.7
Results of running the EarlyBidder against seven copies of ATTac-01 over the course of 197 games. The three different versions of ATTac-01 had slightly different *flight-lookahead* settings.

Agent	Score	Trip Value
EarlyBidder	2869 ± 69	10079 ± 55
ATTac(2)	2614 ± 38	9671 ± 32
ATTac(3)	2570 ± 39	9641 ± 32
ATTac(4)	2494 ± 68	9613 ± 55

From the results in Table 6.7 it is clear that ATTac-01 does better when committing to its flight purchases later in the game (ATTac(2) as opposed to ATTac(4)). Additionally, in comparison with Table 6.6, the configuration of agents represented here does significantly better overall. That is, having many copies of ATTac-01 in the pool does not cause them to suffer. It also does not cause EarlyBidder to suffer; in fact with all other agents playing ATTac, EarlyBidder comes out on top. It gets a significantly higher value for its clients and only pays slightly more than the ATTac-01 agents (as computed by value minus score).

The results in this section suggest that the unpredictability of the closing prices is one of the determining factors between the effectiveness of the two strategies (assuming nobody else is using the open-loop strategy). We speculate that with large price fluctuations from game to game, the closed-loop strategy (ATTac) should do better, but with stable prices, the open-loop strategy could do better.

6.5 Summary

This chapter presented examples of the effective use of adaptivity and machine learning in the creation of autonomous bidding agents. The flexibility engendered by these types of approaches is necessary in economies where an agent does not know ahead of time what price patterns will arise. TAC prices are unpredictable in this way, in part because each agent entered in the competition is created by a different research group using different methods and focusing on different research challenges. Thus, the competing agents' strategies are complex and unpredictable. Many real markets, in which the strategies of the other bidders are not known a priori, are also unpredictable for similar reasons.

Section 6.1 chronicled ATTac-00's ability to adapt to unpredictable hotel prices by revising its predictions over the course of a few games with identical agents. Specifically, ATTac-00 determined empirically which hotels were likely to skyrocket in the finals of TAC-00.

Then, Sections 6.2–6.4 presented and evaluated ATTac-01's bidding strategy, which is based on learned hotel price distributions. This learning was accomplished using a novel boosting-based learning algorithm that took as input training data from hundreds of TAC game instances involving tens of different agents over the course of several months.

Both of these agents were successful in the TAC competitions, finishing at the top of the standings in TAC-00, TAC-01, and TAC-03. More significantly, the controlled experiments presented in this chapter isolate the adaptivity and learning ability of these agents as keys to their success.

In addition to its emphasis on adaptivity and learning, this chapter served to present the ATTac trading agents. In particular, a high-level overview of the ATTac algorithm was presented in Table 6.3, and ATTac's bidding approach for hotels, based on an average marginal utility calculation, was explained in Table 6.4.

Chapter 7 includes ATTac's approach to the TAC flight and entertainment ticket markets, as well as several bidding strategy case studies of other TAC agents pertaining to all three types of TAC markets: flights, hotels, and entertainment tickets.

7 Market-Specific Bidding Strategies

The preceding chapters examined some general issues (price prediction, bidding under uncertainty, and learning) that arise in a broad range of trading environments. Although many of the models, methods, and analyses presented rely on particular features or experience from the TAC travel environment, most of the concepts and insights developed cut across market mechanisms and subject domains.

In this chapter we undertake a deeper examination of the respective TAC markets, and present some of the techniques developed by TAC agents specifically addressing the particulars of those markets. Recall that the three categories of travel goods are exchanged through qualitatively different market mechanisms:

- Flights are sold via a *posted-price mechanism.*
- Hotels are sold via *multiunit, simultaneous ascending auctions* (SimAAs).[1]
- Entertainment tickets are traded via *continuous double auctions* (CDAs).

To deal with this diversity of markets, agents must consider specialized techniques that take into account the form of auction mechanism, as well as domain-specific context relating to particular combinations of travel goods and agent preferences that characterize the TAC scenario.

The analysis of particular TAC markets presented below illustrates the kind of market-specific reasoning agent designers have employed in developing successful strategies for the TAC travel game. Despite the specificity of the TAC context, general lessons emerge here as well. To a large degree, models and techniques developed for TAC markets also apply directly to other instances of these mechanism types: posted-price, SimAA, and CDA. At a higher level, concepts and insights deriving from the in-depth analysis of specific markets can also be applied analogously to a broad class of trading domains.

7.1 Flight Buying

The three components of bidding decisions we have described throughout the book are what goods to offer to trade, at what price, and when. Most of the

1. The more standard abbreviation is "SAA", but in this book SAA is already taken to abbreviate sample average approximation.

models and algorithms presented thus far address the problems of *what goods* and *what price*. For flight purchases in TAC, the key question is *when*. What price is not an issue at all, since the agent decides simply whether to accept the posted price or not. What flights *is* an issue, though the standard method of solving an acquisition problem given current and predicted prices appears to address this choice quite adequately. Thus, our investigation of TAC flight buying presents a case study in bid timing.

Posted-Price Mechanisms

The hallmark of a posted-price mechanism is that a designated party sets a price that the other parties can "take or leave". Posted-price markets may differ regarding limits on quantity, the process or frequency by which prices change, or other features. In the case of TAC flight markets, TACAir submits sell bids for flights to and from the destination city on each day. Because the quantity supplied by TACAir is effectively unlimited (in practice, a large number sure to exceed the demand of TAC agents)—and no agents are allowed to sell flights—the TACAir *posted price* prevails at auction. Agents are notified of posted prices through price quotes, and can buy any quantity of flights by submitting bids at or above these prices.

TACAir updates prices according to a known stochastic process, as specified in Section 2.1. The process has both revealed and hidden state, but is not affected at all by the actions (i.e., flight purchases) of the TAC agents. In this sense, the flight auctions qualify as second-price pseudo-auctions, the abstract model studied in Chapter 5.

Flight Purchase Tradeoffs

The fundamental issue regarding TAC flight decisions is a natural one: balancing concern about future price increases with the benefit of delaying commitment to travel on particular days. If flight prices were nonincreasing, agents would simply delay purchases until the end of the game, when all uncertainty about hotel markets (i.e., what rooms each agent wins) has been resolved. By committing to a flight any earlier, an agent risks finding that its choice was suboptimal, based on subsequent shifts in hotel prices or availability. An extreme (but not unusual) instance of this risk is that it may end up wasting the flight entirely if it cannot obtain hotel rooms to compile a feasible trip on the corresponding days.

In the first TAC tournament (TAC-00), the random walk of flight prices was unbiased: perturbations were distributed $\sim U[-10, 10]$. Thus, at any time prices were equally likely to go up or down,[2] so agents were just as well off delaying any intended purchase. Indeed, this was the conclusion reached by almost all TAC-00 agents, and therefore all flight purchasing took place just before game end.

The modification of flight price dynamics for TAC-01 was designed to introduce a substantive tradeoff. Sure enough, the TAC entrants modified their flight-buying strategies in response. For example, postcompetition analysis revealed that two TAC-01 finalists (Caisersose and livingagents) always acquired all their flights immediately, on average purchasing them about one minute into the game. Urlaub01 was even faster on average (46 seconds), even though it occasionally picked up some extra flights late into the game. ATTac made its flight-bidding decisions based on a cost-benefit analysis, described in some detail below. This led to some immediate purchases and others spread out in the game, with an overall mean time of about two minutes into the game. The remaining agents in the finals deliberated longer, with Tacsman buying its flights on average over four minutes after game start.

Experience in TAC-02 and TAC-03 confirmed the substantive tradeoff in flight purchasing. Vetsikas and Selman [2003] established through extensive experimentation with WhiteBear that agents could gain by explicitly projecting the price dynamics of individual flight tickets. Nevertheless, fixed policies remained prevalent, and most flight purchases still occurred at the beginning of the game (e.g., Walverine purchased all of its flights within the first four seconds in TAC-02 games). In order to accentuate this tradeoff further, and encourage a wider spread of flight purchase activity (specifically, less purchasing up-front), the TACAir flight-pricing policy was changed once more in 2004. The 2004 rules, which prevail today, yield a more varied set of flight price trajectories, including a significant fraction expected to decrease in early stages of the game. As noted in Section 2.3, the changes led designers of existing agents (e.g,. WhiteBear [Vetsikas and Selman, 2005], and Walverine as described in the case study below) to reconsider their flight strategies. New agents such as Mertacor [Toulis et al., 2006] also devoted special attention to flight price timing.

2. A minor exception is when the price is right at its lower or upper limit—an event sufficiently infrequent to be negligible in the current discussion.

Flight-Pricing Analysis

Efforts to make deliberate decisions about the flight purchase tradeoff start with a model of flight price evolution. As described in Section 2.1, flight prices follow a random walk with a bias that is determined by a hidden parameter that is chosen randomly at the start of the game. Specifically, for flight f the hidden parameter x_f is chosen from the integers in $[-10, 30]$, and the perturbation at any time t is then generated stochastically as a function of x_f and t according to Equations (2.1) and (2.2). Whereas flight price perturbations are designed to increase in expectation given no information about the hidden parameter, conditional on this parameter, prices may be expected to increase, decrease, or stay constant.

An agent can model this process by maintaining a distribution $\Pr(x_f)$ for each flight f. The distribution is initially uniform on [-10,30], then updated using Bayes' rule given the observed perturbations Δ at each iteration:

$$\Pr(x_f \mid \Delta) = \alpha \Pr(x_f) \Pr(\Delta \mid x_f),$$

where α is a normalization constant.

Given this distribution over the hidden x_f parameter, the expected perturbation for the next iteration, $E[\Delta' \mid x_f]$, is simply the average of the upper and lower perturbation bounds as defined by Equation (2.2). Averaging over the given distribution over x_f, we have $E[\Delta'] = \sum_{x_f} \Pr(x_f) E[\Delta' \mid x_f]$.

The distribution over x_f can also be used to project the point at which the flight price will reach its minimum. For each value of x_f, we can use Monte Carlo simulation to derive a distribution over minimum future prices. The overall distribution is then weighted by $\Pr(x_f)$ to calculate the expected value of the minimum flight price. RoxyBot (and heuristics in the experiments of Section 5.5) used this method to time flight purchases, deciding to purchase a desired flight only if its price is near its expected minimum.

Flight Cost-Benefit Analysis: ATTac Case Study

ATTac-01 based its flight-bidding decisions on a cost-benefit analysis of the underlying timing tradeoff. The cost of postponing the purchase of flights is due to the fact that prices tend to increase over time, whereas the benefit of postponing commitments to flights is that additional information about the eventual hotel prices becomes known.

In this section, we describe how ATTac computes the incremental cost of postponing bidding for a particular flight, and the respective value of delaying commitment. During each bidding cycle, ATTac begins by computing a target set of goods given its current holdings and an average of its predicted hotel price distributions. This target set is either the optimal acquisition, if unique, or an arbitrarily selected optimal acquisition. After estimating both the cost and the benefit of delaying the purchase of each flight in this optimal acquisition, ATTac purchases exactly those flights for which the calculated cost of postponing commitment is greater than or equal to the calculated benefit.

ATTac evaluates the *cost* of postponement of each relevant flight by estimating the flight's future prices. These estimates are computed using an approximate analog of Bayesian updating, as described above, defined with respect to the 2001 flight-price process. The horizon of future times to consider is governed by ATTac's *flight-lookahead* parameter. With a value of l, ATTac defines the cost of postponement to be the average predicted increase of the flight costs $1, 2, \ldots, l$ minutes in the future. Because flight prices tend to increase over time, a higher value of *flight-lookahead* leads to a higher estimated cost of postponing flight purchases, and thus a tendency to buy flights earlier. Recall that the experiment reported in Table 6.7 varied the value of *flight-lookahead* from 2 to 4, indicating that a value of 2 worked best. In TAC-01, ATTac started with *flight-lookahead* set to 3, but changed to 2 by the end of the finals in order to delay its flight commitments further.

ATTac's algorithm for determining the *benefit* of postponing commitment is similar to its hotel-bidding algorithm (see Table 6.4). The former is detailed, with explanations, in Table 7.1. Recall that ATTac predicts hotel prices in the form of distributions. Given these distributions over hotel prices, for each unit i of each flight f it computes the benefit of postponing commitment by sampling future hotel prices and determining, on average, how much better off it would be if it could buy a flight other than $f.i$ right now (i.e., at that flight's current price). If $f.i$ is included in an optimal acquisition in every scenario, then there is no value in delaying commitment and it can be purchased immediately. However, if there are many scenarios in which $f.i$ is not included in an optimal acquisition, there is potential gain by delaying the purchase. In practice, this benefit can be computed by estimating the loss in expected value if the agent is *forced* to purchase the flight now, as opposed to merely having the opportunity to do so.

Heuristic Flight Timing: Walverine Case Study

Prior to 2004, Walverine purchased flights as soon as they were identified to be in the target set (i.e., an optimal acquisition). Consequently, it bought flights

Table 7.1
ATTac's algorithm for estimating the value of postponing flight commitments.

- Suppose the agent currently owns k units of a flight f, with current price p_f, and the target optimal acquisition calls for owning $k + n$ units.
- Repeat until time bound:
  1. Generate a random closing order for all open hotels.
  2. Conditioned on this order, sample hotel closing prices from predicted price distributions.
  3. Encode the agent's current holdings, the sampled hotel prices, and the current flight and entertainment prices in pricelines P.
  4. for $i = 0, \ldots, n$
     (a) Define P_{fi} to be the same as P except that an additional i units of flight f are obtainable at zero cost. Thus if the agent already holds k units of f, $\vec{p}_f$ is replaced by a vector with $k + i$ zeros (instead of just k zeros) and p_f thereafter.
     (b) Compute $U_i = \text{ACQ}(P_{fi}) - ip_f$
       –Estimate ACQ(P_{fi}) with the LP relaxation (see Appendix B).
       –U_i is thus the optimal acquisition value if the agent is *forced* to buy i additional units of flight f. Additional units can also be acquired as needed.
       –Note that $U_0 \geq U_1 \geq \cdots \geq U_n$ since it is never worse to retain extra flexibility.
- The value of waiting to buy unit i is the average of $U_{i-1} - U_i$. For example, if all samples lead to the conclusion that the ith flight should be bought, then $U_i = U_{i-1}$ and there is no benefit to postponing commitment.

for all clients immediately after the first price quote, and additional flights later in the game whenever changing conditions warranted. In response to the rule change in 2004, Walverine adopted an explicit approach to addressing the flight purchase tradeoff. Rather than construct a direct measure of costs and benefits like ATTac, Walverine incorporates key situation features as factors in a heuristic flight timing decision process.

First, Walverine estimates the underlying flight process parameters and computes the expected price perturbation using Bayesian updating (described above). Next, the agent determines its target flight holdings (as well as other goods), by solving its version of the acquisition problem.

Given the set of flights in its target set, Walverine decides which to purchase *now* as a function of the expected perturbations, current holdings, and marginal values of those flights. The strategy is designed to postpone purchase of flights whose prices are not quickly increasing, allowing for flexibility in avoiding expensive hotels as hotel price information is revealed.

The flight purchase strategy can be described in the form of a decision tree as depicted in Figure 7.1. First, Walverine compares the expected perturbation $(E[\Delta'])$ with a threshold $T1$, postponing purchase if the prices are not expected to increase by $T1$ or more. If $T1$ is exceeded, Walverine next compares the expected perturbation with a second higher threshold, $T2$, and if the prices are expected to increase by more than $T2$ Walverine purchases all units of that flight that are in the target set.

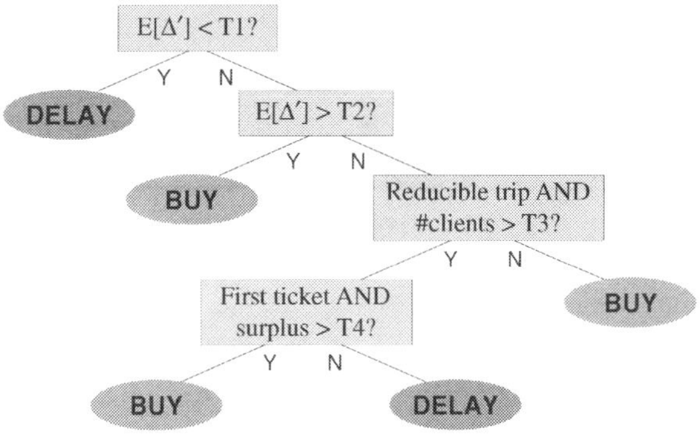

Figure 7.1
Walverine's decision tree for deciding whether to delay flight purchases.

If $T1 < E[\Delta'] < T2$, the Walverine flight delay strategy is designed to take into account the potential benefit of avoiding travel on high-demand days. Walverine checks whether each flight constitutes one end of a *reducible* trip: one that spans more than a single day. If the trip is not reducible, Walverine buys all units. If reducible, Walverine considers the number of clients it plans (according to the optimal acquisition) to accommodate on the day that would be avoided by shortening the trip, that is, the day of an inflight or the day before an outflight. If its own demand for that day is below a third threshold, $T3$, Walverine purchases all the units. Otherwise (reducible and demand greater than $T3$), Walverine delays the purchases, except possibly for one unit of the flight, which it will purchase if its marginal surplus exceeds yet another threshold, $T4$.

Though the strategy described above is based on sound calculations and tradeoff principles, it is difficult to justify particular settings of the four threshold parameters without making numerous assumptions and simplifications. The Walverine designers treat these as parameters to be explored empirically, along with the other strategy parameters, as detailed in Section 8.4.

7.2 Hotel-Bidding Strategies

Our discussion of bidding strategies in Chapter 5 was motivated largely by issues present in simultaneous auctions. In TAC, these issues surface primarily in dealing with hotel markets. Our treatment of hotel bidding to this point has focused on the problems of predicting prices and optimizing bids with respect to these price predictions. Although this approach does cover an important fraction of the simultaneous-auction bidding problem, as we have noted, it leaves aside the *strategic* element, whereby agents consider the influence of their actions on markets, or more generally how agents jointly choose actions anticipating those of others. The direct effects of an agent's own bids on prices can indeed be represented using nonlinear price predictions. The role of strategic analysis would be to model these effects based on assumptions about the strategies or strategy-selection procedures of other agents.

In this section, we address the strategic dimension of TAC hotel auctions, both abstractly and through specific algorithms. We start with the canonical simultaneous ascending auction (SimAA) model, surveying the known strategic properties of this mechanism. Although TAC hotel auctions are not pure SimAAs, they share many characteristics. We then turn to the particular problem of TAC hotel bidding, building on discussions elsewhere in this book. Many of the ideas developed in Chapter 5 come directly from the TAC hotel-bidding strategies employed by RoxyBot. Section 6.3 presents a comprehensive description of ATTac's hotel-bidding strategy. Here we provide a detailed account of the models and algorithms employed by Walverine for hotel bidding.

Simultaneous Ascending Auctions

A *simultaneous ascending auction* [Cramton, 2006] sells items from a set G of related goods to I agents through an array of single-item ascending auctions, one for each good. The auctions proceed concurrently, and bidding is organized in rounds. At any given time, the price quote, BID, is defined to be the highest bid received thus far, or zero if there are no bids as of yet. The ask quote, ASK, is BID plus a fixed increment. To be admissible, a new bid must beat the quote by offering at least ASK. If an auction receives multiple admissible bids in a given round, it admits the highest (breaking ties arbitrarily). An auction is *quiescent* when a round passes with no new admissible bids. When all are simultaneously quiescent, the auctions close and their respective goods are allotted as per the last admitted bids. Because no good in a SimAA is committed until all are, an agent's bidding strategy in one auction cannot be contingent on the outcome in another. Thus, an agent bidding for a package of goods inherently runs the risk that it will purchase some but not all goods in the package. This is the well-known *exposure problem*, introduced in Chapter 3 and studied in Chapter 5. Any design of bidding strategies for SimAAs must be evaluated in terms of how it deals with exposure.

Perhaps the most natural starting approach to bidding in SimAAs is a strategy called *straightforward bidding* (SB).[3] A straightforward bidder solves an acquisition problem, under the projection that *current prices* will prevail. It then places incremental bids on the goods in the target set that it is currently not winning. In other words, SB bids like TargetPrice (Section 5.3), taking as input the current *BID* prices for goods it is winning (since it need not increment the price in order to acquire these), and ASK for goods it is not winning.

The straightforward bidding strategy is quite simple, involving no anticipation of future prices. For the extreme case of substitutable preferences where agents value only single goods (i.e., the value of a package is just that of its most valued good), such anticipation is unnecessary, as the agent would not wish to change its bid even after observing the bids of other agents [Bikhchandani and Mamer, 1997]. When all agents have single-good value, and value every good equally (e.g., Example 5.8), the situation is equivalent to a problem in which all buyers have an inelastic demand for a single unit of a homogeneous commodity. For this problem, Peters and Severinov [2006] show that straightforward bidding is a perfect Bayesian equilibrium. Up to discretization effects, the SimAA outcomes are efficient when agents follow straightforward bidding. Still assuming single-good value, it can also be shown [Bertsekas, 1992; Wellman et al., 2001a] that the final prices differ from the minimum equilibrium prices by at most $\kappa \equiv \min(|G|, I)$, and that the value of the allocation, defined to be the sum of the bidders' surpluses, differs from the optimal by at most $\kappa(1+\kappa)$.

Unfortunately, the nice properties of straightforward bidding with single-good value do not generalize when agents have more complicated preferences, specifically allowing complementarity. Indeed, the resulting price vector can differ from the minimum equilibrium price vector, and the allocation value can differ from the optimal by arbitrarily large amounts [Wellman et al.,

3. We adopt the terminology introduced by Milgrom [2000]. The same strategy is also referred to as "myopic best response", or "myopically optimal", or even "myoptimal" [Kephart et al., 1998].

2001a]. However, whereas the case against SB is quite clear, auction theory [Krishna, 2002] to date has relatively little to say about how one *should* bid in simultaneous markets with complementarities. In fact, determining an optimal strategy even when it is known that other agents are playing SB turns out to be an unsolved and surprisingly difficult problem, sensitive to the smallest details of agents' preferences [Reeves et al., 2005].

The gap in our knowledge about SimAA strategy is especially striking given the ubiquity of simultaneous auctions in economic settings. Indeed, as argued throughout this book, markets for interdependent goods operating simultaneously and independently represent the normal state of affairs. Even for some markets that are expressly designed, most famously the US FCC spectrum auctions starting in the mid-1990s [McAfee and McMillan, 1996], variants of the SimAA have been deliberately adopted, despite awareness of strategic complications [Milgrom, 2000]. Simulation studies of scenarios based on the FCC auctions have shed light on some strategic issues [Csirik et al., 2001], as have accounts of some of the strategists involved [Weber, 1997], but the general setup is still too complex to admit definitive strategic recommendations.

Recent research has explored extensions of SB with features to mitigate the exposure problem. One modifies SB to approximately account for sunk costs, recognizing that goods an agent is already winning impose no incremental costs if other agents do not submit additional bids [Reeves et al., 2005]. Another adopts a key element of the trading agent architecture presented in Chapter 3, namely the use of price predictions. This idea can be implemented as an extension to SB [MacKie-Mason et al., 2004], resulting in a strategy that bids just like TargetPrice, that is, selecting a target set of goods to bid on based on price predictions. Performance depends on the specific price prediction, so it is necessary to develop prediction methods that support effective bidding in a range of environments. Especially effective is a strategy that generates probabilistic price predictions that are *self-confirming*, in the sense that when all agents bid based on such a strategy, the predictions are correct [Osepayshvili et al., 2005]. Although this strategy is not optimal, experimental analysis suggests that it is quite robust (in equilibrium within a large set of known strategies), and likely to be difficult to improve upon for bidding in SimAAs under broad classes of preferences exhibiting complementarity.

The abstract SimAA mechanism differs from the TAC hotel auctions in several ways. TAC hotel auctions are multiunit, and clear at the price of the lowest winning bid. Rather than wait until all are quiescent, one random auction closes each minute. In that respect they represent a hybrid between simultaneous and sequential auctions. Thus, although the TAC hotel auctions present some of the same issues as SimAAs, they are sufficiently different to warrant specialized techniques that go beyond the SimAA strategies studied in the literature.

TAC Hotel Bidding: Walverine Case Study

In Chapter 5 we presented several approaches to bidding under uncertainty and evaluated them on the task of TAC hotel bidding. The bidding heuristics defined there take as input a distribution over prices. If the input prices are linear, the agent in effect behaves competitively, ignoring the potential effect of its own bids on these prices. Nonlinear price predictions can in principle represent such own price effects, and the bidding heuristics of Chapter 5 exploit this information if available in the input distributions.

In Section 6.3, we described how ATTac adjusts its (linear) predicted hotel price distributions to anticipate the extra cost of additional rooms. ATTac models own price effects by fitting an exponential function to available pricing data, and incorporates the nonlinear adjusted prediction in its bidding. In this section, we present another method for generating and using nonlinear price distributions, this time based on the hotel-bidding strategy of Walverine. Walverine adheres to the basic structure of price prediction followed by optimization. Its prediction, however, is not described directly as a distribution over prices, but rather in terms of a distribution from which other bids in the auction are drawn. In essence, Walverine assumes that other agents bid marginal values based on linear price predictions. Walverine itself, however, places bids that maximize expected surplus given this distribution of other agents' bids. As part of its algorithm, Walverine also *shades* its bids downward to reflect the possibility that one of its own unit offers will be the lowest winning and thus set the price.

Generating Bid Distributions

As for its basic price-prediction algorithm (see Section 4.4), Walverine models the seven other agents as 56 individual clients. It generates a distribution of marginal valuations assuming each of the possible preferred travel-day pairs, (IAD, IDD), and sums over the ten cases to generate an overall distribution R for the representative client.

Let S and T stand for Shanties and Towers, respectively, and let h, i denote a room in hotel $h \in \{S, T\}$ on day i. For a given (IAD, IDD) pair, we estimate the value of (h, i) as the difference in expected net valuation between the best trip assuming room (h, i) is free, and the best trip of the alternative hotel type h'. In other words, the value of a given room is estimated to be the price above which the client would prefer to switch to the best trip using the alternate hotel type.

Let $r^*(IAD, IDD, h)$ denote the optimal trip for the specified day preferences, conditional on staying in hotel h. We can calculate this trip by taking into account the flight prices, prices for hotel h, day deviation penalties, and expected entertainment value. Note that the optimal trip for preferences (IAD, IDD) must be either $r^*(IAD, IDD, T)$ or $r^*(IAD, IDD, S)$. Let σ_h denote the net valuation of $r^*(IAD, IDD, h)$, based on the factors above but *not* accounting for the hotel premium, *HP*.

Setting the price of (h, i) to zero and that of all other hotels to predicted prices, we calculate best packages $r^*(IAD, IDD, h)$, $r^*(IAD, IDD, h')$ and their associated net valuations σ_h and $\sigma_{h'}$. If $(h, i) \notin r^*(IAD, IDD, h)$, we say that R_h is zero; otherwise it is the expected difference in net valuations:

$$\begin{aligned} R_S &= \max(0, \sigma_S - \sigma_T - HP), \\ R_T &= \max(0, \sigma_T - \sigma_S + HP). \end{aligned}$$

Since $HP \sim U[50, 150]$, these expressions represent uniform random variables:

$$\begin{aligned} \sigma_S - \sigma_T - HP &\sim U[\sigma_S - \sigma_T - 150, \sigma_S - \sigma_T - 50], \\ \sigma_T - \sigma_S + HP &\sim U[\sigma_T - \sigma_S + 50, \sigma_T - \sigma_S + 150]. \end{aligned} \tag{7.1}$$

For each (IAD, IDD) we can thus construct a cumulative distribution $R_{IAD,IDD}$ representing the marginal valuation of a given hotel room. In general, $R_{IAD,IDD}$ will include a mass at zero, representing the case where the room is not used even if free. Thus, we have

$$R_{IAD,IDD}(x) = \begin{cases} 0 & \text{if } x < \max(0, \alpha) \\ \frac{x-\alpha}{\beta-\alpha} & \text{if } \max(0, \alpha) \leq x \leq \beta \\ 1 & \text{if } x \geq \beta \end{cases},$$

where α and β are the lower and upper bounds, respectively, of the corresponding uniform distribution of Equation (7.1).

The overall valuation distribution for a representative client is the sum over arrival/departure preferences,

$$R(x) = \frac{1}{10} \sum_{(IAD,IDD)} R_{IAD,IDD}(x).$$

Finally, it will also prove useful to define a valuation distribution conditional on exceeding a given value q. For $x \geq q$,

$$R(x \mid q) = \frac{R(x) - R(q)}{1 - R(q)}. \tag{7.2}$$

Computing Optimal Bids

After estimating a bid distribution, Walverine's *optimal bid-shading algorithm* derives an optimal set of bids with respect to this distribution. The calculation makes use of an order statistic, $R_{k,n}(x)$, which represents the probability that a given value x would be kth highest if inserted into a set of n independent draws from R.

$$R_{k,n}(x) = [1 - R(x)]^{k-1} R(x)^{n-k+1} \binom{n}{k-1}$$

We can also define the conditional order statistic, $R_{k,n}(x \mid q)$, by substituting the conditional valuation distribution (Equation (7.2)) for R in the definition above.

Once hotel auctions start issuing price quotes, we have additional information about the distribution of bids. If H is the hypothetical quantity won for Walverine at the time of the last issued quote, the current ASK tells us that there are $16 - H$ bids from other clients at or above ASK, and $56 - (16 - H) = 40 + H$ at or below (assuming a bid from every client, including zero bids). We therefore define another order statistic, B_k, corresponding to the kth highest bid, sampling $16 - H$ bids from $R(\cdot \mid ASK)$ as defined by Equation (7.2), and $40 + H$ bids from R.

Note that these order statistics are defined in terms of other agents' bids, but we are generally interested in the kth highest value in an auction overall. Let n_b be the number of our bids in the auction greater than b. We define B_k so as to include our own bids, and employ the $(k - n_b)$th order statistic on others, $R_{k-n_b,n}(b)$, in calculating B_k.

Given our definitions, the probability that a bid b will be the kth highest is the following:

$$B_k(b) = \sum_{i=0}^{k-n_b-1} R_{i,16-H}(b) \cdot R_{k-n_b-i,40+H}(b \mid ASK). \qquad (7.3)$$

We characterize the expected value of submitting a bid at price b as a combination of the following statistics, all defined in terms of B_k:

- $B_{16}(b)$: Probability that b will win and set the price.
- $B_{15}^{+} \equiv \sum_{i=1}^{15} B_i(b)$: Probability that b will win but not set the price
- $M_{15} \equiv \{x \mid \sum_{i=1}^{15} P_i(x) = .5\}$: Median price if we submit an offer b.
- $M_{16} \equiv \{x \mid \sum_{i=1}^{16} P_i(x) = .5\}$: Median price if we do not bid.

Before proceeding, Walverine assesses the quality of its model, by computing the probability that the 16th bid would be above the quote given these distributions. If this probability is sufficiently low, $B_{16}^{+}(ASK) < .02$, then Walverine deems its model of other agents' bidding to be invalid and reverts to its point price prediction based on competitive equilibrium analysis (Section 4.4). In that case, Walverine conservatively bids its marginal values given this prediction, that is, it plays the StraightMV heuristic.

If the conditional bid distribution passes the test, based on these statistics we can evaluate the expected utility EU of a candidate bid for a given unit, taking into consideration the marginal value μ of the unit to Walverine, and the number of units n_b of this good for which it is bidding greater than b. The expected utility of a bid should reflect the expected price that will be paid for the unit, as well as the expected effect the bid will have on the price paid for all our higher bids in this auction. Lacking an expression for expected prices conditional on bidding, we employ as an approximation the median price statistics, M_{15} and M_{16}, defined above.[4]

$$\begin{aligned} EU(b) &= B_{16}(b)\,[(\mu - b) - n_b(b - M_{16})] \\ &\quad + B_{15}^{+}(b)\,[(\mu - M_{15}) - n_b(M_{15} - M_{16})] \end{aligned}$$

Walverine's proposed offer for this unit is the bid value maximizing expected utility,

$$b^* = \arg\max_b EU(b), \qquad (7.4)$$

which we can calculate by enumerating candidate bids (restricted to integers).

4. Offline analysis using Monte Carlo simulation verified that the approximation is reasonable.

Beat-the-Quote Adjustments

Upon calculating desired offer prices for all units of a given hotel, Walverine assembles them into an overall bid vector for the auction, taking the *beat-the-quote rule* (BTQ) into consideration. BTQ dictates that if the hypothetical quantity won for an agent's current bid is H, any replacement bid for that auction must represent an offer to buy at least H units at a price at least $ASK + 1$. For example, suppose the current bid offers to pay $(200, 150, 50)$ for three units, respectively, of a given hotel room. If $ASK = 100$, then the agent is winning its first two units (i.e., $H = 2$). To satisfy BTQ, the agent's new bid must be at least $(101, 101)$.

Let $b = (b_1, \ldots, b_8)$ be the agent's current bid for the eight potentially valuable units in this auction ($b_i = 0$ corresponds to no offer for that unit), and let b' be the proposed new bid, derived according to the optimization procedure above (Equation (7.4)). To ensure satisfaction of BTQ, the agent could submit the modified bid

$$b'' = (\max(b'_1, ASK + 1), \ldots, \max(b'_H, ASK + 1), b'_{H+1}, \ldots, b_8).$$

But this may not be a wise solution. Consider $b = (200, 150, 50, 0, \ldots)$ as in the example above, but with $ASK = 150$ (equal to the agent's lowest winning bid), and desired new bid $b' = (500, 0, \ldots)$. In this situation, the agent would like to revise upward its offer for the first unit, but would prefer that its offer of 150 for the second unit were outbid by another agent. Considering that other agents also follow BTQ, there will likely be several new bids at a price of $ASK + 1$ in the next round of bidding, meaning that an unrevised bid of 150 stands a much better chance of being outbid than does a revised bid of 151. In this case, the agent must balance the desirability of revising its bid for the first unit against its aversion to increasing its offer for the second.

Walverine decides whether to revise its bid based on a crude comparison of these factors. It assesses the value of bidding in terms of the magnitude of its desired price changes that are allowed by BTQ, and the cost of bidding in terms of the amount by which BTQ requires bidding above actual value. If this latter value exceeds the former, or a constant threshold, then Walverine refrains from submitting a revised bid. Otherwise it submits b''. This procedure serves the same purpose as ATTac's more direct comparison of the expected values of the current and proposed bid, as described in Section 6.3.

Discussion

Optimizing bids with respect to a model of other agents' behavior can only be effective in proportion to the accuracy of the model. Informal analysis based on game data from the TAC-02 finals reveals that Walverine's distributions systematically underestimate the actual values of bids. It appears that the distributions are fairly accurate during the initial stages of the game, when the modeling assumptions hold (zero holdings, all auctions open). The deterioration in accuracy of these distributions is not a fatal problem, however, as the agent reverts to bidding marginal values when the observed price quote is judged too unlikely with respect to its estimates.

Efforts to devise alternative bid estimation schemes did produce a more accurate model. Surprisingly, bidding based on the original, nominally less accurate distributions produced superior results, to both straight marginal-value bidding and bidding based on the more accurate new distribution. However, mean-difference tests did not reveal any of these differences to be statistically significant.

7.3 Trading Entertainment Tickets

Most TAC designers treat entertainment trading as a task only loosely coupled to flight and hotel bidding.[5] The markets are clearly interdependent, as the value of an entertainment ticket depends on what other tickets the agent holds, as well as the possible travel packages it can assemble for its clients. The relationship is relatively weak, however, since unlike flights and hotels, entertainment does not affect trip feasibility: it merely provides a value bonus. Often a ticket not used for one client can be given to another, or sold to another agent. Furthermore, entertainment markets are open throughout the game, and are not subject to time-dependent price movements or rigid clearing schedules like the other goods.

A typical functional organization of a TAC agent is illustrated by the architecture diagram for Walverine [Cheng et al., 2005], presented in Figure 7.2. Note especially the partition of bidding decisions into one strategy for flight and hotel acquisition, and another for entertainment trading. An optimization server (OPT) supports the key bid determination problems (see Section 3.2), given information about transactions, and actual and predicted prices. There

5. An exception is RoxyBot-06, which made its entertainment-bidding decisions in conjunction with its flight and hotel-bidding decisions, all within its sample average approximation module.

is no direct communication between the flight/hotel and entertainment modules; rather, all information is passed implicitly through the optimizer. That is, answers to bid determination problems submitted by one module reflect state information set by the other in performing its own optimization queries.

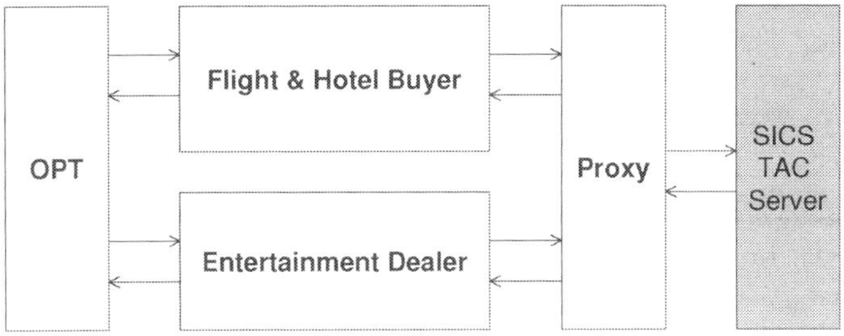

Figure 7.2
Functional architecture for Walverine, illustrating the modular separation of entertainment trading.

Continuous Double Auctions

Entertainment is the sole TAC good that agents may sell as well as buy. A market allowing offers on both the buy and sell sides is called *two-sided*, and its associated mechanism is a *double auction*. The entertainment auctions are also *continuous*, in that they match offers and release updated price quotes whenever a new bid is admitted.

The *continuous double auction* (CDA) mechanism [Friedman, 1993] is a simple and well-studied auction institution, employed commonly in commodity and financial markets. The CDA has also been widely investigated in experimental economic studies, and notably in the Santa Fe Double Auction Tournament [Rust et al., 1994]. As discussed in Section 2.3, the winning trader in this competition held back until most of the other agents revealed private information through their bids, then "stole the deal" by sniping at an advantageous price. Agents capable of more elaborate reasoning failed to make such sophistication pay off. This outcome is consistent with observations that even extremely naive strategies—exhibiting what Gode and Sunder [1993] dubbed *zero intelligence* (ZI)—achieve virtually efficient outcomes in this environment. Such results suggested a strong limit on the potential returns of sophisticated reasoning.

Over the last 15 years, CDA markets have served as a basis for many further studies of trading agents. Cliff [1998] provides an extensive bibliography covering the early line of this work, including his own evolutionary studies of “ZI plus” agents. One particularly influential trading strategy was proposed by Gjerstad and Dickhaut [1998], later revised and termed the *heuristic belief learning* (HBL) model [Gjerstad, 2004]. An HBL agent maintains a belief state over acceptance of hypothetical buy or sell offers, constructed from historical observed frequencies. It then constructs optimal offers with respect to these beliefs and its underlying preferences. The timing of bid generation is stochastic, controlled by a *pace* parameter, which may depend on absolute time and the order book state. Gjerstad [2004] demonstrates that pace is a pivotal strategic variable, and that there is surprisingly large potential advantage to strategic dynamic behavior despite the eventual convergence to competitive prices and allocations. In extensive simulated trials, Tesauro and Das [2001] found that a modified version of HBL outperformed a range of other strategies, including ZI, ZI plus, and the sniping strategy that won the original Santa Fe tournament. The strategy also compared favorably with human traders [Das et al., 2001]. Further extension of HBL to optimize bidding over time [Tesauro and Bredin, 2002] also provides improvements, and this enhanced HBL currently represents the apparent leading contender among generic CDA strategies.

Researchers continue to search through the strategy space in quest of better CDA bidding strategies. Competitions in financial domains, such as those employing the Penn Exchange Simulator [Kearns and Ortiz, 2003], enable comparison of a wide variety of CDA bidding strategies [Sherstov and Stone, 2004]. In abstract CDA domains, methods combining evolutionary algorithms and game-theoretic solution concepts are gaining attention [Phelps et al., 2006; Vytelingum et al., 2006].

TAC Entertainment Strategies

Despite the great research interest in CDAs—as well as commercial interest given their ubiquity in financial markets—the literature offers no definitive answer to the problem faced by TAC entertainment traders. Entrants through the years have tried a variety of approaches; we illustrate a few of these below.

ATTac Case Study

At the core of ATTac’s strategy for bidding on entertainment (as for other goods) is a calculation of the average marginal utility of each ticket. For each ticket, ATTac estimates the expected utility of having one more and one fewer of the ticket by sampling from its learned distribution model of hotel prices (see Chapter 6). These calculations yield bounds on its buy and sell offer prices. Details of ATTac's entertainment-ticket average marginal utility calculations are given in Table 7.2 in a notation and style similar to ATTac's hotel and flight-bidding algorithms (Tables 6.4 and 7.1 respectively). Note that this algorithm is exactly AverageMU (specialized for the TAC context), but applied to derive bounds rather than actual bids.

Table 7.2
ATTac's algorithm for calculating value of entertainment tickets.

Repeat until time bound:

1. Generate a random closing order for all open hotels.
2. Conditioned on this order, sample hotel closing prices from predicted price distributions.
3. For each type of ticket t, considered one at a time:
   - Suppose the agent currently owns k units of ticket t.
   - Encode the agent's current holdings, the sampled hotel prices, and the current flight and entertainment prices in pricelines P.
     - –Since tickets are considered sequentially, if the determined buy or sell bid for a previously considered ticket leads to a price that would clear according to the current quotes, assume the transaction goes through before constructing P by reflecting the revised number of owned tickets in $\vec{p}_t$.
   - for $i = k - 1, k, k + 1$
     - –Estimate $U_{ti} = \text{ACQ}(P(t, i))$ using the LP relaxation.
     - –Thus U_{ti} is the utility of owning exactly i units of ticket t with no further possibility of buying or selling it.
     - –Note that $U_{t,k-1} \leq U_{tk} \leq U_{t,k+1}$ since it is never worse to own extra tickets.

The value of buying ticket t is the mean of $U_{t,k+1} - U_{tk}$ over all the samples; the value of selling is the mean of $U_{tk} - U_{t,k-1}$.

Given these average marginal utilities, the actual bid prices are a linear function of time remaining in the game: ATTac settles for a smaller and smaller profit from ticket transactions as the game goes on. In particular, ATTac's bidding strategy for the entertainment tickets hypothesizes that for each ticket, the potential buy/sell price remains constant over the course of a single game (but may vary from game to game). So as to avoid overbidding/underbidding for that price, ATTac gradually increases/decreases its offer over the course of the game. The initial bids are always as optimistic as possible, but by the end of the game, ATTac is willing to settle for deals that are minimally profitable. In addition, this strategy serves to hedge against ATTac's early uncertainty in its final allocation of goods to clients.

Like many other agents, ATTac considers entertainment bids in a separate thread from its flight and hotel bid computations. ATTac constructs new entertainment bids every 20 seconds, an interval designed to strike a balance between responsiveness and generating enough samples to obtain reasonable marginal utility estimates. In each entertainment-bidding cycle, ATTac places a buy bid for each type of entertainment ticket, and a sell bid for each type of entertainment ticket that it currently owns. In all cases, the prices depend on the amount of time left in the game (T_l), becoming less aggressive as time goes on (see Figure 7.3).

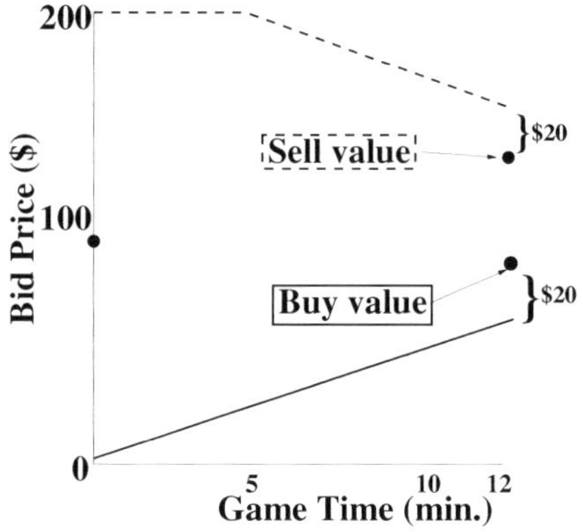

Figure 7.3
ATTac's bidding strategy for entertainment tickets. The black circles indicate the calculated values of the tickets to ATTac. The lines indicate the bid prices corresponding to those values. For example, the solid line (which increases over time) corresponds to the buy price relative to the buy value.

For each owned entertainment ticket t, let μ_t^- be its average marginal utility (i.e., "Sell value" in Figure 7.3). ATTac offers to sell t for $\min(200, \mu_t^- + \delta)$ where δ decreases linearly from 100 to 20 based on T_l.[6] If the current bid price (BID) is greater than the computed sell price, then ATTac raises its sell price to $BID - 0.01$.

Similarly, ATTac bids to buy each type of entertainment ticket t (including those that it is also offering to sell) based on the increased value that would be derived by owning t. Let μ_t^+ be the average marginal utility of an additional

6. Recall that 200 is the maximum possible value of t to any client under the TAC parameters.

unit of t ("Buy value" in Figure 7.3). Then, ATTac offers to buy t for $\mu_t^+ - \delta$, where δ decreases linearly from 100 to 20 based on T_l. As an additional hedge, ATTac offers to buy entertainment tickets for up to 10, even when they have no (or very low) apparent marginal utility as a "bargain" that may eventually lead to profitable arbitrage.

All of the parameters described in this section were chosen without detailed experimentation based on the intuition that, unless opponents know and explicitly exploit these values (which itself may not be easy or even possible), ATTac's performance is not very sensitive to them.

RoxyBot Case Study

Early versions of RoxyBot employed standard bidding heuristics for trading entertainment, using adaptive estimates of prices in the entertainment auctions. For each entertainment ticket e, the agent maintains an estimate $p_{e,\text{buy}}$ of the price at which it could buy a ticket, and a corresponding estimate $p_{e,\text{sell}}$ of the price at which it could sell a ticket.

To revise its estimates based on market updates, RoxyBot uses an approach inspired by the ZI plus traders mentioned above. Specifically, the agent applies a Widrow-Huff updating process, with rate parameters α and β. Suppose at update time there has been a recent trade of ticket e at price p_e. Then RoxyBot adjusts its estimates in the direction of the trade price,

$$p_{e,\text{buy}} \leftarrow (1 - \alpha)p_{e,\text{buy}} + \alpha p_e$$
$$p_{e,\text{sell}} \leftarrow (1 - \alpha)p_{e,\text{sell}} + \alpha p_e.$$

Otherwise, RoxyBot updates its estimate based on the current price quote:

$$p_{e,\text{buy}} \leftarrow (1 - \beta)p_{e,\text{buy}} + \beta ASK$$
$$p_{e,\text{sell}} \leftarrow (1 - \beta)p_{e,\text{sell}} + \beta BID.$$

In tournament play in 2000, RoxyBot set the rate parameters as follows: $\alpha = 0.1$ and $\beta = 0.05$.

Suppose RoxyBot currently holds k units of entertainment ticket e. It constructs a buyer priceline with k zeros, followed by $p_{e,\text{buy}}$, and ∞s thereafter. Its seller priceline is simply $p_{e,\text{sell}}$ followed by zeros. Hence, RoxyBot considers it possible to buy or sell at most a single unit at any particular time. Since entertainment auctions clear continuously, this assumption should not limit its trading opportunities.

Walverine Case Study

Walverine's approach to entertainment trading can be considered a polar opposite of the competitive analysis approach it takes to hotel buying. Equilibrium analysis has little to say about the dynamics of prices produced through CDAs, yet these transient behaviors seem particularly salient for effective entertainment trading. Thus, for this domain, we employ no model of the market, and no explicit calculations of the expected outcomes of alternative bid choices. Instead, Walverine adopts a *model-free*, empirical approach called *Q-learning*—a variety of *reinforcement learning* [Sutton and Barto, 1998].

Learning Framework The idea of applying Q-learning to TAC strategies was proposed by Boadway and Precup [2001], and employed in their TAC-01 entry, jboadw. This agent attempted to learn a policy for the entire TAC game, but this proved too ambitious given the time available for development and training. Inspired by their example, the Walverine-02 designers sought to pursue this approach for the much more limited TAC task of entertainment trading.

The aim of Q-learning is to estimate a function $Q : S \times A \rightarrow \Re$, representing the value of taking a given action in a given state. Value is typically measured by (discounted) cumulative future rewards, and the function can be represented in tabular or implicit form. From the Q function one can derive an optimal policy, namely that performing the maximally valued action in any given state. The recurrence (Bellman) equation relating values of adjacent states provides the basis for updating Q from experience of taking actions and observing state transitions and rewards.

Walverine's entertainment component considers each auction independently. It approximates the state of an entertainment auction as the combination of six features: BID, ASK, number of tickets held, marginal value of first unit (μ_1), marginal value of zeroth unit (μ_0), and game time. The state space is discretized into value sets of size 6, 6, 3, 7, 7, and 3, for the respective dimensions. Marginal values provided by Walverine's optimizer summarize client preferences and provide the necessary link to its flight/hotel module.

The reward from entertainment has two components: cash flow from trading and the entertainment value accrued to clients at the end of the game.

In each entertainment auction, Walverine maintains an offer to buy one unit, and an offer to sell one unit (at a higher price, of course). Rather than take the offer prices as actions, however, we define the action space in terms of *offsets from marginal value*. That is, the action buy(x) means to revise its current unit buy offer to the price $\mu_1 - x$. Similarly, sell(x) corresponds to a sell offer at $\mu_0 + x$. We defined eight discrete offset values. However, rather than consider all 64 buy/sell combinations, Walverine alternates between buy and sell decisions, considering only the eight available options for each case.

Learning Results Walverine's learning procedure encodes Q as a table. The agent maintains two tables: one for entertainment events on days $\{1,4\}$, and the other for days $\{2,3\}$. Within each category (six auctions apiece), the learning agent shares its trading experience. Given the size of each table (6291 states and 16 actions[7]), Walverine required a great deal of training experience. The Q-learning algorithm operated over data gathered from 14,839 games, including matches against other TAC participants during preliminary rounds, as well as many instances of self-play. Walverine employed a variety of entertainment trading policies while gathering experience, including a hand-coded strategy based on the one reportedly employed by livingagents in TAC-01 [Fritschi and Dorer, 2002]. Once it had accumulated sufficient data, the environment included some instances of Walverine based on preliminary learned policies, with various exploration-exploitation control methods.

Figure 7.4 displays a learning curve representing the evolution of Walverine's entertainment performance during the training period. We take as a baseline the value of the null (no-trading) strategy, which was determined experimentally to provide an entertainment reward (through retaining endowed tickets) of 1019 on average. As a second baseline, we evaluate the performance of the aforementioned livingagents entertainment strategy, embedded in Walverine. The performance axis of Figure 7.4 measures Walverine's learned entertainment strategy compared to this second baseline. In each interval of training games represented, we evaluate the policy learned based on games prior to that interval (thus the first interval represents the no-trading baseline). The evaluation consists of self-play games with half the agents following the learned entertainment policy and the other half following the livingagents entertainment strategy. By the time of the TAC-02 finals, Walverine had reached within 50 points of the hand-coded strategy.

It is important to note that Walverine itself underwent many changes during the learning process, which undoubtedly confounds the results. Moreover,

7. There are 15,876 distinct combinations of state variables, but many of these do not represent legal states. In all of its training, Walverine actually experienced 2588 and 2602 states, respectively, in the two auction categories.

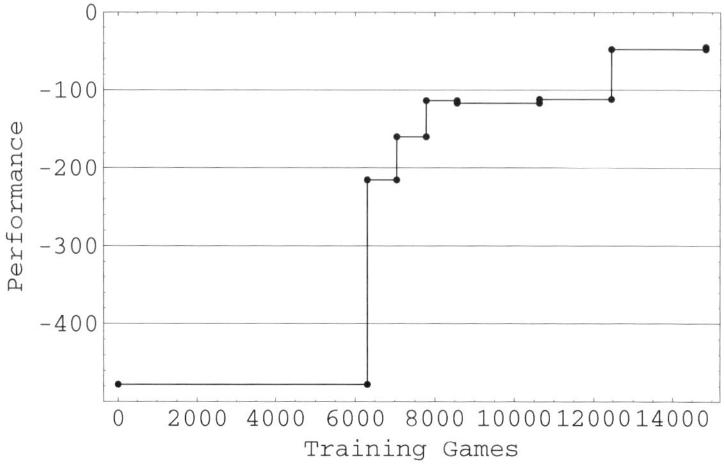

Figure 7.4
Walverine-02's entertainment learning curve.

the policies evaluated in Figure 7.4 retain an exploration element, except the last interval, which is pure exploitation.

In the TAC-02 finals, Walverine averaged an entertainment reward of 1409, nearly 400 over the nonbidding baseline. A summary of entertainment performance by agent is included in Appendix A, Table A.6. Interestingly, WhiteBear, the high scorer in TAC-02 (and again in TAC-04), was extremely successful on entertainment, achieving an average reward of 1623. The WhiteBear designers Vetsikas and Selman [2003] report employing a simple entertainment-bidding procedure, and so the high payoff achieved remains somewhat mysterious. Walverine adopted a version of the WhiteBear entertainment strategy in 2005, and this was likely a significant contributor in its improvement from TAC-04 to TAC-05.

7.4 Discussion

All three TAC markets present agents with interesting tradeoffs and challenging prediction and optimization problems. Some of the complexity of TAC decision making can be attributed to domain-specific features of the TAC scenario. However, we have seen that even the simplified generic versions of these markets (posted-price, SimAA, CDA) pose unsolved problems. Many

TAC agents adopt techniques from the literature on the generic problems to the TAC setting. For instance, we noted the adaptation of ZI plus for entertainment trading by RoxyBot [Greenwald and Boyan, 2005]. Similarly, elements of straightforward bidding, as well as heuristic belief learning or related price-prediction approaches can be found in the hotel and entertainment modules of several TAC agents.

Despite the elaborate and often sophisticated algorithms incorporated in TAC agent designs, there is substantial room for improvement. For example, whereas flight price estimation can be considered a solved problem, there is no direct evidence that any TAC agent addresses the bid-timing tradeoffs optimally (or even near-optimally). Similarly, we doubt we have seen the last word about hotel price prediction, especially for the challenging problem of modeling own price effects and other agents' behavior. The techniques and analysis of Chapter 5 provide a fine means to judge the quality of one-shot hotel bidding given price predictions, but as yet there has been little headway on extending this line of work to explicitly address the dynamic nature of TAC hotel markets. Finally, there is evidence from analysis of the overall entertainment market that some potential gains from trade are "left on the table". It appears likely that better entertainment strategies could significantly enlarge the surplus, or do a better job on behalf of particular agents. To date we lack a precise understanding of what about the more successful entertainment strategies makes them so, and how much further improvement is possible.

We stress the limitations of current approaches and knowledge in order to highlight the opportunities available for further research to produce superior strategies, for TAC as well as the more general versions of these markets. Despite ongoing improvement of TAC agents and improved understanding of the general bidding problems, the potential for new ideas is far from exhausted.

8 Experimental Methods and Strategic Analysis

It is an inescapable conclusion that there are many ways to play the TAC travel game. Indeed, we have seen many candidate approaches for each of several subtasks: price prediction, bidding under uncertainty, timing commitments, and so on. Each TAC agent brings to bear its own suite of solutions to such problems, and whereas we can put forth analytical and empirical evidence that certain techniques are more effective than others, no clearly dominant overall strategy has emerged. Some narrow subproblems can be considered "solved" (e.g., allocation, flight price estimation), and these are widely regarded as building blocks for effective trading behavior in TAC. However, there is as yet no definitive solution to any of the larger, more fundamental bidding strategy choices faced by TAC agents.

Successful agent designers combine analytical modeling and experimentation to evaluate candidate techniques and guide innovation. Since analytical models of the TAC environment necessarily simplify the actual game, conducting experimental trials is essential in order to validate strategy ideas and tune parameters. Since these (offline) experiments incorporate assumptions about other agents' behavior, designers also depend on online experiments (e.g., preliminary tournament rounds) to test their designs in the most realistic setting available.

In this chapter, we explore issues in the conduct and analysis of trading agent experiments. We emphasize in particular the challenge posed by *strategic interactions*—where the performance of a strategy generally depends on other agents' behavior. We present an empirical methodology based on *game theory*, illustrated through a case study of variations on Walverine. In the course of describing the experiments, we develop general techniques for mitigating the combinatorial explosion of agent strategies, and for reducing variance due to stochastic sampling.

8.1 Strategic Interactions

When the effectiveness of one's strategy depends on strategic choices made by others, each combination of strategies—a *strategy profile*—may have special characteristics. Consequently, an experimenter must carefully consider the context in which to test a strategic hypothesis. In this section, we first establish that strategic interactions are in fact prevalent in TAC. Next we consider principles for selecting appropriate experimental contexts, concluding that game-theoretic stability provides a compelling criterion.

Strategic Interactions in TAC Travel

That strategic choices interact—a defining property of multiagent domains—has been frequently noted in the TAC literature, and is documented throughout this book.

A report on the first TAC tournament [Stone and Greenwald, 2005] observes that the strategy of bidding high prices for hotels performed reasonably in preliminary rounds, but poorly in the finals when more agents were high bidders (thus raising final prices to unprofitable levels). Stone et al. [2001] evaluate their agent ATTac-00 in controlled experiments (Section 6.1), measuring relative scores in a range of contexts, varying the number of other agents playing high- and low-bidding strategies. A report on the 2001 competition [Wellman et al., 2003b], supported by the experiment summarized in Table 6.6, concludes that the top scorer, livingagents, would perform quite poorly against copies of itself. The designers of SouthamptonTAC [He and Jennings, 2002] observed the sensitivity of their agent's TAC-01 performance to the tendency of other agents to buy flights in advance, and redesigned their agent for TAC-02 to attempt to classify the competitive environment faced and adapt accordingly [He and Jennings, 2003]. As detailed in Chapter 6, ATTac-01 explicitly takes into account the identity of other agents in training its price-prediction module [Stone et al., 2003]. To evaluate alternative learning mechanisms through post-competition analysis, the ATTac designers recognized the effect of the strategies on the outcomes being learned, and thus adopted a carefully phased experimental design in order to account for such effects (Section 6.4).

Chapter 5 explores in depth several heuristics for hotel bidding based on predicted prices. In particular, in the first experiment reported in Section 5.5, where there are two copies of four bidding heuristics, the behavior of TargetMV and TargetMV* is indistinguishable. But in the second experiment, where there are four copies of these two heuristics, TargetMV is significantly better. These results confirm that absolute performance of a strategy indeed depends on what the other agent plays. Wellman et al. [2003a] examined the efficacy of bid shading in Walverine, varying the number of agents employing shading or not, and derived an equilibrium shading probability based on these results.

By far the most extensive experimental TAC analysis reported prior to the study in this chapter was performed by Vetsikas and Selman [2003, 2005].

As described in Section 2.3, the WhiteBear designers systematically explored candidate choices for several components of the agent's strategy. They carefully selected contexts in which to evaluate prespecified hypotheses about specific choices. The authors grant much of the credit for WhiteBear's success in 2002–04 to this deliberate experimental methodology.

Game-Theoretic Analysis

The typical objective of trading agent experimentation is to establish that a proposed strategy possesses some advantageous characteristic(s) compared to alternatives in a given setting, or to develop a model of performance as a function of environmental features. Because TAC is a multiagent environment, and hence characterized by strategic interactions, any simulation involving the strategy of interest will be sensitive to the configuration of other agents' strategies. Determining the combinations of agent behaviors to simulate is therefore a crucial issue in experimental design.

The issue of strategic interaction arises naturally in many other areas of multiagent systems (MAS) research. Although it appears that much MAS research pursues this determination in an ad hoc manner, the issue is often recognized, and several approaches address it directly. In a *factorial* design, for example, all combinations of agent strategies are simulated. Exhaustive search is infeasible, however, when there are large numbers of possible strategies or a large population of agents. Even when feasible, in interpreting the experiments the analyst must render judgments about the degree to which the various configurations are relevant in order to draw conclusions about proposed strategies.

One appealing way to determine a relevant set of agent strategies is to generate a population iteratively through some evolutionary process. The evolutionary approach was pioneered in computational agent research by Axelrod's famous iterated prisoner's dilemma tournament [Axelrod, 1984], and has become a standard method among researchers in agent-based computational economics [Tesfatsion and Judd, 2006]. Evolutionary search techniques provide (at least) two useful functions in MAS experimentation:

1. *Generating strategies*, given a set of primitive building blocks, employing stochastic local search from an initial population. Techniques for strategy generation are typically based on genetic algorithms or genetic programming [Mitchell, 1996].
2. *Finding stable profiles* by evolving populations of strategies, for example using replicator dynamics [Taylor and Jonker, 1978].

Beyond the examples provided, there are alternative means as well to support both of these functions. Any structured search technique (employing genetic operators or not) is a candidate method for exploring a space of available strategies. Evolutionary stability is one of several criteria that might be employed to evaluate the plausibility of populations. It is uniquely compelling only to the extent that the evolutionary dynamic employed is itself a plausible model of how agent strategies might adapt over time.

Game theory is another source of stability criteria often employed in MAS research. Informally, a profile of strategies is *stable* if no agent has an incentive to deviate from its assigned strategy. This criterion, when formalized precisely, defines a *Nash equilibrium* (Definition 8.3 below). The adequacy of solution concepts like Nash's for prescriptive or descriptive modeling is widely debated in game theory and the social sciences (e.g., see Kreps [1990]). Without engaging in that discussion, we note that the *in*stability of a profile should be considered evidence against its plausibility—rational agents would surely seek to deviate from such profiles. Thus, we adopt standard game-theoretic solution concepts (in particular, Nash equilibrium and approximations thereof) as a starting point.

Although evolutionary and game-theoretic stability (i.e., equilibrium) concepts sometimes coincide [Friedman, 1991], this is not always the case. Classic game theory generally tends to avoid assuming any particular dynamic model, which may be viewed as a strength or weakness depending on one's perspective and the particular issues at hand. What game theory does provide is a rigorous mathematical framework for formalizing interactions among rational agents, and a rich set of solution concepts useful for characterizing alternative strategic configurations.

Whereas game theory is now quite commonly employed by MAS researchers in theoretical investigations, it has been less frequently applied in experimental studies. Reeves [2005, Section 3.9] surveys some of the emerging efforts. One can interpret many MAS studies as including game-theoretic perspectives implicitly if not explicitly. The Walverine studies reported here are part of a broader research effort to develop a general empirical game-theoretic methodology [Wellman, 2006].

8.2 Hierarchical Game Reduction

One of the most daunting challenges in MAS experimentation is dealing with the combinatorial explosion of potentially relevant strategic contexts in which to evaluate alternative designs. Practical empirical analysis inevitably accepts incomplete exploration and approximate results. In this section, we describe one approach to simplify analysis by approximating the game under consideration by a smaller, computationally more tractable game.

Motivation

Suppose that we manage to narrow down the candidate TAC agent variants to a reasonable number of strategies (say 40). Because the performance of a strategy for one TAC agent depends on the strategies of the other seven, we wish to undertake a game-theoretic analysis of the situation. Determining the payoff for a particular strategy profile is expensive, however, as each game instance takes nine minutes to run, plus another minute or two to calculate scores, compile results, and set up the next simulation. Moreover, since the environment is stochastic, numerous samples (say 12) are required to produce a reliable estimate for even one profile. At roughly two hours per profile, exhaustively exploring profile space will require 2×40^8 or 13 trillion hours simply to estimate the payoff function representing the game under analysis. Since TAC Travel is symmetric, we can exploit that fact to reduce the number of distinct profiles to $\binom{47}{8}$, which will require 628 million hours. That is quite a bit less, but still much more time than we have.

The idea of *hierarchical game reduction* is that although a strategy's payoff does depend on the play of other agents (otherwise we are not in a game situation at all), it may be relatively insensitive to the exact numbers of other agents playing particular strategies. For example, consider a profile where k agents play strategy s, and the rest play s'. In many natural games, the payoff for the respective strategies in this profile will vary smoothly with k, differing only incrementally for contexts with $k \pm 1$. If such is the case, we sacrifice relatively little fidelity by restricting attention to subsets of profiles, for instance those with only even numbers of any particular strategy. To do so essentially transforms the I-player game to an $I/2$-player game over the same strategy set, where the payoffs to a profile in the reduced game are simply those from the original game where each strategy in the reduced profile is played twice.

The potential savings from reduced games are considerable, as they contain combinatorially fewer profiles. The 4-player approximation to the TAC game (with 40 strategies) comprises 123,410 distinct profiles, compared with 314 million for the original 8-player game. In case exhaustive consideration of the 4-player game is still infeasible, we can approximate further by a corresponding 2-player game, which has only 820 profiles. Approximating by a 1-player game is tantamount to ignoring strategic effects, considering only the 40 profiles where the strategies are played against themselves. In general, an I-player symmetric game with S strategies includes $\binom{I+S-1}{I}$ distinct profiles. Figure 8.1 shows the exponential growth in both I and S.

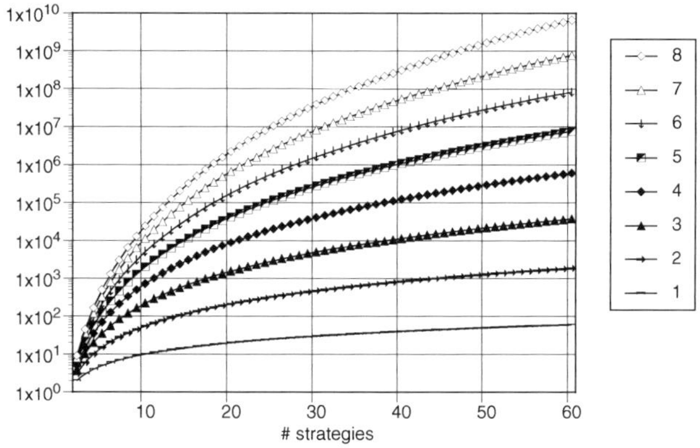

Figure 8.1
Number of distinct profiles (log scale) of a symmetric game, for various numbers of players and strategies.

Game Theory: Basic Definitions

We develop our hierarchical reduction concepts in the framework of *symmetric normal-form games.*

DEFINITION 8.1 NORMAL-FORM GAME: $\Gamma = \langle I, \{S_i\}, \{u_i()\}\rangle$ is an *I-player normal-form game*, with *strategy set* S_i the available strategies for player i, and the *payoff function* $u_i(s_1, \ldots, s_I)$ giving the utility accruing to player i when players choose the *strategy profile* $(s_1, \ldots, s_I)$.

DEFINITION 8.2 SYMMETRIC GAME: A normal-form game is *symmetric* if the players have identical strategy spaces ($S_1 = \cdots = S_I = S$) and

$u_i(s_i, s_{-i}) = u_j(s_j, s_{-j})$, for $s_i = s_j$ and $s_{-i} = s_{-j}$ for all $i, j \in \{1, \ldots, I\}$. Thus we can write $u(t, s)$ for the payoff to any player playing strategy t when the remaining players play profile s. We denote a symmetric game by the tuple $\langle I, S, u() \rangle$.

Agent i may choose its strategy probabilistically. Let $\Delta(S_i)$ denote the set of probability distributions over the *pure strategies* S_i. The payoff for playing mixed strategy $\sigma_i \in \Delta(S_i)$ when other agents play $\sigma_{-i} \in \Delta(S_{-i})$ is defined as the expectation of u with respect to the respective probability distributions.

We are particularly interested in *Nash equilibrium* (NE) strategy profiles, where all agents play strategies that are best responses to the others. Such configurations are stable because no agent has an incentive to deviate.

DEFINITION 8.3 NASH EQUILIBRIUM: A strategy profile σ constitutes an NE of game Γ if for every player i, $\sigma_i' \in \Delta(S_i)$, $u_i(\sigma_i, \sigma_{-i}) \geq u_i(\sigma_i', \sigma_{-i})$.

If the strategy σ satisfying Definition 8.3 is pure, it is termed a *pure-strategy Nash equilibrium* (PSNE).

It is also useful to define an approximate solution concept, the ϵ-NE, where ϵ is the maximum benefit for deviation to any agent.

DEFINITION 8.4ϵ-NASH EQUILIBRIUM: A strategy profile σ constitutes an ϵ-NE of game Γ if for every player i, $\sigma_i' \in \Delta(S_i)$, $u_i(\sigma_i, \sigma_{-i}) + \epsilon \geq u_i(\sigma_i', \sigma_{-i})$.

Hierarchy of Reduced Games

The idea of a *reduced game* is to coarsen the profile space by restricting the degrees of strategic freedom. Although the original set of strategies remains available, the number of agents playing any strategy must be a multiple of q.

DEFINITION 8.5 REDUCED GAME: Let $\Gamma = \langle I, S, u() \rangle$ be an I-player symmetric game, with $I = pq$ for integers p and q. The *p-player reduced version of* Γ, written $\Gamma\downarrow_p$, is given by $\langle p, S, \hat{u}() \rangle$, where

$$\hat{u}_i(s_1, \ldots, s_p) = u_{q \cdot i}(\underbrace{s_1, \ldots,}_{q} \underbrace{s_2, \ldots,}_{q} \ldots, \underbrace{s_p, \ldots}_{q}).$$

In other words, the payoff function in the reduced game is obtained by playing the specified profile in the original q times.

Every profile in the reduced game is one in the original game, of course, and any profile in the original game can be reached from a profile contained in the reduced game by changing at most $p(q-1)$ agent strategies.

The premise of this approach is that the reduced game will often serve as a good approximation of the full game it abstracts. One way to measure approximation quality is to evaluate solutions of the reduced game in the context of the original. Specifically, we ask: If the agents play a reduced-game equilibrium in the original game, how much can a single agent gain from deviating from such a profile? If the answer is zero, then the equilibria coincide. More generally, the smaller the gain from deviating, the more faithful the reduced game approximation.

Let us denote by $\epsilon_\Gamma(s)$ the potential gain to deviating from strategy profile s in game Γ. For game $\Gamma = \langle I, \{S_i\}, \{u_i()\}\rangle$,

$$\epsilon_\Gamma(s) = \max_{i\in I} \max_{s'\in S_i} u_i(s', s_{-i}) - u_i(s_i, s_{-i}). \tag{8.1}$$

This usage follows the notion of approximate equilibrium introduced above. Profile s is an $\epsilon_\Gamma(s)$-NE of Γ, with 0-NE corresponding to exact NE. Henceforth, we drop the game subscript when understood in context.

In the worst case, an equilibrium of the reduced game may be arbitrarily far from equilibrium with respect to the full game, and an equilibrium of the full game may not have any near neighbors in the reduced game that are close to equilibrium there. Wellman et al. [2005b] provide evidence that the hierarchical reduction provides an effective approximation in several natural game classes. Intuition suggests that it should apply for TAC, and the level of agreement between TAC$\downarrow_2$ and TAC$\downarrow_4$ seen in our results below tends to support that assessment.

8.3 Control Variates

Interpreting results based on experimental trials must be mindful of stochastic factors contributing to these results. This is especially important for drawing conclusions about TAC tournament outcomes, which typically comprise a relatively small number of games. For example, the randomly generated client preferences for an agent in a particular game instance may be unusually favorable (e.g., short trips and high hotel premiums) or unfavorable, in either case exerting a significant influence on scores. Given a sufficient number of samples, the average score will converge to the true expectation with respect to these stochastic factors. In any finite data set, we can improve our statistical estimate (i.e., reduce the effective variance) by adjusting it based on the known correlation of scores with these stochastic factors.

One well-known variance reduction method is the introduction of *control variates* [Ross, 2002], which improves the estimate of the mean of a random function by exploiting correlation with observable random variables. In our case the function is the entire game server plus eight agents playing a particular strategy profile, evaluating to a vector of eight scores. Random factors in the game include hotel closing order, flight prices, entertainment ticket endowment, and, most critically, client preferences. The idea is to replace sampled scores with scores that have been "adjusted for luck". For example, an agent whose clients had abnormally low hotel premiums would have its score adjusted upward as a handicap. Or in a game with very cheap flight prices, all the scores would be adjusted downward to compensate. Such adjustments reduce variance at the cost of potentially introducing bias. Fortunately, the bias goes to zero as the number of samples increases [L'Ecuyer, 1994].

In this section, we describe in detail our application of control variates to the TAC environment. Adjustments based on control variates are applied to all the experimental data presented in this chapter. For the actual TAC tournaments (comprehensive data provided in Appendix A), we report scores in their official unadjusted form, along with separate adjustments computed according to the methods below.

Application to TAC (2004–)

For adjusting TAC scores based on the 2004 rules, we have identified the following control variables (for a hypothetical agent A):

- ENT: Sum of A's clients' entertainment premiums ($8 \times 3 = 24$ values). $E[\text{ENT}] = 2400$.
- FLT: Sum of initial flight quotes (eight values; same for all agents). $E[\text{FLT}] = 2600$.
- WTD: Weighted total demand: Total demand vector (for each night, the number of the 64 clients who would be there that night if they got their preferred trips) dotted with the demand vector for A's clients. $E[\text{WTD}] = 540.16$.

- HTL: Sum of A's clients' hotel premiums (eight values). $E[\text{HTL}] = 800$.

The expectations are determined analytically based on specified game distributions [Reeves, 2005].

Given the above, we adjust an agent's score by subtracting

$$\begin{aligned}\beta_{\text{ENT}}(\text{ENT} - E[\text{ENT}]) &+ \beta_{\text{FLT}}(\text{FLT} - E[\text{FLT}]) \\ &+ \beta_{\text{WTD}}(\text{WTD} - E[\text{WTD}]) \\ &+ \beta_{\text{HTL}}(\text{HTL} - E[\text{HTL}]),\end{aligned}$$

where the βs are determined by performing a multiple regression from the control variables to score using a data set consisting of 2190 games played with various combinations of Walverine variants. Using adjusted scores in lieu of raw scores reduces overall variance by 22% based on a sample of 9000 all-Walverine games. This is the adjustment we applied in the extensive analysis of Walverine experiments reported in this chapter.

We have also estimated the coefficients based on the 107 games in the TAC-04 semifinals and finals. For comparison, the regression coefficients for the two data sets are reported in Table 8.1. Although the numeric values differ, it is clear from both data sets that it improves an agent's score somewhat to have clients with high entertainment premiums, it hurts performance to be in a game with high flight prices, it hurts to have clients that prefer long trips (particularly when other agents' clients do as well), and finally, having clients with high hotel premiums improves score.

Table 8.1
Control variable coefficients, derived by regression over two different data sets.

coefficient	all-Walverine	2004 tournament
β_{ENT}	0.296	0.349
β_{FLT}	–2.014	–1.721
β_{WTD}	–1.921	–2.305
β_{HTL}	0.645	0.916

We employ the coefficients derived from the 2004 tournament to adjust the TAC-04 scores (see Appendix A, Table A.10), and the coefficients from the all-Walverine data set for adjusting TAC-05 and TAC-06 scores (Tables A.12 and A.15 in Appendix A).

Client Preference Adjustment (2001–03)

For the years 2001–03, we applied a similar adjustment based on a set of control variables limited to statistics on the agent's own client preferences. We tested a few candidate variables for significance over the TAC-01 seeding round games, employing the variables in a linear regression along with indicator 0-1 variables for each of the agent identities. After a very small amount of trial and error, we came up with the following significant measures:

1. Total client preferred travel days
2. Total entertainment values (ENT)
3. Ratio of "easy" days (1 and 4) to hard (2 and 3) in preferred trip intervals

Applying the resulting regression model to the finals data yields the "client preference adjustment" that we have reported for the TAC-01 through TAC-03 tournaments. Although these do not modify the official tournament results, we consider the adjusted scores statistically more reliable than raw scores. For TAC-01, if the scores were adjusted based on these factors, there would be two changes in the rankings (see Appendix A, Table A.4). First, right at the top, it turned out that livingagents had somewhat more favorable client data than did ATTac, and so in the adjusted rankings ATTac would come out in front. Caisersose had by far the least favorable inputs, and so it too would rise by one spot. No other changes in final rankings would result. For TAC-02, applying the adjustment would lead to a realignment of third through fifth place (Table A.6). The most substantial effect appears in TAC-03, where adjustment would shuffle the top five finalists (Table A.8).

8.4 Walverine Parameters

As noted above, TAC experiments typically aim to assess the effects of specified strategy choices. To facilitate implementation of variations and organize the search for effective strategies, experimenters expose *strategy parameters* representing the available choices. The combinations of possible settings of these parameters define an overall *strategy space* under consideration.

The WhiteBear designers [Vetsikas and Selman, 2003, 2005] have been most explicit in organizing their experimental regimen around a parametric strategy space. Specific experiments are designed to compare versions of WhiteBear differing only in the settings of one or two parameters. Similarly, most of the experiments reported elsewhere in this book evaluate particular agent designs, where one element (parameter) varies while others are held constant. For example, one of the controlled experiments evaluating ATTac-01's learning algorithm (Section 6.4) considered seven different settings for the price-prediction module, keeping the rest of ATTac-01 fixed.

The design and development of Walverine included considerable testing and experimentation, much of it conducted in an ad hoc manner over the first couple of years the agent participated in TAC. In preparation for TAC-04, the agent's designers initiated a more systematic search over Walverine's strategy space. We describe some of the key strategy parameters in this section. In the next, we present the results of this experimentation, illustrating the game-reduction techniques described above as well as the more general empirical game-theoretic approach. Although the search had not progressed sufficiently to provide much guidance for TAC-04, the method was used to select the version of Walverine entered in TAC-05, and confirm the persistence of this choice for TAC-06.

Flight Purchase Timing

Walverine's approach to flight purchasing is described in Section 7.1. As explained there, the agent decides whether to delay the purchase of a given flight by stepping through a decision tree (Figure 7.1) evaluating relevant timing factors. The tree employs thresholds (labeled $T1, \ldots, T4$) on these factors at each choice point. These thresholds are essentially free parameters in the Walverine design, and thus are exposed as strategy selections.

Hotel Bid Shading

As described in Section 7.2, Walverine computes, for each hotel auction, the bid value maximizing expected utility based on a model of other agents' marginal value distributions. Because this optimization is based on numerous simplifications and approximations, we include several parameters to control its use.

Through a *shading mode* parameter, bid optimization can be turned off, in which case Walverine bids according to StraightMV. Another parameter defines a *shade percentage*, specifying a fixed fraction to bid below marginal value. There are two modes corresponding to the optimal shading algorithm, differing in how they model the other agents' value distributions. In the first, the distributions are derived from the simplified competitive analysis described in Section 7.2. For this mode, the parameter *shade model threshold* turns off bid optimization in case the model appears too unlikely given the price quote. Specifically, Walverine calculates $B_{16}^{+}(ASK)$, the probability that the 16th highest bid is greater than or equal to the quote according to the modeled value distributions, and if too low (below .02 in the baseline setting) refrains from using the model. For the second shading mode, instead of the competitive model Walverine employs empirically derived distributions keyed on the hotel closing order.

Entertainment Trading

For entertainment, there is a single parameter selecting among a discrete set of policies. As a baseline, one setting selects the strategy employed by livingagents in TAC-01 [Fritschi and Dorer, 2002]. As described in Section 7.3, Walverine applied reinforcement learning to derive policies from scratch, expressed as functions of marginal valuations and various additional state variables. The policy employed by Walverine in TAC-02 was derived by Q-learning over a discretized state space. For TAC-03 Walverine learned an alternative policy, this time employing a neural network to represent the value function. Analysis of other agents indicated that WhiteBear performs particularly well in entertainment trading. Therefore, the Walverine developers also implemented an entertainment module based on the WhiteBear policy, adapted for the Walverine architecture.

Other Parameters

As described in Section 4.4, Walverine predicts hotel prices based on competitive equilibrium analysis, and uses these predictions to decide which flights to acquire. The result, however, does not account for uncertainty in the predictions. The agent applies a simple method to hedge its price estimates, by assigning an *outlier probability* to the event that a hotel price will be much greater than predicted [Cheng et al., 2005]. It can hedge to a greater or lesser degree by modifying this outlier parameter.

Given a price distribution, there are two broad approaches to bid optimization, as described in Section 5.4: optimize bids with respect to the distribution itself, or collapse the distribution into its expectation (see Section 5.4). The former approach is more accurate in principle, and the results of Section 5.5 suggest that it can be advantageous for TAC hotel bidding. However, due to necessary compromises in implementation and possible differences in the rest of the agent, such results have not always been observed in related TAC experiments (see Section 6.4, as well as the study by Greenwald and Boyan [2004]). Thus, we include a parameter controlling which method Walverine employs in its flight acquisition decisions.

We have also discussed the use of pricelines, accounting for potentially nonlinear prices for goods. The parameterized Walverine includes an option for optimizing packages with respect to pricelines. A further parameter selects how price predictions and optimizations account for outstanding hotel bids in determining current holdings. In one setting current bids for open hotel auctions are ignored, and in another the current hypothetical winnings are treated as actual holdings.

8.5 TAC Experiments

To apply reduced-game analysis to the TAC domain, we identified a restricted set of strategies, defined by setting parameters for Walverine. We considered a total of 40 distinct strategies, covering variant policies for bidding on flights, hotels, and entertainment. Table 8.2 describes a subset of the strategies included in our analysis, in terms of the Walverine parameters discussed in Section 8.4.[1] These strategies were selected based on their success in one or more of the reduced games, which perhaps accounts for their similarity.

We collected data for a large number of games: over 91,000, representing over two years of (almost continuous) simulation.[2] Each game instance provides a sample payoff vector for a profile over our restricted strategy set.

Table 8.3 shows how our data set is apportioned among the 1-, 2-, and 4-player reduced games. We are able to exhaustively cover the 1-player game, of course. We could also have exhausted the 2-player profiles, but chose to skip some of the less promising ones (fewer than one-quarter) in favor of

1. Interpreting the flight parameters in Table 8.2 requires some additional explanation. Strategies 3–10 and 29–34 included bugs in Walverine's flight purchase delay algorithm that made their flight-timing choices somewhat unpredictable. Strategies 16–28 included a less significant bug that improperly handled boundary conditions and rounded expected perturbations so that they appeared 0.25 lower on average. Strategies 1, 2, and 11–15 did not delay flight purchases at all.

2. Our simulation testbed comprises two dedicated workstations to run the agents, another RAM-laden four-CPU machine to run the agents' optimization processes, a share of a fourth machine to run the TAC game server, and background processes on other machines to control the experiment generation and data gathering. As of the start of the TAC-05 finals (when the first decisive analysis took place), the database contained about 47,000 games. We continued to run the testbed over the following year, in preparation for TAC-06 and this analysis. The subsequent simulations added new profiles and further samples per profile, but no new strategies.

Table 8.2
A selected subset of the strategies included in our Walverine experiments. Walverine-04 corresponds to strategy 17, and Walverine-05 to strategy 37.

Strategy	Flights				Hotels	Entertainment
	$T1$	$T2$	$T3$	$T4$		
3	0.25	0.50	3	200	optimal shading	Q-learned neural net
4	0.25	1.00	3	200	optimal shading	Q-learned neural net
6	0.50	1.00	3	100	optimal shading	Q-learned neural net
16	0.25	0.50	3	200	optimal shading	Q-learned neural net
17	0.25	1.00	3	200	optimal shading	Q-learned neural net
34	0.75	1.50	2	200	50% shading	Q-learned neural net
35	0.50	1.25	3	200	optimal shading	Q-learned neural net
37	0.50	1.25	3	200	optimal shading	WhiteBear
39	0.75	1.50	2	200	optimal shading	WhiteBear
40	0.75	1.50	3	200	10% shading	WhiteBear

devoting more samples elsewhere. The available number of samples could not cover the 4-player games, but as we see below, even 2.9% is sufficient to draw conclusions about the possible equilibria of the game. Spread over the 8-player game, however, 91,000 instances would be insufficient to explore much, and so we refrain from any sampling of the unreduced game.

Table 8.3
Profiles evaluated, reduced TAC games (TAC$\downarrow_p$).

p	Profiles			Samples/Profile	
	total	evaluated	%	min	mean
4	123,410	3626	2.9	15	25.1
2	820	646	78.8	20	40.0
1	40	40	100.0	30	90.8

In the spirit of hierarchical exploration, we sample more instances per profile as the game is further reduced, obtaining more reliable statistical estimates of the coarse backbone relative to its refinement.

Search through Profile Space

One important part of the experimental procedure not described thus far is how we chose which agent strategy configurations to sample, and to what extent. Indeed, the process is manually controlled, informed by standard analysis routines but somewhat ad hoc. Nevertheless, we describe our basic approach, and raise the issue as an important area for future research in empirical game-theoretic methodology.

The relevant question at any point in the sampling process is: "What profile to sample next?" We can choose to generate (i) an additional sample of a profile already evaluated, (ii) a first sample for an unevaluated profile comprised of existing strategies, or (iii) a first sample for a profile including a new strategy. Since the profile space explodes in the number of strategies, we are generally conservative, becoming more amenable to adding new strategies as the existing strategy base appears to us relatively well understood. In many cases, we introduced new strategies based on discovering new ideas for agent components, or problems with some of the existing elements.

We followed a much more structured process for introducing new profiles of existing strategies. In general, profiles are introduced with a view toward refuting candidate equilibria. Specifically, we tend to seek profiles that represent deviations from an existing pure profile or two-strategy mixture with small ϵ bound. By interleaving game analysis with sampling, we can identify prospective profiles routinely. Since there will generally be many choices of how to deviate, we require secondary criteria as well. For instance, we prefer profiles that deviate from multiple candidates, or have many evaluated neighbors already in the data set.

Note that the foregoing selection can be applied with respect to the game at any level of reduction. We have interleaved consideration of TAC$\downarrow_1$, TAC$\downarrow_2$, and TAC$\downarrow_4$, devoting more effort toward the finer-grained games as the coarser levels become better defined (i.e., once deviations from candidates of more severely reduced games have been thoroughly explored).

With respect to profiles already sampled, our highest priority is to maintain a minimum number of samples (see Table 8.3) for any evaluated profile. Next, whenever we explore new deviations from a candidate, we also allocate some samples to the candidate itself, and some to profiles that currently seem to be the best deviations.

Although the process described here is informal and could benefit from analysis and optimization, it contains several important qualitative features. Given the size of the search space, uniform exploration is infeasible. Consequently, we require guidance to focus on the parts of profile space most relevant to strategic analysis. The criteria we adopted balance exploration of new directions with better understanding of areas with established promise. We suspect that existing methods can be employed to improve and automate our sampling process. For example, the information-theoretic criteria proposed by Walsh et al. [2003], for allocating additional samples given a completely evaluated empirical game, could perhaps be extended to cases with missing profiles.

One-Player Game

The 1-player game (TAC $\downarrow_1$) would typically not merit the term "game", as it assumes each strategy plays only among copies of itself. Thus, its analysis considers no strategic interactions. To "solve" the game, we simply evaluate which has the greatest expected payoff. For our experiment, we obtained 30–300 samples of each of the 40 1-player profiles, one for each strategy.

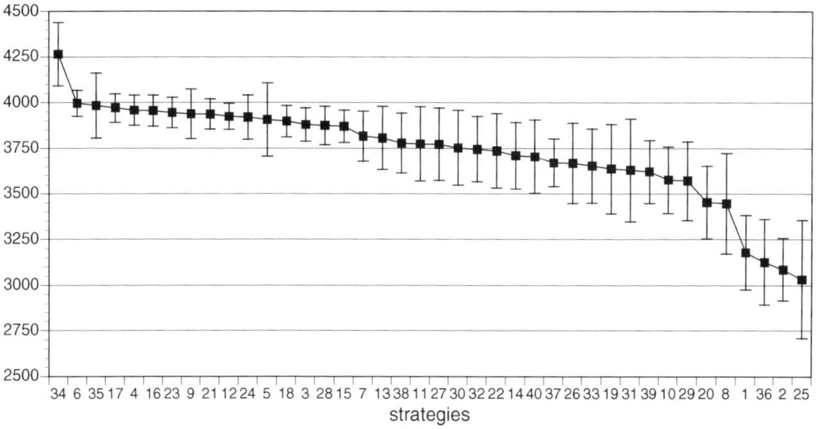

Figure 8.2
Average payoffs for strategy profiles in TAC$\downarrow_1$. Error bars delimit 95% confidence intervals.

Figure 8.2 displays the average payoffs for each 1-player profile, sorted from best to worst, left to right. We tended to take more samples of the more promising profiles, but cannot statistically distinguish every profile in the ranking. Nevertheless our top strategy, number 34, performs dramatically—269 points—better than the next best, number 6. It is instructive to consider why strategy 34 fares so well in self-play. It happens to be the only strategy in the pool that simply shades its hotel bids downward by a large fixed percentage (50%), in effect bidding as would StraightMV but divided by two. The effect when all agents do this is to dramatically lower hotel prices, hence the high scores overall.

In the absence of further data (or reflection), we might propose strategy 34, the unique PSNE of the 1-player game, as a strong general strategy. In fact, however, this strategy is quite vulnerable in environments with other agents. The other agents benefit from the weak contention for hotels, and since they do not adhere to the 50% shading, can obtain more than their proportional share at advantageous prices. Strategy 34 is thus unable to get the hotels it wants. By exploring a reduction less extreme than TAC$\downarrow_1$ we can start to consider some of these strategic interactions.

Two-Player Game

The 2-player game, TAC$\downarrow_2$, comprises 820 distinct profiles: $40 \times 39/2 = 780$ where two different strategies are played by four agents each, plus the 40 profiles from TAC$\downarrow_1$ where all agents play the same. We can identify PSNE simply by examining each strategy pair (s, s'), and verifying whether each is a best response to the other. In doing so, we must account for the fact that our sample data may not include evaluations for all possible profiles.

DEFINITION 8.6: Profiles can be classified into four disjoint categories, defined below for the 2-player pure-strategy case. (The generalization to I-player is straightforward.)

1. If (s, s') has not been empirically evaluated, then $\hat{u}(s, s')$ is undefined, and we say (s, s') is *unevaluated.*
2. Otherwise, and for some t, $\hat{u}(t, s') > \hat{u}(s, s')$ or $\hat{u}(t, s) > \hat{u}(s', s)$. In this case, we say (s, s') is *refuted.*
3. Otherwise, and for some t, (t, s') is unevaluated or (s, t) is unevaluated. In this case, we say (s, s') is a *candidate.*
4. Otherwise, we say (s, s') is *confirmed.*

Based on our TAC$\downarrow_2$ simulations, we have confirmed five PSNE: (3,28), (4,9), (5,24), (6,40), and (16,34). We have refuted 641 profiles, and the remaining 174 are unevaluated.

The definitions above say nothing about the statistical strength of our confirmation or refutation of equilibria. For any particular comparison, one can perform a statistical analysis to evaluate the weight of evidence for or against stability of a given profile. For instance, we could construct diagrams of the form of Figure 8.2, but representing the payoff in response to a particular strategy, rather than in self-play. Such a plot of responses to strategy 24 would indicate, for example, that 4 is quite nearly as good as 5, and so the confirmation of (5,24) as a PSNE is statistically weak.

We can also measure the *degree* of refutation in terms of the ϵ measure defined by Equation (8.1). Since the payoff function is only partially evaluated, for any profile we have a *lower bound* on ϵ based on the deviation profiles thus far evaluated. We can generalize the classifications above (refuted, candidate, confirmed) in the obvious way to hold with respect to any given ϵ level. For example, profile (17,18) is confirmed at $\epsilon = 0.08$, (4,24) at $\epsilon = 1.8$, and (6,17) at $\epsilon = 6.2$, but all other non-PSNE profiles are refuted at $\epsilon > 20$. Figure 8.3 presents the distribution of ϵ levels at which the 646 evaluated 2-player profiles have been refuted. For example, over half have been refuted at $\epsilon > 240$, and all but 18 at $\epsilon > 80$. These 18 pure profiles remain candidates (in fact all confirmed) at $\epsilon = 40$.

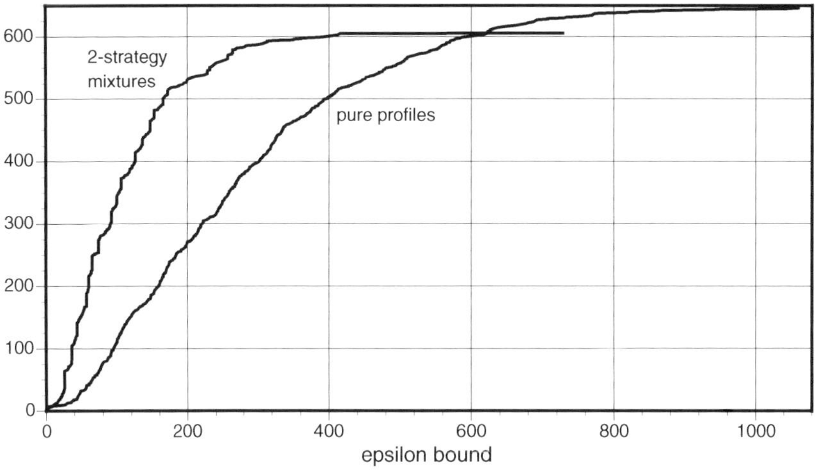

Figure 8.3
Cumulative distribution of ϵ bounds in $\text{TAC}_{\downarrow 2}$.

We can also evaluate symmetric profiles by considering mixtures of strategies. Although we do not have the full payoff function, we can derive ϵ bounds on mixed profiles, as long as we have evaluated pure profiles corresponding to all combinations of strategies *supported* (i.e., are played with positive probability) in the mixture. For example, we can derive such bounds for all 606 *pairs* of strategies for which we have evaluated 2-player profiles. The distribution of bounds for these pairs are also plotted in Figure 8.3. Note that the ϵ bound for a strategy pair is based on the *best* mixture possible of that pair, and so the refutation levels tend to be smaller than for pure strategies. Indeed, three pairs—(16,34), (4,9), (6,40)—participate in confirmed equilibria at $\epsilon = 1.0$, and a total of nine pairs remain candidates at $\epsilon = 10$, with eight confirmed at that level.

We apply the term *k-clique* to a set of k strategies such that all profiles involving these strategies are evaluated. A clique defines a subgame of the original game, which can be evaluated by standard methods. We applied iterative elimination of dominated strategies to all the maximal cliques of the 2-player game, ranging in size up to $k = 27$. This indeed pruned many strategies and induced new subsumption relations among the cliques, leaving us with only one maximal clique, of size 20. The 20-strategy game proved insoluble given the standard algorithm (Lemke-Howson, [McKelvey and McLennan, 1996]) and available computation, so we pruned another strategy, which was almost dominated in that there exists another strategy no worse by more than 11.3 against any profile. This yields a 19-strategy subgame for which any NE must be an 11.3-NE of the original [Cheng and Wellman, 2007]. Applying the Lemke-Howson algorithm to this subgame, we identified 31 candidate symmetric equilibria (not refuted by strategies outside the cliques), with distinct supports (i.e., sets of supported strategies) ranging in size from two to nine.

Because any equilibrium of the full game must also be an equilibrium in any subgame encompassing its support, this exercise allows us to prune broad regions of profile space from consideration.[3] For instance, the subgame results effectively refute 5058 strategy triples (out of 9880 total, or 51%) as comprising support for symmetric equilibria. Similarly, we refute 30,138 strategy quadruples (33%). Given the importance of small supports in recent approaches to deriving equilibria [Porter et al., 2004], or approximate equilibria [Lipton et al., 2003], focusing search in these regions can be helpful.

Finally, we can account for statistical variation in the estimated payoffs by employing sensitivity analysis in our ϵ calculations. Specifically, we interpret each payoff value in the estimated game as normally distributed with mean and variance given by the sample. We then apply Monte Carlo methods to generate a distribution of ϵ values for a given profile, one corresponding to each draw of a payoff function from the specified distributions. Naturally, even our confirmed equilibria are refuted with substantial probability, and thus have positive ϵ in expectation. The most robustly stable profile we have identified thus far is a mixture of (6,9,21), with a mean ϵ value of 77.

3. Pruning is strictly justified only under the assumption that we have identified *all* symmetric equilibria of the clique subgames. The Lemke-Howson algorithm does not guarantee this, but in every case for which we were able to check using more exhaustive methods [McKelvey and McLennan, 1996], in fact all such equilibria were found.

Four-Player Game

Our analysis of the 4-player game, TAC$\downarrow_4$, parallels that of the 2-player game, though based on a sparser coverage of the profile space.

Although our coverage of TAC$\downarrow_4$ is far from exhaustive, in some areas of the strategy space the evaluated profiles are relatively dense. For instance, there are 25 5-cliques, that is, (overlapping) sets of five strategies for which we have sampled all possible profiles. We used replicator dynamics to derive a symmetric mixed equilibrium for each of these clique games, and for eight of these the profile is a candidate equilibrium with respect to the entire data set (i.e., no beneficial deviations are found among the evaluated profiles). These candidates are presented in Table 8.4.

Table 8.4
Candidate equilibria in TAC$\downarrow_4$, as determined by replicator dynamics applied to clique subgames. Each column represents a symmetric mixed profile, with dashes indicating that a strategy was not included in the corresponding clique.

Strategy	mixed profiles							
3	.171	0	.136	—	—	—	—	—
4	0	0	.675	—	—	—	—	—
5	—	—	—	0	0	—	—	—
6	—	—	—	—	—	0	—	—
7	.128	—	—	.260	—	—	—	—
9	—	—	—	—	.384	—	—	—
16	.701	.744	.064	.622	.390	.224	0	.085
17	0	.225	0	—	—	0	.399	0
18	—	—	—	—	—	—	.087	—
21	—	—	—	0	0	—	—	—
23	—	.031	—	—	—	—	—	—
24	—	—	.125	.118	.226	.177	.304	—
37	—	—	—	—	—	—	—	.199
39	—	—	—	—	—	.599	.210	.170
40	—	—	—	—	—	—	—	.546

Another form of analysis considers the maximum benefit from deviation (ϵ bounds) established for the various TAC$\downarrow_4$ profiles. As indicated in Table 8.3, we evaluated 3626 TAC$\downarrow_4$ profiles. Of these, 191 are TAC$\downarrow_2$ profiles with no evaluated neighbors in TAC$\downarrow_4$ (i.e., no deviations tested). Although these are technically PSNE candidates, we distinguish them from the PSNE candidates that have actually survived some challenge. There are two of these, (3,5,17,37) and (9,21,21,37), though both are far from confirmed. The best confirmed approximate equilibrium is (16,37,40,40), which is confirmed at $\epsilon = 11.5$.

The vast majority of other profiles are refuted at high ϵ values. We plot the distribution of ϵ bounds in Figure 8.4. Among the 3435 profiles for which some deviation is evaluated, 97.7% of them are refuted at $\epsilon > 50$. Over half are refuted at $\epsilon > 230$.

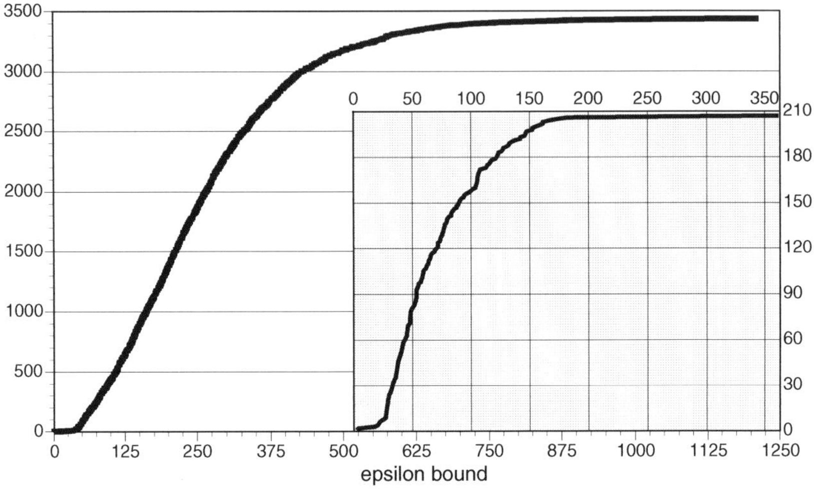

Figure 8.4
Cumulative distribution of ϵ bounds in TAC$\downarrow_4$. Main graph: pure profiles. Inset: two-strategy mixtures.

Figure 8.4 also shows, inset, the distribution of ϵ bounds over the 207 strategy pairs for which we have evaluated all combinations in TAC$\downarrow_4$ (i.e., the 2-cliques). Among these are one confirmed equilibrium (16,17) at $\epsilon = 2.5$ and another (3,37) at $\epsilon = 3.9$, with all other pairs refuted at $\epsilon > 17$.

One way to assess a strategy is to consider its versatility across contexts, as indicated by the frequency with which the best deviation from a profile is to that agent. Among the 3435 evaluated TAC$\downarrow_4$ profiles with deviations, in 642 of them (18.7%), the best deviation is to strategy 37. The next "most-deviated-to" strategy (40) covers 412 (12.0%), and no others account for more than 9%. Note that one must interpret such numbers with much caution, since the potential deviations are not evaluated with equal frequency. Moreover, any figure of merit that aggregates across profiles is suspect, as the distribution of available profiles is not uniform, and different profiles are not equally relevant to such an evaluation.

Finally, given data in both TAC$\downarrow_2$ and TAC$\downarrow_4$, we can perform some comparisons to investigate how well the 2-player game approximates the higher-fidelity 4-player game. The plot of Figure 8.5 includes a point for each 2-clique in TAC$\downarrow_4$, measuring on the x-axis the instability (ϵ) in the 4-player game one obtains by playing the most stable mixture of the two strategies according to the TAC$\downarrow_2$ analysis. The y-axis measures the corresponding ϵ for playing according to the TAC$\downarrow_4$ analysis. The plot suggests a rough correlation, though there are clearly many cases where the TAC$\downarrow_2$ solution is far from the best for TAC$\downarrow_4$. Although we do not have analogous measures relating TAC$\downarrow_4$ and TAC$\downarrow_8$ (i.e., the full 8-player game), we believe the approximation is considerably more accurate for this finer-grain comparison.

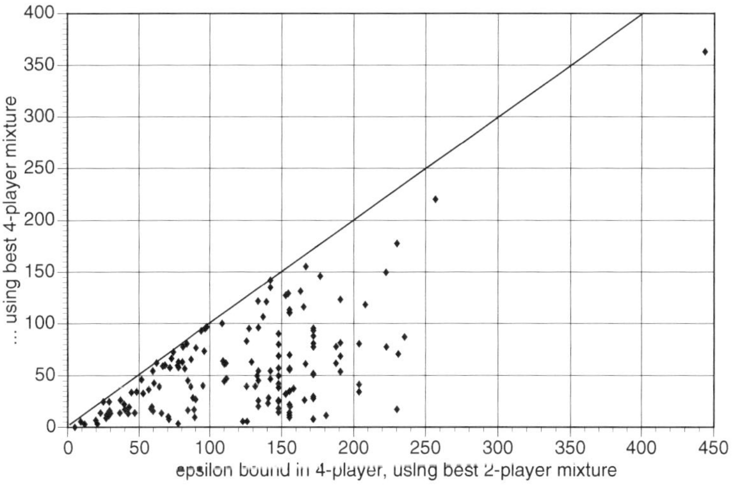

Figure 8.5
ϵ bounds in the 4-player game achieved by playing the best mixture from the 2-player game, vs. playing that best in the 4-player. All points must be southeast of the diagonal by definition.

Selecting Walverine-05

Given all this simulation and analysis, how should one determine the "best" strategy to play in TAC? We do have strong evidence for expecting that all but a fraction of the original 40 strategies will turn out to be unstable within this set. The supports of candidate equilibria tend to concentrate on a fraction of the strategies, suggesting we may limit consideration to this group. Thus, the

Walverine designers employed the preceding analysis primarily to identify promising strategies, and then refined this set through further evaluation in preliminary rounds of the actual TAC tournament.

For the first stage—identifying promising strategies—the 1-player game is of little use. Even discounting strategy 34 (the best strategy in the 1-player game, specially crafted to do well with copies of itself) our experience suggests that strategic interaction is too fundamental to TAC for performance in the 1-player game to correlate more than loosely with performance in the unreduced game. The 4-player game accounts for strategic interaction at a fine granularity, being sensitive to deviations by as few as two of the eight agents. The 2-player game could well lead us astray in this respect. For example, that strategy 34 appears in a PSNE of TAC$\downarrow_2$ is likely an artifact of the coarse granularity of that approximation to TAC.

Nonetheless, given the high correlation between the 2- and 4-player game and the relative completeness and analytical convenience of the TAC$\downarrow_2$ data set, the Walverine designers focused on the 2-player game for identifying the final Walverine candidate strategies, augmenting their selections with strategies that appear promising in TAC$\downarrow_4$. Informally, criteria for picking strong strategies include presence in many equilibria and how strongly the strategy is supported. Details of the selection procedure are provided by Wellman et al. [2006].

As the TAC-05 tournament approached, the Walverine designers chose $\{4, 16, 17, 35\}$ as the most promising candidate strategies from TAC$\downarrow_2$, and added $\{3, 37, 39, 40\}$ based on their promise in TAC$\downarrow_4$. Figure 8.6 reveals strategies 37 and 40 to be the top two candidates after the seeding rounds. Recall that these two strategies were most frequently the best deviation target in the data set. In the semifinals, Walverine alternated playing 37 and 40, with 37 coming out on top, 4182 to 3945 ($p = .05$). Based on this, Walverine played strategy 37 in the TAC-05 finals. The results are described in Appendix A, Section A.6.

Based on continuing simulations over the same strategy set during the next year, and a similar winnowing process in the preliminary rounds, strategy 37 was selected for play in TAC-06 as well. (See Appendix A, Section A.7.)

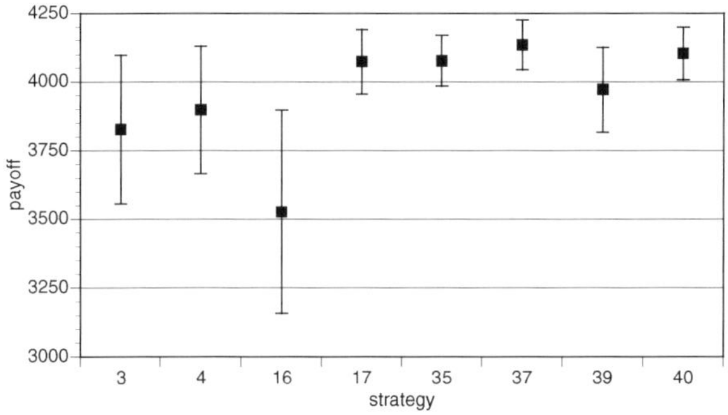

Figure 8.6
Performance of eight Walverine variants in the TAC-05 seeding rounds (507 games).

8.6 Discussion

Whereas a full-blown game-theoretic analysis of domains as complex as TAC is not tractable, empirical methods combining Monte Carlo simulation with game-theoretic reasoning can be a powerful approach to identifying stable strategy profiles. Combined with rigorous testing and evaluation of strategy ideas in fixed environments, game-theoretic reasoning can address the implications of strategic interactions with other agents.

The methods of this chapter have been applied to a variety of trading agent domains. Empirical game-theoretic analysis of a class of simultaneous ascending auction scenarios helped to identify and validate a new strategy for dealing with the exposure problem in these games [Osepayshvili et al., 2005]. For the TAC supply chain management game [Arunachalam and Sadeh, 2005], such analysis verified that aggressive early procurement was a stable (but very destructive) behavior given the 2003 rules, and that a preemptive tactic by one agent was an effective remedy [Wellman et al., 2005a]. Further, attempts at revising the game rules to deter this behavior through storage costs were unsuccessful, and empirical game-theoretic methods demonstrated that no reasonable setting of these costs would have impeded aggressive early procurement [Vorobeychik et al., 2006].

Through an extensive case study of a parameterized Walverine, we illustrated several techniques for exploring a large profile space: hierarchical reduction, reducing variance through control variables, and bounding approximate equilibria in an incomplete game. The success of Walverine-05 in TAC-05 and TAC-06 offers some validation of the approach, but more important is that the empirical game provides guidance to TAC experimenters regarding the relevant contexts in which to evaluate their agent designs. As trading agent researchers develop new ideas—price prediction algorithms, bidding heuristics, and so on—systematic exploration of the widened strategy profile space will help distinguish the most significant advances.

9 Conclusion

This book began with an argument that research situated within the setting of a trading agent *competition* could provide unique insights into the prospects of creating autonomous bidding agents. To that end, a community of agent researchers commenced in 2000 an in-depth exploration of the TAC travel scenario, used as the central domain throughout this book.

Recognizing that a key feature of TAC is that it is formulated as a *competition*, it is incumbent upon us to assess the impact of this feature on our research. In this concluding chapter, we offer some observations about our experiences regarding the use of competitions in multiagent research (Section 9.1). The points presented are important for understanding the context of the research results detailed in this book, and are also potentially useful for colleagues in other areas who are considering formulating new research competitions. We then conclude in Section 9.2 with a brief high-level summary of the book's main contributions and a look toward the future of trading agent research.

9.1 Multiagent Competitions and Research

Competitions are becoming increasingly prevalent in the research world. For one example, the annual Loebner competition[1] challenges entrants to create a computer program whose verbal responses in conversation are judged to be most "human-like". For another example, the biannual planning systems competition [McDermott, 2000; Younes et al., 2005] compares the performance of AI planning systems in a variety of planning domains.

Unlike TAC, in both the Loebner and planning competitions programs are judged and/or scored independently; an entrant's absolute score does not depend on the behavior of the other entrants. However, there have also been several competitions in multiagent domains, in which the agents *do* interact directly. Examples include Axelrod's iterated prisoner's dilemma (IPD) tournament [Axelrod, 1984]; the Santa Fe double auction tournament [Rust et al., 1994]; and the RoShamBo (rock/paper/scissors) programming competition [Billings, 2000]. All three of these competitions led to interesting outcomes despite the fact that entered programs faced very limited input spaces (e.g., in RoShamBo, the agent's only inputs are the sequence of rock/paper/scissors se-

1. `http://www.loebner.net/Prizef/loebner-prize.html`

lections made by others) and chose among relatively few possible actions. The static versions of these games are well understood, and for IPD and RoShamBo the dynamic (iterated) versions have known game-theoretic solutions.

The TAC multiagent domain is comparatively much more complicated and difficult to analyze. In this regard, TAC is more similar to the ongoing series of robot soccer competitions, RoboCup [Kitano et al., 1997]. In both, the agents face complex sensations (e.g., price quotes) with a good deal of hidden state and, for all intents and purposes, continuous action spaces. But most importantly, the success of agent strategies depends a great deal on the strategies of the other competitors.

These features are also shared by the second market game more recently included in the broader TAC enterprise, namely the TAC supply chain management (TAC/SCM) game [Arunachalam and Sadeh, 2005; Eriksson et al., 2006]. The supply chain domain presents interesting challenges not emphasized by TAC Travel, such as multiattribute (e.g., prices, quantities, due dates, etc.) negotiation, and combining trading with production planning and delivery scheduling. At the same time, it shares some key elements (as do most market domains), such as price prediction and bid optimization. All three authors have participated in TAC/SCM and most of the points we raise below from the perspective of TAC Travel apply to our TAC/SCM experience as well.

As a research initiative, TAC has helped advance the state of the art, by providing new and challenging domains for studying issues within the field of artificial intelligence, such as autonomous bidding, multiagent learning, and decision making under uncertainty. However, these domains can be studied outside the competition setting. In this section, we examine the potential pitfalls as well as the benefits of holding periodic large-scale competitions, drawing on our experiences as participants and organizers. We proceed under the premise that scientific progress (as opposed to, for example, entertainment) is the primary goal.

Pitfalls

There are many ways in which an organized competition can divert effort away from fundamental research goals. Here we list some of the possible hazards, and where possible, indicate how TAC has tried to avoid them. As often potential benefits and pitfalls stem from common features, it is up to the participants and organizers to sway the balance toward the benefits.

Obsession with Winning One of the most obvious potential pitfalls of competitions is that entrants try to win them at the expense of all else, including science, especially if there are monetary prizes involved. It is desirable, of course, that developers put forth their best efforts to maximize their agents' performance. A focus on winning, however, leads entrants to maximize their relative rank rather than absolute expected score. This can distort the agents' incentives—leading them to take excessive risks, for example. Worse, an obsession with winning will lead some to protect their most successful ideas from disclosure, thus defeating the public research goals of the enterprise. To avoid this pitfall, TAC designers structure the tournament to minimize the potential benefit of excessive risk-taking (e.g., by including sufficient games). In the TAC domain, the goal of maximizing absolute score appears to be tightly aligned with the goal of maximizing relative rank. In addition, TAC refrains from awarding any monetary prizes, and instead tries to cultivate the practice of disseminating new ideas rapidly. The final round each year includes a forum for poster presentations about each agent, and participants are encouraged to post design descriptions and share ideas with others, potentially leading to publications based on their efforts. Since most participants are academic researchers, their natural incentive structures support emphasizing scientific objectives. Nevertheless, success in the tournament is often considered (e.g., by journal and conference referees) as evidence for merit of the research ideas, and so the tournament outcome is consequential. Overall, the research competition must strike a balance: promoting competitive spirit while trying to prevent that spirit from taking over completely.

Domain-Dependent Solutions Another potential pitfall is the tendency to get bogged down in the low-level details of the domain. If the competition is to serve scientific interests, the successful solutions should exhibit techniques that are generally applicable beyond the particular domain in question. Whereas attention to domain-specific features is necessary to create an effective agent, ad hoc methods should not be sufficient to produce a winning entry. One way to encourage generalizable solutions is to repeat the competition regularly, perhaps with occasional modest rule changes. Maintaining a modular high-level agent architecture facilitates modification of the agent over time, and incorporation of ideas and techniques proven effective by other agents in past competitions. For example, TAC-00 agents explored a variety of approaches to the TAC-specific bid determination problems defined in Chapter 3, and by TAC-01 many of the agents were building upon the previous year's published approaches. As reported in Chapter 4, by TAC-02 most agents had defined a distinct price-prediction module, thus supporting the use of general bidding heuristics (as in Chapter 5), not limited to the specifics of TAC. The rule change in 2004 further rewarded generality and modularity, favoring designs that could take advantage of flexibility in flight purchase timing (or could be easily extended to do so). Overall, successful TAC agents employ a mix of domain-dependent and general-purpose methods (as illustrated by the generic problems and case studies discussed in Chapter 7), maintaining flexibility while still enabling fine-tuned performance.

Barrier to Entry As a competition repeats from year to year, it is natural that experienced participants develop an advantage over newcomers. As time goes on, however, the cumulative effect can erect an imposing barrier to entry. For example, in the world of computer chess, the leaders in the field invested large amounts of time and money building specialized hardware expressly for the purpose. It became virtually impossible for a newcomer to get up to speed in a reasonable amount of time.[2] Because the rules of chess are well-defined and unchanging, a successful approach in one competition is likely to remain successful even if left unchanged. A policy of occasional rule changes thus also helps to lower barriers to entry. For example, the 2001 TAC rule change—from having all of the hotel auctions close at the end of the game to having them close randomly over the course of the game—posed a new and important challenge that had to be addressed by the veteran competitors as well as by the newcomers. Any disadvantage faced by newcomers can also be reduced considerably to the extent that competitors publish their techniques and even make portions of their code available. The TAC agent repository (`http://www.sics.se/tac/showagents.php`) facilitates such sharing, of components for agent development or entire agents for experimental comparisons and analysis.

Inflexible Rules While it is essential that the rules be well-defined, if participants focus on exploiting minute aspects of those rules it can undermine the underlying research goals. Thus, the TAC GameMaster reserves the right to disqualify agents "violating the spirit of fair play". While this approach has the potential to lead to some heated arguments, in our experience, it has been helpful to establish that human judgment will ultimately govern conduct in the interest of the competition.

Invalid Evaluation Conclusions Lazy observers of a competition may con-

2. In the case of chess, commodity hardware has now advanced to the point that, arguably, specialized hardware no longer confers a significant advantage.

clude that if agent A beats agent B, then all of the techniques used by A are superior to those used by B. Of course, this conclusion is invalid. Unless the agents are identical except in one respect, no individual aspect of either can conclusively be credited or blamed for the result. Rather, proper credit assignment can be rendered only through carefully designed controlled experiments. This book has presented several examples where advances in trading agent design are validated by extensive experimental regimens designed to isolate the techniques of interest.

Benefits

If a competition is successful in avoiding the pitfalls, the research community can enjoy the countervailing benefits. Here we list some of those benefits, illustrating them with specific examples from TAC whenever possible.

Research Inspiration Although competitive spirit is blamed for a potential pitfall above (obsession with winning), the motivating force behind competition is also a great source of research inspiration. Several research innovations have been the direct result of preparations for competitions. Ideas first developed as solutions to challenging problems within a specific competition domain can be expressed subsequently as general-purpose techniques and methodological frameworks. For example, the evaluation of abstract, general bidding heuristics presented in Chapter 5 began as a comparison between the bidding heuristics used by ATTac-01 (AverageMU) and RoxyBot-02 (BidEvaluator). Indeed, trading agent research inspired by TAC experience is the reason for this book's existence.

Requirement for Complete Agents Although many of the research contributions emerging from competition efforts pertain to specific techniques and solutions to subproblems, the fact that these were made to work within an overall system—that is, a complete autonomous agent—lends substantial credibility to the results. In addition to optimizing component models and algorithms, agent developers must confront the challenging issues of "closing the loop", that is, putting all the pieces together, from processing information about the environment, to taking actions. No matter how sophisticated an agent's high-level design, if the low-level issues are not resolved, the agent cannot perform. Whereas this need for closing the loop may impede excellent component ideas from being recognized as such, the discipline of working out integration issues can provide crucial insights about the workable definitions of these subproblems.

Deadlines Competitions not only require complete working systems, they also set hard deadlines for their creation. The deadline focuses the energy of entrants on the most crucial issues. Moreover, having a common discrete deadline serves a synchronizing function, enabling the participants to compare their approaches at set times.

Common Platform for Exchanging Ideas Competitions can bring together a group of people who have all tried to solve the same problems in the same general domain, but may not share a common language for expressing and comparing approaches and techniques. For example, in the design of the original planning competition, one main challenge was finding the commonalities and compatibilities among different planning representations [McDermott, 2000]. After several iterations, the relationships of various planning systems are better understood, and ideas from many systems have been unified in the Planning Domain Definition Language (PDDL) that grew directly out of the competition. In addition to a common platform for implementation, a competition offers a common reference point for comparing approaches. For example, the analysis of hotel price-prediction approaches in Chapter 4 employed the TAC-02 semifinals and finals as a test set for measuring prediction quality.

Continually Improving Solutions When holding repeated competitions with the same platform, there is likely to be a continual improvement in solutions from event to event. All entrants know that in order to have a chance of winning a competition, they must be able to outperform the previous champion. Therefore, they are motivated to develop a method that improves over previous solutions. Of course, this benefit only applies if the same, or similar, rules are used as the basis for competition year after year. In the AAAI robot competitions [Arkin, 1998], there are some new tasks to be solved every year (in recent years there have also been some repeated tasks). While the new tasks encourage new entrants, in successive competitions, there is no basis for measuring improvement from year to year. Note the tradeoff between maintaining constant rules to facilitate measuring progress, and changing rules to promote generality in solutions and reduce barriers to entry. The TAC organization has managed this tradeoff by making occasional changes (in 2001 and 2004), but leaving the game unchanged for multiple iterations between changes.

Excitement for Students at all Levels The inherent excitement of the TAC competitions encourages students at all levels to become involved in serious research. Competition entries often come from teams of professors, graduate students, and undergraduates working together. Getting students involved in competitions is an excellent way of exposing them to cutting-edge research problems and collaborative research practice. In addition, competitions can be an attractive vehicle for undergraduate and graduate project classes. Courses around the world have employed TAC to teach about artificial intelligence or electronic commerce. Students in these classes have genuinely enjoyed putting in the time and effort needed to create working agents, and watching them perform. Several TAC entries over the years got their start as student projects, either from classroom efforts or individual directed research.

Wide Pool of Agents Created After each competition, all of the entrants have created agents capable of performing in the given domain. If these agents are made available in some way, they can subsequently be used for controlled testing of research contributions. For example, in order to test an isolated aspect of one's agent, say technique x, one could play the agent first with technique x active, and then without, thus establishing the effects of technique x. However, as discussed in Chapter 8, it is important to carefully select the context of *other* agents in which to perform this test. In that case study, the pool of agents was limited to variations of one team's entry, Walverine. The set of agents that competed in prior TAC tournaments is a potentially richer source of strategies to employ in controlled testing. The TAC agent repository mentioned above stores many versions of prior entries, from both TAC games (Travel and SCM). Jordan et al. [2007] have exploited this repository for empirical game-theoretic analysis of TAC/SCM agents and Pardoe and Stone [2006] have used it for controlled testing of their adaptive TAC/SCM agent.

Generate Realistic Populations Another related benefit of competitions is that realistic agent populations, constituting small economies in the case of TAC, can be studied. Presumably there are many groups in the financial industry who have created or are creating automatic trading agents. However, they generally do not share information about their techniques, or often even let on that they are building agents at all. Therefore, there may be significant innovations that are hidden from the public domain. Research competitions provide incentives for participants to innovate in a common problem domain, and in an open forum, so that the broader community can study and learn from these efforts.

Encourage Robust and Flexible Software Competitions are by their nature one-shot events. If software fails for any reason, much hard work can be wasted. Thus it is important to test systems thoroughly, under as many conditions as possible, prior to the event. In addition, since the rules of a competition may change slightly from year to year, it is always beneficial to create software that can be easily adapted to such changes.

In our experience, the benefits of the trading agent competition far outweigh the pitfalls. These competitions have been a source of inspiration in our own research, enabling the very writing of this book. As evidenced by the bibliography, numerous other participants have also published articles based on research originally motivated by TAC competitions.[3] Again, the competition results themselves are not scientifically conclusive; but the competition process coupled with subsequent experimentation and analysis can yield myriad lessons for trading agent design and analysis.

9.2 Concluding Remarks

In the seven years since its introduction in 2000, a tremendous amount of effort has gone into organizing and competing in TAC. Is this effort justified?

Not surprisingly, we would argue that the attention and energy focused on TAC by the trading agent research community has been worthwhile. As a result of this endeavor, we have at our disposal a bonanza of new trading agent techniques: bidding heuristics, price-prediction methods, learning algorithms, and optimization models. These techniques have all been vetted in a challenging and competitive benchmark environment, refined, and compared with alternatives. Experimental analysis of TAC strategies has produced a treasure trove of data, resolving empirical questions of efficacy and pointing trading agent researchers in promising new directions.

Even more significant than the individual techniques, in our view, are the broader lessons we can extract from the TAC experience. One might have predicted that the competition would converge on a single best-practice solution, with slight variations, or would devolve into a contest among incomparable ad hoc programs. Instead, what we observe is the emergence of a common (if not universal) trading agent architecture, with an interesting diversity of competing approaches explored for the various subproblems. Specific TAC techniques have evolved along distinct threads through generations of the tournament, but—aided by common functional structure—with substantial cross-fertilization across entrants.

3. For an up-to-date and comprehensive listing of TAC-related publications, see `http://tac.eecs.umich.edu/researchreport.html`.

In Chapter 3, we characterized the basic underlying architecture of an autonomous bidder, and exploited its structure to organize the presentation of specific trading agent techniques. Our coverage of techniques for the major trading agent subtasks, specifically price prediction (Chapter 4, and particular machine-learning approaches in Chapter 6) and bidding under uncertainty (Chapter 5), encompasses state-of-the-art methods for dealing with these problems in interdependent markets. In presenting this material, we aimed to convey the general applicability of these techniques, while grounding their motivation and evaluation in the specific TAC domain. Even the most TAC-specific bidding strategies (Chapter 7) can be related to the research literature on more generic market mechanisms.

Ultimately, the value of TAC-derived agent design ideas will be determined by their applicability to real-world trading environments. The TAC travel game is not entirely realistic—certainly not as a model of real-world travel markets. Given the prime motivation of fostering research, the game design reflects the balance of many factors: making it interesting and engaging, making it simple to understand and play, yet making it challenging enough to expand the boundaries of knowledge. Ensuring that the game stressed motivating research questions, while maintaining simplicity, sometimes ran counter to the goal of modeling reality.

For example, the periodic closing of randomly selected hotel auctions is a reasonable measure to promote early bidding, but one not commonly (if ever) seen in real-world market mechanisms. The more fundamental features of the TAC environment, however, *are* characteristic of real markets. Even if the random-closing element is not literally there, the need to maintain active bids in a dynamic market, with recourse to alternatives in other ongoing and subsequent markets, is ubiquitous in real-world trading.

Thus, we consider the body of techniques distilled from trading agents competing in TAC to provide a firm engineering foundation for autonomous bidding in real-world domains. Continued research and practice in TAC Travel, TAC/SCM, and other trading environments will refine and validate (and likely supersede) this body of knowledge, rendering more accessible and routine the art of trading agent design.

Although automated trading in electronic markets has not yet fully taken hold, the trend is well underway. Through TAC, the trading agent community has demonstrated the potential for autonomous bidders to make pivotal trading decisions in a most effective way. Such agents promise to accelerate the automation of trading more broadly, and thus shape the future of commerce.

A Tournament Data

This appendix presents comprehensive data from the history of TAC tournaments. Each TAC tournament is organized as a series of competition phases. Although the precise structure varies from year to year, it generally includes preliminary rounds (qualifying and/or seeding) held over an extended period (e.g., a few weeks), followed a short time later by semifinals and finals collocated with an academic research conference. At the conference, in parallel with the final phase of the tournament, entrants discuss their designs and disseminate research results, through oral presentations, posters, and informal exchanges. Since 2003, TAC has been held in conjunction with the *Workshop on Trading Agent Design and Analysis* (TADA), which includes papers about TAC as well as other studies contributing to trading agent research. Although attending TAC is encouraged, entrants may also participate remotely without traveling to the conference venue.

The main purpose of the preliminary rounds is to encourage competitors to create functional agents well in advance of the finals, thus ensuring a competitive field by the main event. During the preliminary rounds, agents are randomly scheduled to participate in a large number of games running around the clock. Any agent that is in reasonable working order satisfies the qualification criteria and proceeds to the seeding round. The seeding round serves to winnow the field (if necessary) to the number of slots available for semifinalists, and is sometimes used to group the agents into heats. Often in preliminary rounds games are weighted in a progressive manner, thus encouraging teams to experiment early on but create a stable agent by the end of the round. As a (not incidental) side effect, the preliminary rounds provide a source of realistic game data that is often exploited by designers taking a statistical approach.

From 2000–02, the semifinals and finals were held on a single day. This format severely limited the number of games that could be played. On the other hand, it allowed the culmination of the tournament to take place in a workshop environment with most of the participants present. The single-day format also ensured that agents would remain more or less unchanged during these rounds. Starting in 2003, the final phase of the tournament (including both semifinal and final rounds) was extended to three days,[1] with the TADA workshop held on the first day. The games during this phase are displayed in an open exhibit

1. The organizers also enacted a rule prohibiting modification of an agent during a tournament day.

area, so TAC, TADA, and conference attendees can observe the competition.

For each year of the tournament, we provide some basic data about the version of the rules in force, who operated the competition, and where the finals were held. We list the participating agents by name and affiliation, and provide citations to published descriptions. For some years we also include narrative descriptions of the tournament progression. We further present tournament results, tabulating scores for each agent in the various rounds of the tournament. In these tables, agents are sorted by performance in the final round, then (for those not in the finals) semifinals, etc. Adjustment factors (where reported) are based on the control variates method described in Section 8.3.

A.1 2000

Rules: 2000

GameMaster: Michael Wellman

Operations: University of Michigan

Finals Date: 8 July

Locale: Fourth International Conference on Multiagent Systems (ICMAS-00), Boston, Massachusetts, USA

The first TAC event attracted 16 entrants from six countries (Japan, Russia, Sweden, Switzerland, Turkey, United States). The agents and their designers' affiliations are listed in Table A.1. Twenty agents played in the preliminary rounds—a few teams entered more than one, which was allowed this first year. Only the top scoring agent from each team was considered for qualification.

The preliminary rounds were conducted over the period 22–30 June, comprising 55–80 games per agent, with the lowest ten scores dropped. Twelve semifinalists were selected based on their performance in the preliminary round, with one slot reserved for each country represented in the agent pool. The 12 semifinalists played six games each in a round-robin style. The top eight agents proceeded to a final round of seven games. The official final scores include the 13 games played by each of the finalists. Scores for all rounds are presented in Table A.2.

Further details of the TAC-00 agents and tournament results are reported by Stone and Greenwald [2005]. Boman [2001] provides some further contemporaneous observations on the event.

Table A.1
TAC-00 participants.

Agent	Affiliation	Reference
ALTA	Artificial Life, Inc.	
Aster	InterTrust Technologies	
ATTac	AT&T Labs — Research	[Stone et al., 2001]
Codex	Marc Ringuette	
DAIHard	U Tulsa	
EPFLAgent	Swiss Federal Inst Technology	
EZAgent	North Carolina State U	
Gekko	USC/ISI	
harami	Bogazici U	
Kuis	Kyoto U	
Nidsia	Dalle Molle Inst. for AI (IDSIA)	[Fornara and Gambardella, 2001]
RiskPro	Royal Inst Technology & Stockholm U	
RoxyBot	Brown U	[Greenwald and Boyan, 2005]
T1	Swedish Inst Comp Sci & Industrilogik	
UATrader	U Arizona	
umbctac	U Maryland Baltimore Cty	

A.2 2001

Rules: 2001
GameMaster: Michael Wellman
Operations: University of Michigan
Finals Date: 14 October
Locale: Third ACM Conference on Electronic Commerce (EC-01), Tampa, Florida, USA

The TAC-01 qualifying round ran from 10–17 September and included 28 agents, each of which played in about 270 games. Several groups entered more than one agent in the qualifying round; however, only one agent per group was allowed to proceed to the seeding round. The top 12 agents automatically qualified, and all others with positive scores were invited to participate in the seeding round and finals.

For the resulting field of 17 teams (see Table A.3), a seeding round was held from 24 September until 5 October to determine how the semifinal groups would be formed. In addition to the qualifying teams, two additional agents were included in the seeding rounds for calibration purposes. First, ATTac-00 (Section 6.1) is a copy of the highest-scoring agent from the TAC-00 finals. To account for the rule changes between TAC-00 and TAC-01, ATTac-00 was

Table A.2
TAC-00 scores, all rounds.

Agent	Preliminary	Semifinals	Finals
ATTac	3921	3139	3398
RoxyBot	4464	3011	3283
Aster	4047	3010	3068
umbctac	3433	3189	3051
ALTA	3456	2653	2198
DAIHard	3719	2542	1873
RiskPro	3571	1515	1570
T1	3060	1678	1270
Gekko	3324	1479	—
Kuis	2853	1309	—
Nidsia	1577	1011	—
EZAgent	2392	687	—
UATrader	2452	—	—
Codex	1830	—	—
harami	1608		—
EPFLAgent	500	—	—

modified with a one-line change that caused it to place all of its bids before the first hotel closed as opposed to during the last minute of the game.

Second, dummy_buyer, the default agent provided by the TAC organizers to play in test games that did not have a full slate of players, was included in the seeding round's pool as a benchmark. Whereas most of the other agents' behaviors were modified between (and during) the qualifying and seeding round, this dummy agent was left unchanged. Indeed, we observed substantial deterioration in the dummy agent's standing as the preliminary rounds progressed.

One entrant (bang) withdrew from the competition after the seeding round. The remaining 16 eligible teams were grouped into two semifinal heats. The top four and bottom four teams from the seeding round formed one group, with the rest of the teams (places 5–12) forming the other.

The semifinals and finals were held together on 14 October. Each of the semifinal heats consisted of 11 games among identical agents. The top four teams from each heat advanced to the finals. The finals consisted of 24 games among the same eight agents. Right from the beginning, it became clear that livingagents was the team to beat in the finals. They jumped to an early lead in the first two games, and by eight games into the round, they were more than 135 points per game ahead of the next team (SouthamptonTAC). After another eight games, they were more than 250 points ahead of their two closest competitors (ATTac and WhiteBear).

Table A.3
TAC-01 participants. ATTac-00 and dummy_buyer were inserted in the seeding round for calibration purposes only.

Agent	Affiliation	Reference
006	Swedish Inst Comp Sci	[Aurell et al., 2002]
arc-2k	Chinese U Hong Kong	
ATTac	AT&T Labs — Research	[Stone et al., 2003]
ATTac-00	AT&T Labs — Research	[Stone et al., 2001]
bang	NCST Bangalore	
Caisersose	U Essex	
dummy_buyer	U Michigan	
harami	Bogazici U	
jboadw	McGill U	[Boadway and Precup, 2001]
livingagents	Living Systems AG	[Fritschi and Dorer, 2002]
PainInNEC	NEC Research	
polimi_bot	Politecnico di Milano	
Retsina	Carnegie Mellon U	
RoxyBot	Brown U	[Greenwald, 2002]
SouthamptonTAC	U Southampton	[He and Jennings, 2002]
Tacsman	Stanford U	
umbctac	U Maryland Baltimore Cty	
Urlaub01	Penn State U	
WhiteBear	Cornell U	

At that point, ATTac began making a comeback. With one game to be played, ATTac was only an average of 22 points per game behind. It thus needed to beat livingagents by 514 points in the final game to overtake it, well within the margins observed in individual game instances.

As the game completed, ATTac's score of 3979 was one of the first to be posted by the server. The other agents' scores were reported one by one, until only the livingagents score was left. After agonizing seconds, the TAC server posted a final game score of 4626, securing a win for livingagents.

A listing of TAC-01 scores (all rounds, plus control variates adjustment for final-round scores) are presented in Table A.4. The seeding round comprised approximately 315 games per agent. In the semifinal heats, each agent played only 11 games. Each agent in the finals played 24 games.

Lanzi and Strada [2002] present a statistical analysis of the TAC-01 tournament results.

A.3 2002

Rules: 2001

Table A.4
TAC-01 scores, all rounds.

Agent	Seeding	Heat 1	Heat 2	Finals	(adjust)
livingagents	3012	3660	—	3670	–66
ATTac	2686	—	3249	3622	42
WhiteBear	3120	3485	—	3513	–72
Urlaub01	3076	3485	—	3421	–2
Retsina	2675	—	3294	3352	–30
SouthamptonTAC	3164	3615	—	3254[a]	–64
Caisersose	2870	—	3038	3074	202
Tacsman	2984	—	2966	2859	–11
006	1115	3241	—	—	—
PainInNEC	2575	—	2906	—	—
polimi_bot	2858	—	2835	—	—
umbctac	2765	—	2773	—	—
RoxyBot	2732	—	2112	—	—
arc-2k	–36	1746	—	—	—
jboadw	1307	1717	—	—	—
harami	2156	94	—	—	—
ATTac-00	2412	—	—	—	—
dummy_buyer	1673	—	—	—	—
bang	1306	—	—	—	—

[a] SouthamptonTAC's final score was adversely affected by a crash in one game, leading to a loss of over 3000 points. Discounting that game would have led to an average score of 3531.

GameMaster: Joakim Eriksson
Operations: Swedish Institute of Computer Science
Finals Date: 28 July
Locale: Eighteenth National Conference on Artificial Intelligence (AAAI-02), Edmonton, Alberta, Canada

The entrant field for TAC-02 (Table A.5) increased to 19 agents, from nine different countries. Many agent developers took advantage of the new software libraries provided by the Swedish Institute of Computer Science (SICS), now handling operations. Capsule descriptions of 16 TAC-02 agents appear in the survey article by Greenwald [2003a].

The TAC-02 seeding rounds were held during the period 1–12 July, each agent playing 440 games. Weights increased each day, so that later games counted more than earlier, and the lowest ten scores for each agent were dropped. The top 16 agents advanced to the semifinals, held on 28 July in Edmonton, Canada. There were two semifinal heats: H1 comprising agents seeded 1–4 and 13–16, with the 5–12 seeds placed in heat H2. The top four

Table A.5
TAC-02 participants.

Agent	Affiliation	Reference
006	Swedish Inst Comp Sci	[Aurell et al., 2002]
ATTac	AT&T Labs — Research	[Stone et al., 2003]
BigRed	McGill U	
cuhk	Chinese U Hong Kong	
harami	Bogazici U	
kavayaH	Oracle India	[Putchala et al., 2002]
livingagents	Living Systems AG	[Fritschi and Dorer, 2002]
PackaTAC	N Carolina State U	
PainInNEC	NEC Research (et al.)	
RoxyBot	Brown U	[Greenwald and Boyan, 2004]
SouthamptonTAC	U Southampton	[He and Jennings, 2003, 2004]
Thalis	U Essex	[Fasli and Poursanidis, 2003]
tniTac	Poli Bucharest	
TOMAhack	U Toronto	
tvad	Technion	
umbctac	U Maryland Baltimore Cty	[Ding et al., 2003]
Walverine	U Michigan	[Cheng et al., 2005]
WhiteBear	Cornell U	[Vetsikas and Selman, 2003]
zepp	Poli Bucharest	

teams from each heat (14 games, lowest score dropped) proceeded to the finals, which ran for 32 games the same day.

The scores for all rounds (and adjustments for final scores) are presented in Table A.6. We include a separate evaluation of entertainment reward (trip entertainment value plus cash flow from entertainment trading) in the finals, as discussed in Section 7.3.

Note that ATTac was the highest scorer in the seeding round. A bug in the process of retraining its price predictor for the final tournament caused it to falter in the semifinals (see Section 6.4).

A.4 2003

Rules: 2001
GameMaster: Joakim Eriksson
Operations: Swedish Institute of Computer Science
Finals Date: 11–13 August
Locale: Eighteenth International Joint Conference on Artificial Intelligence (IJCAI-03), Acapulco, Mexico

Table A.6
TAC-02 scores, all rounds. Seeding rounds are weighted as described in text.

Agent	Seeding	Heat 1	Heat 2	Finals	(adjust)	entertainment
WhiteBear	2966	—	3324	3413	66	1623
SouthamptonTAC	3129	3397	—	3385	–48	1464
Thalis	3000	—	3199	3246	–36	1393
umbctac	3118	3208	2773	3236	55	1327
Walverine	2772	—	3287	3210	67	1409
livingagents	3091	3310	—	3181[a]	–20	1362
kavayaH	2549	3200	—	3099	–60	1460
cuhk	3055	—	3266	3069	–24	1452
PackaTAC	2835	—	3250	—	—	—
RoxyBot	2855	—	3160	—	—	—
006	2847	—	3146	—	—	—
tniTac	2232	3108	—	—	—	—
ATTac	3131	3065	—	—	—	—
TOMAhack	2809	—	2843	—	—	—
tvad	2618	2724	—	—	—	—
PainInNEC	2319	2193	—	—	—	—
zepp	2098	—	—	—	—	—
harami	2064	—	—	—	—	—
BigRed	696	—	—	—	—	—

[a] livingagents missed two games due to a bug. Discounting those games would have led to an average score of 3393.

Table A.7 lists the agents that participated in the TAC-03 tournament. Eleven out of 15 entrants were agents with TAC experience, or represented institutions that had previously entered TAC agents. The version of ATTac entered in this tournament was ATTac-01.

Scores (all rounds) are presented in Table A.8. The semifinal round comprised 60 games for the 15 teams (each playing 32) on 11–12 August. Due to network problems encountered in the semifinals, NNN was advanced to the finals. Each of the nine finalists played 24 games on 13 August.

A.5 2004

Rules: 2004

GameMaster: Amy Greenwald

Operations: Swedish Institute of Computer Science

Finals Date: 20–22 July

Locale: Third International Joint Conference on Autonomous Agents and Multiagent Systems (AAMAS-04), New

Table A.7
TAC-03 participants.

Agent	Affiliation	Reference
ATTac	AT&T Labs — Research	[Stone et al., 2003]
CUP	PUC Rio de Janeiro	
EPFLAgentas	Swiss Federal Inst Technology	
Leprechaun	U Mannheim	
MISS	U Southampton	
NNN	Hebrew U	
PackaTAC	N Carolina State U	
RoxyBot	Brown U	
TeamHarmony	Hokkaido U	[Onodera et al., 2003]
Thalis	U Essex	
tniTac	Poli Bucharest	
umbctac	U Maryland Baltimore Cty	
Walverine	U Michigan	[Cheng et al., 2005]
WhiteBear	Cornell U	[Vetsikas and Selman, 2005]
zepp	Poli Bucharest	

York, New York, USA

Table A.9 lists the agents entered in the TAC-04 tournament.

Scores (all rounds) are presented in Table A.10. In the semifinal round (20–21 July), 11 agents played 50 games each. The eight finalists played 35 games on 22 July. The fact that the control variate adjustments (see Section 8.3) are all quite positive indicates that the stochastic factors (flight prices, client preferences) were generally unfavorable during the final round. A sensitivity analysis of the TAC-04 finals supporting the robustness of WhiteBear's victory is presented by Reeves [2005, Chapter 6].

A.6 2005

Rules: 2004
GameMaster: Ioannis Vetsikas
Operations: Swedish Institute of Computer Science
Finals Date: 1–3 August
Locale: Nineteenth International Joint Conference on Artificial Intelligence (IJCAI-05), Edinburgh, Scotland, UK

Table A.11 lists the agents entered in the TAC-05 tournament.

The TAC-05 seeding round comprised 688 games, conducted over two

Table A.8
TAC-03 scores, all rounds.

Agent	Seeding	Semifinals	Finals	(adjust)
ATTac	3735	3474	3200	–55
PackaTAC	3668	3354	3163	–111
WhiteBear	3796	3729	3142	2
Thalis	3140	3104	3133	15
umbctac	3565	3536	3108	60
NNN	3454	2756	3071	–17
Walverine	3536	3356	3005	42
RoxyBot	3386	3219	2799	128
zepp	2741	3066	1714	–63
tniTac	2640	3044	—	—
TeamHarmony	3039	2889	—	—
Leprechaun	2694	2643	—	—
EPFLAgentas	2824	2591	—	—
MISS	1607	1749	—	—
CUP	2179	1483	—	—

Table A.9
TAC-04 participants.

Agent	Affiliation	Reference
006	Swedish Inst Comp Sci	[Aurell et al., 2002]
Agent-at-CSE	Chinese U Hong Kong	
LearnAgents	PUC Rio de Janeiro	[Sardinha et al., 2005]
NNN	Hebrew U	
RoxyBot	Brown U	
smacAgent	U Lille	
TeamHarmony	Hokkaido U	[Onodera et al., 2003]
UMTac	U Macau	
UUTac	U Utrecht	
Walverine	U Michigan	[Cheng et al., 2005]
WhiteBear	Cornell U	[Vetsikas and Selman, 2005]
zepp	Poli Bucharest	

weeks in July. Ten agents proceeded to the semifinals (1–2 August), playing 56 games each. The top eight agents played a final round of 80 games on 3 August. Official results are presented in Table A.12.

Unfortunately, the first 22 games of the final round were tainted, due to a serious malfunction by RoxyBot.[2] Since games with erratic agent behavior

2. The misbehavior was due to a simple human error: instead of playing a copy of the agent on each of the two game servers per the tournament protocol, the RoxyBot team accidentally set both copies of the agent to play on the same server. RoxyBot not only failed to participate in the first server's games (scoring 0) but placed double bids (e.g., buying twice the desired flights) in games

Table A.10
TAC-04 scores, all rounds.

Agent	Seeding	Semifinals	Finals	(adjust)
WhiteBear	3980	4334	4122	88
Walverine	3845	4031	3849	72
LearnAgents	3549	3931	3737	102
006	3781	4067	3708	108
NNN	3859	3688	3666	32
UMTac	3556	3654	3281	90
Agent-at-CSE	3543	3723	3263	85
RoxyBot	3337	3431	2015	102
UUTac	2800	3306	—	—
TeamHarmony	3068	3200	—	—
zepp	1737	2371	—	—
smacAgent	2227	—	—	—

Table A.11
TAC-05 participants.

Agent	Affiliation	Reference
006	Swedish Inst Comp Sci	[Aurell et al., 2002]
cuhk	Chinese U Hong Kong	
Dolphin	U Southampton	
e-Agent	U Campinas	
Freud		
kin_agent	U Macau	
LearnAgents	PUC Rio de Janeiro	
Mertacor	Aristotle U Thessaloniki	
RoxyBot	Brown U	
Walverine	U Michigan	[Wellman et al., 2006]
WhiteBear	Cornell U	[Vetsikas and Selman, 2005]

add noise to the scores, the TAC operators published unofficial results with the errant RoxyBot games removed (Table A.13).[3]

A.7 2006

Rules: 2004
GameMaster: Alberto Sardinha
Operations: Swedish Institute of Computer Science

---

on the other server, thus accruing negative scores.

3. Walverine's missed games occurred during those games, whereas the network problems experienced by LearnAgents happened later and thus are still reflected in the revised results.

Table A.12
TAC-05 scores, all rounds.

Agent	Seeding	Semifinals	Finals	(adjust)
Mertacor	4033	4024	4126	–102
WhiteBear	4169	4138	4106	–113
Walverine	4062	4072	4059[a]	–45
Dolphin	3450	3936	4023	–88
006	3931	3839	3972	–80
LearnAgents	3941	3953	3899[b]	–61
e-Agent	2871	3483	3451	–55
RoxyBot	3803	3933	3168	–72
kin_agent	3645	3149	—	—
Freud	3572	2710	—	—
cuhk	3353	—	—	—

[a] Walverine missed two final-round games due a network glitch.
[b] LearnAgents experienced network problems for a few games, lowering its score.

Table A.13
Scores, adjustments, and 95% mean confidence intervals on control-variate adjusted scores for the 58 games of the TAC-05 finals, after removing the first 22 tainted games.

Agent	Finals (22 games removed)	(adjust)	95% C.I.
Walverine	4157	–25	± 138
RoxyBot	4067	–37	± 167
Mertacor	4063	–89	± 152
WhiteBear	4002	–100	± 130
Dolphin	3993	–94	± 149
006	3905	–62	± 141
LearnAgents	3785	–66	± 280
e-Agent	3367	–25	± 117

Finals Date: 9–11 May

Locale: Fifth International Joint Conference on Autonomous Agents and Multiagent Systems (AAMAS-06), Hakodate, Hokkaido, Japan

Table A.14 lists the agents entered in the TAC-06 tournament. Note that WhiteDolphin is a merger of WhiteBear and Dolphin, and L-Agent is a version of LearnAgents.

The TAC-06 results are presented in Table A.15. Since there were only eight entrants, the tournament did not include a semifinal round. The finals comprised 165 games over three days, with the 80 games on the last day weighted 1.5 times as much as the 85 over the first two days. Note that the

Table A.14
TAC-06 participants.

Agent	Affiliation	Reference
006	Swedish Inst Comp Sci	[Aurell et al., 2002]
kin_agent	U Macau	
L-Agent	Carnegie Mellon U	
Mertacor	Aristotle U Thessaloniki	
RoxyBot	Brown U	[Lee et al., 2007]
UTTA	U Tehran	
Walverine	U Michigan	[Wellman et al., 2006]
WhiteDolphin	U Southampton	

relatively large number of final-round games translates to correspondingly small adjustments based on control variates.

Table A.15
TAC-06 scores, seeding and final rounds.

Agent	Seeding	Finals	(adjust)
RoxyBot	4148	4032	–5
Walverine	3992	4032	–17
WhiteDolphin	3901	3936	–2
006	3882	3902	–27
Mertacor	3509	3880	–16
L-Agent	3284	3860	7
kin_agent	3897	3725	0
UTTA	1726	2680	–14

After its glowing performance in the preliminary rounds, on the first day of the finals, RoxyBot finished third, behind Mertacor and Walverine—the top scorers in 2005. As it happens, RoxyBot's new optimization routine, which was suited for stochastic flight, hotel, and entertainment price predictions, was accidentally fed deterministic predictions (i.e., point price estimates) for entertainment prices. Moreover, these predictions were fixed, rather than adapted based on recent game history.

On days 2 and 3, RoxyBot ran properly, basing its bidding in all auctions on stochastic information. Moreover, the agent was upgraded after day 1 to bid on flights not just once, but twice, during each minute. This enabled the agent to delay its bidding somewhat at the end of a game for flights whose prices are decreasing. No doubt this minor modification enabled RoxyBot to emerge victorious in 2006, edging out Walverine by a whisker, below the integer precision reported in Table A.15. The actual margin was 0.22—a mere 22 parts in 400,000. Adjusting for control variates spreads the top two finishers a bit further. Accounting for RoxyBot's difficulties on day 1 of the finals, the difference between first and second place is not as close as it looks.

B Integer Linear Programming Formulations

The problem of bidding in the simultaneous auctions that characterize TAC can be formulated as a two-stage stochastic program, in which bids are placed in the first stage and winnings are allocated in the second stage. In this appendix, we present the implementation details of an integer linear program (ILP) encoded in RoxyBot-06 that approximates an optimal solution to this stochastic program.[1]

In addition, we present integer linear programming (ILP) solutions to:

1. the TAC completion problem, an essential component of RoxyBot-00;
2. the TAC acquisition problem, necessary to compute marginal values (indeed, the LP relaxation of an ILP was used extensively by ATTac-01 in computing average marginal utilities, which requires solving multiple acquisition problems); and
3. the TAC allocation problem, used in the evaluation of candidate bids by RoxyBot-02.

B.1 The Sample Average Approximation of the TAC Travel Bidding Problem

We formulate this ILP assuming current prices are known, and future prices are uncertain in the first stage but revealed in the second stage. Note that whenever prices are known, it suffices for an agent to make decisions about the quantity of each good to buy, rather than about bid amounts, since choosing to bid an amount that is greater than or equal to the price of a good is equivalent to a decision to buy that good.

Unlike in the main body of the book, this ILP formulation of bidding in TAC assumes linear prices. Table B.1 lists the price constants and decision variables for each auction type. For hotels, the only decisions pertain to buy offers; for flights, the agent decides how many tickets to buy now and how many to buy later; for entertainment events, the agent chooses sell quantities as well as buy quantities.

1. Lee et al. [2007] provide a precise specification of RoxyBot-06's bidding ILP. The formulation here is slightly simplified, but we expect it would perform comparably in TAC.

Table B.1
Auction types and associated price constants and decision variables.

Hotels	Price	Variable (bid)
bid now	$\mathcal{Y}_{as}$	ϕ_{apq}

Flights and Events	Price	Variable (qty)
buy now	$\mathcal{M}_a$	μ_a
buy later	$\mathcal{Y}_{as}$	υ_{as}

Events	Price	Variable (qty)
sell now	$\mathcal{N}_a$	ν_a
sell later	$\mathcal{Z}_{as}$	ζ_{as}

Index Sets

$a \in A$ indexes the set of goods, or auctions.
$a_f \in A_f$ indexes the set of flight auctions.
$a_h \in A_h$ indexes the set of hotel auctions.
$a_e \in A_e$ indexes the set of event auctions.

$c \in C$ indexes the set of clients.

$p \in P$ indexes the set of prices.

$q \in Q$ indexes the set of quantities
(i.e., the units of each good in each auction).

$s \in S$ indexes the set of scenarios.

$t \in T$ indexes the set of trips.

Constants

$\mathcal{G}_{at}$ indicates the quantity of good a required to complete trip t.

$\mathcal{M}_a$ indicates the current buy price of a_f, a_e.

$\mathcal{N}_a$ indicates the current sell price of a_e.

$\mathcal{Y}_{as}$ indicates the future buy price of a_f, a_h, a_e in scenario s.

$\mathcal{Z}_{as}$ indicates the future sell price of a_e in scenario s.

$\mathcal{H}_a$ indicates the hypothetical quantity won of hotel a_h.

$\mathcal{O}_a$ indicates the quantity of good a the agent owns.

$\mathcal{U}_{ct}$ indicates client c's value for trip t.

Decision Variables

$\Gamma = \{\gamma_{cst}\}$ is a set of Boolean variables indicating whether or not client c is allocated trip t in scenario s.

$\Phi = \{\phi_{apq}\}$ is a set of Boolean variables indicating whether to bid price p on the qth unit of a_h.

$M = \{\mu_a\}$ is a set of integer variables indicating how many units of a_f, a_e to buy now.

$N = \{\nu_a\}$ is a set of integer variables indicating how many units of a_e to sell now.

$Y = \{\upsilon_{as}\}$ is a set of integer variables indicating how many units of a_f, a_e to buy later in scenario s.

$Z = \{\zeta_{as}\}$ is a set of integer variables indicating how many units of a_e to sell later in scenario s.

Objective Function

$$\max_{\Gamma,\Phi,M,N,Y,Z} \sum_{S} \Bigg(\overbrace{\sum_{C,T} \mathcal{U}_{ct}\gamma_{cts}}^{trip\ value} - \overbrace{\sum_{A_f} \left(\overbrace{\mathcal{M}_a\mu_a}^{current} + \overbrace{\mathcal{Y}_{as}\upsilon_{as}}^{future} \right)}^{flight\ cost}$$

$$- \overbrace{\sum_{A_h, Q, p \geq \mathcal{Y}_{as}} \mathcal{Y}_{as}\phi_{apq}}^{hotel\ cost}$$

$$+ \sum_{A_e} \left(\overbrace{\overbrace{\mathcal{N}_a\nu_a}^{current} + \overbrace{\mathcal{Z}_{as}\zeta_{as}}^{future}}^{event\ revenue} - \overbrace{\overbrace{\mathcal{M}_a\mu_a}^{current} - \overbrace{\mathcal{Y}_{as}\upsilon_{as}}^{future}}^{event\ cost} \right) \Bigg) \quad \text{(B.1)}$$

Constraints

$$\sum_{T} \gamma_{cst} \leq 1 \quad \forall c \in C, s \in S \tag{B.2}$$

$$\overbrace{\sum_{C,T} \gamma_{cst} \mathcal{G}_{at}}^{allocation} \leq \overbrace{\mathcal{O}_a}^{own} + \overbrace{(\mu_a + \upsilon_{as})}^{buy} \quad \forall a \in A_f, s \in S \tag{B.3}$$

$$\overbrace{\sum_{C,T} \gamma_{cst} \mathcal{G}_{at}}^{allocation} \leq \overbrace{\mathcal{O}_a}^{own} + \overbrace{\sum_{Q, p \geq \mathcal{Y}_{as}} \phi_{apq}}^{buy} \quad \forall a \in A_h, s \in S \tag{B.4}$$

$$\overbrace{\sum_{C,T} \gamma_{cst} \mathcal{G}_{at}}^{allocation} \leq \overbrace{\mathcal{O}_a}^{own} + \left(\overbrace{\mu_a + \upsilon_{as}}^{buy} \right) - \left(\overbrace{\nu_a + \zeta_{as}}^{sell} \right)$$
$$\forall a \in A_e, s \in S \tag{B.5}$$

$$\sum_{P,Q} \phi_{apq} \geq \mathcal{H}_a \quad \forall a \in A_h \tag{B.6}$$

$$\sum_{P} \phi_{apq} \leq 1 \quad \forall a \in A_h, q \in Q \tag{B.7}$$

Equation (B.2) limits each client to one trip in each scenario. Equation (B.3) prevents the agent from allocating flights that it does not own or buy. Equation (B.4) prevents the agent from allocating hotels that it does not own or buy. Equation (B.5) prevents the agent from allocating event tickets that it does not own or buy and not sell. Equation (B.6) ensures the agent bids on at least HQW units in each hotel auction. Equation (B.7) prevents the agent from placing more than one buy offer per unit in each hotel auction.

An agent might also be constrained not to place sell offers for more units of each good than it owns, and/or not to place buy (sell) offers for more units of each good than the market supplies (demands).

Note that there is no need to explicitly enforce the bid monotonicity constraints in this ILP formulation:

- "Buy offers must be nonincreasing in k, and sell offers nondecreasing."

  The ILP does not need this constraint because prices are assumed to be linear. In effect, the only decisions the ILP makes are how many units of each good to bid on. Hence, the bids (10, 15, 20) and (20, 15, 10) are equivalent.
- "An agent may not offer to sell for less than the price it is willing to buy."

The ILP would never choose to place both a buy offer and a sell offer on a good whose buy price exceeds its sell price because that would be unprofitable.

B.2 TAC Travel Completion Problem

For completion, the constants and variables specialize those of bidding.

Constants

- $\mathcal{G}_{at}$ indicates the quantity of good a necessary to complete trip t.
- $\mathcal{B}_a$ is a constant indicating the buy price at auction a.
- $\mathcal{A}_a$ is a constant indicating the sell price at auction a.
- $\mathcal{O}_a$ indicates the quantity of good a the agent owns.
- $\mathcal{U}_{ct}$ indicates client c's value for trip t.

Variables

- $\Gamma = \{\gamma_{ct}\}$ is a set of Boolean variables indicating whether or not client c is allocated trip t.
- $Y = \{\upsilon_a\}$ is a set of integer variables indicating how many units to buy at auction a.
- $Z = \{\zeta_a\}$ is a set of integer variables indicating how many units to sell at auction a.

Objective Function

$$\max_{\Gamma,Y,Z} \sum_{C,T} \mathcal{U}_{ct}\gamma_{st} - \sum_{A} \mathcal{B}_u \upsilon_u + \sum_{A} \mathcal{A}_a \zeta_a \tag{B.8}$$

The objective function maximizes the difference between the clients' total trip value plus entertainment revenue and the cost of the goods acquired.

Constraints

$$\sum_{T} \gamma_{ct} \leq 1 \qquad \forall c \in C \tag{B.9}$$

$$\sum_{C,T} \mathcal{G}_{at}\gamma_{ct} \leq \mathcal{O}_a + \upsilon_a - \zeta_a \qquad \forall a \in A \tag{B.10}$$

Constraint B.9 limits each client to one trip. Constraint B.10 prevents the agent from allocating goods that it does not own or buy and not sell.

B.3 TAC Travel Acquisition Problem

For acquisition, the index sets, constants, and variables are a subset of those in the formulation of completion.

Objective Function

$$\max_{\Gamma,Y} \sum_{C,T} \mathcal{U}_{ct}\gamma_{st} - \sum_{A} \mathcal{B}_a \upsilon_a \tag{B.11}$$

The objective function maximizes the difference between the clients' total trip value and the cost of the goods acquired.

Constraints

$$\sum_{T} \gamma_{ct} \leq 1 \qquad \forall c \in C \tag{B.12}$$

$$\sum_{C,T} \mathcal{G}_{at}\gamma_{ct} \leq \mathcal{O}_a + \upsilon_a \qquad \forall a \in A \tag{B.13}$$

Constraint B.12 limits each client to one trip. Constraint B.13 prevents the agent from allocating goods that it does not own or buy.

B.4 TAC Travel Allocation Problem

For allocation, the index sets, constants, and variables are a subset of those in the formulation of acquisition.

Objective Function

$$\max_{\Gamma} \sum_{C,T} \mathcal{U}_{ct}\gamma_{ct} \tag{B.14}$$

The objective function maximizes the clients' total trip value.

Constraints

$$\sum_{T} \gamma_{ct} \leq 1 \qquad \forall c \in C \tag{B.15}$$

$$\sum_{C,T} \mathcal{G}_{at}\gamma_{ct} \leq \mathcal{O}_a \qquad \forall a \in A \tag{B.16}$$

Constraint B.15 limits each client to one trip. Constraint B.16 prevents the agent from allocating goods that it does not own.

The TAC allocation problem differs from the general allocation problem in that TAC agents are subject to the further constraint that only one trip can be allocated to each client. Restricting from the multiunit to the single-unit setting, TAC allocation is equivalent to the winner determination problem in combinatorial auctions where bidding is restricted to the XOR bidding language, that is, each bidder can be allocated at most one subset of goods. This latter problem is known to be NP-hard [Lehmann et al., 2006]. Hence, the TAC allocation problem is also NP-hard.

References

Shabbir Ahmed and Alexander Shapiro. The sample average approximation method for stochastic programs with integer recourse. Optimization Online, http://www.optimization-online.org, 2002.

Ronald C. Arkin. The 1997 AAAI mobile robot competition and exhibition. *AI Magazine*, 19 (3):13–17, 1998.

Kenneth J. Arrow and F. H. Hahn. *General Competitive Analysis*. Holden-Day, San Francisco, 1971.

Raghu Arunachalam and Norman M. Sadeh. The supply chain trading agent competition. *Electronic Commerce Research and Applications*, 4:63–81, 2005.

Erik Aurell, Magnus Boman, Mats Carlsson, Joakim Eriksson, Niclas Finne, Sverker Janson, Per Kreuger, and Lars Rasmusson. A trading agent built on constraint programming. In *Eighth International Conference of the Society for Computational Economics: Computing in Economics and Finance*, Aix-en-Provence, 2002.

Robert Axelrod. *The Evolution of Cooperation*. Basic Books, 1984.

Thomas A. Bass. *The Predictors*. Henry Holt and Company, 1999.

Dimitri P. Bertsekas. Auction algorithms for network flow problems: A tutorial introduction. *Computational Optimization and Applications*, 1:7–66, 1992.

Sushil Bikhchandani and John W. Mamer. Competitive equilibrium in an exchange economy with indivisibilities. *Journal of Economic Theory*, 74:385–413, 1997.

Darse Billings. The first international RoShamBo programming competition. *International Computer Games Association Journal*, 23(1):42–50, 2000.

John Birge and Francois Louveaux. *Introduction to Stochastic Programming*. Springer, New York, 1997.

John Boadway and Doina Precup. Reinforcement learning applied to a multiagent system. Presentation at TAC Workshop, 2001.

Magnus Boman. Workshop report: Trading agents. *AgentLink News*, 5:15–16, 2001.

Pete Bonasso and Thomas Dean. A retrospective of the AAAI robot competitions. *AI Magazine*, 18(1):11–23, 1997.

Anil Bose, Prosenjit andMaheshwari and Pat Morin. Fast approximations for sums of distances, clustering and the Fermat-Weber problem. *Computational Geometry: Theory and Applications*, 24:135–146, 2002.

Justin Boyan and Amy Greenwald. Bid determination in simultaneous auctions: An agent architecture. In *Third ACM Conference on Electronic Commerce*, pages 210–212, Tampa, FL, 2001.

Justin Boyan, Amy Greenwald, R. M. Kirby, and Jon Reiter. Bidding algorithms for simultaneous auctions. In *IJCAI-01 Workshop on Economic Agents, Models, and Mechanisms*, pages 1–11, Seattle, 2001.

Shih-Fen Cheng and Michael P. Wellman. Iterated weaker-than-weak dominance. In *Twentieth International Joint Conference on Artificial Intelligence*, Hyderabad, 2007.

Shih-Fen Cheng, Evan Leung, Kevin M. Lochner, Kevin O'Malley, Daniel M. Reeves, and Michael P. Wellman. Walverine: A Walrasian trading agent. *Decision Support Systems*, 39: 169–184, 2005.

Dave Cliff. Evolving parameter sets for adaptive trading agents in continuous double-auction markets. In *Agents-98 Workshop on Artificial Societies and Computational Markets*, pages 38–47, Minneapolis, May 1998.

Adam Cohen. *The Perfect Store: Inside eBay*. Little, Brown, and Company, 2002.

Michael Collins, Robert E. Schapire, and Yoram Singer. Logistic regression, AdaBoost and Bregman distances. *Machine Learning*, 48:253–285, 2002.

Peter Cramton. Simultaneous ascending auctions. In Cramton et al. [2006].

Peter Cramton, Yoav Shoham, and Richard Steinberg, editors. *Combinatorial Auctions*. MIT Press, 2006.

Jánosz A. Csirik, Michael L. Littman, Satinder Singh, and Peter Stone. FAucS: An FCC spectrum auction simulator for autonomous bidding agents. In *Second International Workshop on Electronic Commerce*, volume 2232 of *Lecture Notes in Computer Science*, pages 139–151. Springer-Verlag, 2001.

Rajarshi Das, James E. Hanson, Jeffrey O. Kephart, and Gerald Tesauro. Agent-human interactions in the continuous double auction. In *Seventeenth International Joint Conference on Artificial Intelligence*, pages 1169–1176, Seattle, 2001.

Li Ding, Tim Finin, Yongmei Shi, Youyong Zou, Zhongli Ding, and Rong Pan. Strategies and heuristics used by the UMBCTAC agent in the third Trading Agent Competition. In *IJCAI-03 Workshop on Trading Agent Design and Analysis*, Acapulco, 2003.

Joakim Eriksson and Sverker Janson. The Trading Agent Competition: TAC 2002. *ERCIM News*, 51, October 2002.

Joakim Eriksson, Niclas Finne, and Sverker Janson. Evolution of a supply chain management game for the trading agent competition. *AI Communications*, 19:1–12, 2006.

Maria Fasli and Nikolaos Poursanidis. Thalis: A flexible trading agent. Technical Report CSM-388, University of Essex, Department of Computer Science, 2003.

Nicoletta Fornara and Luca Maria Gambardella. An autonomous bidding agent for simultaneous auctions. In *Fifth International Workshop on Cooperative Information Agents*, number 2182 in Lecture Notes on Artificial Intelligence, pages 130–141, 2001.

Daniel Friedman. Evolutionary games in economics. *Econometrica*, 59:637–666, 1991.

Daniel Friedman. The double auction market institution: A survey. In Daniel Friedman and John Rust, editors, *The Double Auction Market*, pages 3–25. Addison-Wesley, 1993.

Clemens Fritschi and Klaus Dorer. Agent-oriented software engineering for successful TAC participation. In *First International Joint Conference on Autonomous Agents and Multi-Agent Systems*, Bologna, 2002.

Steven Gjerstad. The impact of pace in double auction bargaining. Technical report, University of Arizona, 2004.

Steven Gjerstad and John Dickhaut. Price formation in double auctions. *Games and Economic Behavior*, 22:1–29, 1998.

Dhananjay K. Gode and Shyam Sunder. Allocative efficiency of markets with zero-intelligence traders: Market as a partial substitute for individual rationality. *Journal of Political Economy*, 101:119–137, 1993.

Amy Greenwald. The international trading agent competition: Focus on RoxyBot. *Computing Research News*, 14(5):3, 10, 2002.

Amy Greenwald. The 2002 trading agent competition: An overview of agent strategies. *AI Magazine*, 24(1):83–91, 2003a.

Amy Greenwald. Bidding under uncertainty in simultaneous auctions. In *IJCAI-03 Workshop on Trading Agent Design and Analysis*, Acapulco, 2003b.

Amy Greenwald. Bid determination in simultaneous auctions. Technical Report CS-05-16, Brown University, 2005.

Amy Greenwald and Justin Boyan. Bidding under uncertainty: Theory and experiments. In *Twentieth Conference on Uncertainty in Artificial Intelligence*, pages 209–216, Banff, 2004.

Amy Greenwald and Justin Boyan. Bidding algorithms for simultaneous auctions: A case study. *Autonomous Agents and Multi-Agent Systems*, 10:67–89, 2005.

Amy Greenwald and Peter Stone. Autonomous bidding agents in the trading agent competition. *IEEE Internet Computing*, 5(2):52–60, 2001.

Minghua He and Nicholas R. Jennings. SouthamptonTAC: Designing a successful trading agent.

In *Fifteenth European Conference on Artificial Intelligence*, pages 8–12, Lyon, 2002.

Minghua He and Nicholas R. Jennings. SouthamptonTAC: An adaptive autonomous trading agent. *ACM Transactions on Internet Technology*, 3:218–235, 2003.

Minghua He and Nicholas R. Jennings. Designing a successful trading agent: A fuzzy set approach. *IEEE Transactions on Fuzzy Systems*, 12:389–410, 2004.

Christopher G. Healey, Robert St. Amant, and Jiae Chang. Assisted visualization of e-commerce auction agents. In *Graphics Interface*, pages 201–208, Ottawa, Canada, 2001.

Ronald A. Howard. Bayesian decision models for systems engineering. *IEEE Transactions on Systems Science and Cybernetics*, 1:36–40, 1965.

Patrick R. Jordan, Christopher Kiekintveld, and Michael P. Wellman. Empirical game-theoretic analysis of the TAC supply chain game. In *Sixth International Joint Conference on Autonomous Agents and Multi-Agent Systems*, Honolulu, 2007.

Donald W. Katzner. *The Walrasian Vision of the Microeconomy*. University of Michigan Press, 1989.

Michael Kearns and Luis Ortiz. The Penn-Lehman automated trading project. *IEEE Intelligent Systems*, 18(6):22–31, 2003.

Jeffrey O. Kephart, James E. Hanson, and Jakka Sairamesh. Price and niche wars in a free-market economy of software agents. *Artificial Life*, 4:1–23, 1998.

Hiroaki Kitano, Milind Tambe, Peter Stone, Manuela Veloso, Silvia Coradeschi, Eiichi Osawa, Hitoshi Matsubara, Itsuki Noda, and Minoru Asada. The RoboCup synthetic agent challenge 97. In *Fifteenth International Joint Conference on Artificial Intelligence*, pages 24–29, Nagoya, 1997.

David M. Kreps. *Game Theory and Economic Modelling*. Oxford University Press, 1990.

Vijay Krishna. *Auction Theory*. Academic Press, 2002.

Balachander Krishnamurthy and Jennifer Rexford. *Web Protocols and Practice*. Addison Wesley, 2001.

Pier Luca Lanzi and Alessandro Strada. A statistical analysis of the trading agent competition 2001. *SIGecom Exchanges*, 3(2):1–8, 2002.

Pierre L'Ecuyer. Efficiency improvement and variance reduction. In *Twenty-Sixth Winter Simulation Conference*, pages 122–132, Orlando, FL, 1994.

Seong Jae Lee, Amy Greenwald, and Victor Naroditskiy. RoxyBot-06: An $(SAA)^2$ TAC travel agent. In *Twentieth International Joint Conference on Artificial Intelligence*, Hyderabad, 2007.

Daniel Lehmann, Rudolf Müller, and Tuomas Sandholm. The winner determination problem. In Cramton et al. [2006].

Richard J. Lipton, Evangelos Markakis, and Aranyak Mehta. Playing large games using simple strategies. In *Fourth ACM Conference on Electronic Commerce*, pages 36–41, San Diego, 2003.

Jeffrey K. MacKie-Mason and Michael P. Wellman. Automated markets and trading agents. In Tesfatsion and Judd [2006].

Jeffrey K. MacKie-Mason, Anna Osepayshvili, Daniel M. Reeves, and Michael P. Wellman. Price prediction strategies for market-based scheduling. In *Fourteenth International Conference on Automated Planning and Scheduling*, pages 244–252, Whistler, BC, 2004.

R. Preston McAfee and John McMillan. Analyzing the airwaves auction. *Journal of Economic Perspectives*, 10(1):159–175, 1996.

Drew McDermott. The 1998 AI planning systems competition. *AI Magazine*, 21(2):35–55, 2000.

Richard D. McKelvey and Andrew McLennan. Computation of equilibria in finite games. In *Handbook of Computational Economics*, volume 1. Elsevier, 1996.

Paul Milgrom. Putting auction theory to work: The simultaneous ascending auction. *Journal of Political Economy*, 108:245–272, 2000.

Ross M. Miller. *Paving Wall Street: Experimental Economics and the Quest for the Perfect Market*. Wiley, 2002.

Melanie Mitchell. *An Introduction to Genetic Algorithms*. MIT Press, 1996.

Itsuki Noda, Shóji Suzuki, Hitoshi Matsubara, Minoru Asada, and Hiroaki Kitano. RoboCup-97: The First Robot World Cup Soccer Games and Conferences. *AI Magazine*, 19(3):49–59, 1998.

Kevin O'Malley. Agents and automated online trading. *Dr. Dobb's Journal*, pages 23–28, May 2001.

Kevin O'Malley and Terence Kelly. An API for Internet auctions. *Dr. Dobb's Journal*, pages 70–74, September 1998.

Masaki Onodera, Hidenori Kawamura, Masahito Yamamoto, Koichi Kurumatani, and Azuma Ohuchi. Design of adaptive trading strategy for trading agent competition. In *International Technical Conference on Circuits/Systems, Computers and Communications*, pages 337–340, 2003.

Anna Osepayshvili, Michael P. Wellman, Daniel M. Reeves, and Jeffrey K. MacKie-Mason. Self-confirming price prediction for bidding in simultaneous ascending auctions. In *Twenty-First Conference on Uncertainty in Artificial Intelligence*, pages 441–449, Edinburgh, 2005.

David Pardoe and Peter Stone. TacTex-2005: A champion supply chain management agent. In *Twenty-First National Conference on Artificial Intelligence*, pages 1489–1494, 2006.

Michael Peters and Sergei Severinov. Internet auctions with many traders. *Journal of Economic Theory*, 130:220–245, 2006.

S. Phelps, M. Marcinkiewicz, S. Parsons, and P. McBurney. A novel method for automatic strategy acquisition in n-player non-zero-sum games. In *Fifth International Joint Conference on Autonomous Agents and Multi-Agent Systems*, pages 705–712, Hakodate, 2006.

Ryan Porter, Eugene Nudelman, and Yoav Shoham. Simple search methods for finding a Nash equilibrium. In *Nineteenth National Conference on Artificial Intelligence*, pages 664–669, San Jose, CA, 2004.

Ravi Prakash Putchala, Vincent Naveen Morris, Rajesh Kazhanchi, Laxminarayanan Raman, and Shashank Shekhar. kavayaH: A trading agent developed for TAC-02. Technical report, Oracle India, 2002.

Daniel M. Reeves. *Generating Trading Agent Strategies: Analytic and Empirical Methods for Infinite and Large Games*. PhD thesis, University of Michigan, 2005.

Daniel M. Reeves, Michael P. Wellman, Jeffrey K. MacKie-Mason, and Anna Osepayshvili. Exploring bidding strategies for market-based scheduling. *Decision Support Systems*, 39:67–85, 2005.

Sheldon M. Ross. *Simulation*. Academic Press, third edition, 2002.

Alvin E. Roth and Axel Ockenfels. Last-minute bidding and the rules for ending second-price auctions: Evidence from eBay and Amazon auctions on the Internet. *American Economic Review*, 92:1093–1103, 2002.

Michael H. Rothkopf, Aleksander Pekeč, and Ronald M. Harstad. Computationally manageable combinatorial auctions. *Management Science*, 44:1131–1147, 1998.

Stuart Russell and Peter Norvig. *Artificial Intelligence: A Modern Approach*. Prentice Hall, second edition, 2003.

John Rust, John H. Miller, and Richard Palmer. Characterizing effective trading strategies: Insights from a computerized double auction tournament. *Journal of Economic Dynamics and Control*, 18:61–96, 1994.

Tuomas Sandholm, David Levine, Michael Concordia, Paul Martyn, Rick Hughes, Jim Jacobs, and Dennis Begg. Changing the game in strategic sourcing at Procter and Gamble: Expressive competition enabled by optimization. *Interfaces*, 36:55–68, 2006.

José Alberto R. P. Sardinha, Ruy L. Milidiú, Patrick M. Paranhos, Pedro M. Cunha, and Carlos J. P. Lucena. An agent based architecture for highly competitive electronic markets. In *Eighteenth International FLAIRS Conference*, page 326331, Clearwater Beach, FL, 2005.

Robert E. Schapire and Yoram Singer. BoosTexter: A boosting-based system for text categorization. *Machine Learning*, 39:135–168, 2000.

Robert E. Schapire and Yoram Singer. Improved boosting algorithms using confidence-rated predictions. *Machine Learning*, 37:297–336, 1999.

L. Julian Schvartzman and Michael P. Wellman. Market-based allocation with indivisible bids. *Production and Operations Management*, 16, 2007.

Alexander Sherstov and Peter Stone. Three automated stock-trading agents: A comparative study. In *AAMAS-04 Workshop on Agent-Mediated Electronic Commerce*, New York, 2004.

Hans R. Stoll. Electronic trading in stock markets. *Journal of Economic Perspectives*, 20(1): 153–174, 2006.

Peter Stone and Amy Greenwald. The first international trading agent competition: Autonomous bidding agents. *Electronic Commerce Research*, 5:229–265, 2005.

Peter Stone, Michael L. Littman, Satinder Singh, and Michael Kearns. ATTac-2000: An adaptive autonomous bidding agent. *Journal of Artificial Intelligence Research*, 15:189–206, 2001.

Peter Stone, Robert E. Schapire, Michael L. Littman, János A. Csirik, and David McAllester. Decision-theoretic bidding based on learned density models in simultaneous, interacting auctions. *Journal of Artificial Intelligence Research*, 19:209–242, 2003.

Geoff Sutcliffe. The CADE-17 ATP system competition. *Journal of Automated Reasoning*, 27: 227–250, 2001.

Richard S. Sutton and Andrew G. Barto. *Reinforcement Learning*. MIT Press, 1998.

P. Taylor and L. Jonker. Evolutionary stable strategies and game dynamics. *Mathematical Biosciences*, 40:145–156, 1978.

Gerald Tesauro and Jonathan L. Bredin. Strategic sequential bidding in auctions using dynamic programming. In *First International Joint Conference on Autonomous Agents and Multi-Agent Systems*, pages 591–598, Bologna, 2002.

Gerald Tesauro and Rajarshi Das. High-performance bidding agents for the continuous double auction. In *Third ACM Conference on Electronic Commerce*, pages 206–209, Tampa, FL, 2001.

Leigh Tesfatsion and Kenneth L. Judd, editors. *Handbook of Agent-Based Computational Economics*. Elsevier, 2006.

Panos Toulis, Dionisis Kehagias, and Pericles Mitkas. Mertacor: A successful autonomous trading agent. In *Fifth International Joint Conference on Autonomous Agents and Multi-Agent Systems*, pages 1191–1198, Hakodate, 2006.

Ioannis A. Vetsikas and Bart Selman. A principled study of the design tradeoffs for autonomous trading agents. In *Second International Joint Conference on Autonomous Agents and Multi-Agent Systems*, pages 473–480, Melbourne, 2003.

Ioannis A. Vetsikas and Bart Selman. Autonomous trading agent design in the presence of tradeoffs. In *Seventh International Conference on Electronic Commerce*, pages 293–299, Xi'an, China, 2005.

William Vickrey. Counterspeculation, auctions, and competitive sealed tenders. *Journal of Finance*, 16:8–37, 1961.

Yevgeniy Vorobeychik, Christopher Kiekintveld, and Michael P. Wellman. Empirical mechanism design: Methods, with application to a supply chain scenario. In *Seventh ACM Conference on Electronic Commerce*, pages 306–315, Ann Arbor, MI, 2006.

Perukrishnen Vytelingum, Dave Cliff, and Nicholas R. Jennings. Evolutionary stability of behavioural types in the continuous double auction. In *AAMAS-06 Joint Workshop on Trading Agent Design and Analysis and Agent Mediated Electronic Commerce*, Hakodate, 2006.

Léon Walras. *Elements of Pure Economics*. Allen and Unwin, 1954. English translation by William Jaffé, originally published in 1874.

William E. Walsh, David Parkes, and Rajarshi Das. Choosing samples to compute heuristic-strategy Nash equilibrium. In *AAMAS-03 Workshop on Agent-Mediated Electronic*

Commerce, Melbourne, 2003.

Yun Wan, Satya Menon, and Arkalgud Ramaprasad. A classification of product comparison agents. In *Fifth International Conference on Electronic Commerce*, pages 498–504, Pittsburgh, 2003.

Robert J. Weber. Making more from less: Strategic demand reduction in the FCC spectrum auctions. *Journal of Economics and Management Strategy*, 6:529–548, 1997.

Michael P. Wellman. Methods for empirical game-theoretic analysis (extended abstract). In *Twenty-First National Conference on Artificial Intelligence*, pages 1552–1555, Boston, 2006.

Michael P. Wellman and Peter R. Wurman. A trading agent competition for the research community. In *IJCAI-99 Workshop on Agent-Mediated Electronic Trading*, Stockholm, August 1999.

Michael P. Wellman, William E. Walsh, Peter R. Wurman, and Jeffrey K. MacKie-Mason. Auction protocols for decentralized scheduling. *Games and Economic Behavior*, 35:271–303, 2001a.

Michael P. Wellman, Peter R. Wurman, Kevin O'Malley, Roshan Bangera, Shou-de Lin, Daniel Reeves, and William E. Walsh. Designing the market game for a trading agent competition. *IEEE Internet Computing*, 5(2):43–51, 2001b.

Michael P. Wellman, Shih-Fen Cheng, Daniel M. Reeves, and Kevin M. Lochner. Trading agents competing: Performance, progress, and market effectiveness. *IEEE Intelligent Systems*, 18(6): 48–53, 2003a.

Michael P. Wellman, Amy Greenwald, Peter Stone, and Peter R. Wurman. The 2001 trading agent competition. *Electronic Markets*, 13:4–12, 2003b.

Michael P. Wellman, Joshua Estelle, Satinder Singh, Yevgeniy Vorobeychik, Christopher Kiekintveld, and Vishal Soni. Strategic interactions in a supply chain game. *Computational Intelligence*, 21:1–26, 2005a.

Michael P. Wellman, Daniel M. Reeves, Kevin M. Lochner, Shih-Fen Cheng, and Rahul Suri. Approximate strategic reasoning through hierarchical reduction of large symmetric games. In *Twentieth National Conference on Artificial Intelligence*, pages 502–508, Pittsburgh, 2005b.

Michael P. Wellman, Daniel M. Reeves, Kevin M. Lochner, and Rahul Suri. Searching for Walverine 2005. In *Agent-Mediated Electronic Commerce: Designing Trading Agents and Mechanisms*, number 3937 in Lecture Notes on Artificial Intelligence, pages 157–170. Springer, 2006.

Peter R. Wurman, William E. Walsh, and Michael P. Wellman. Flexible double auctions for electronic commerce: Theory and implementation. *Decision Support Systems*, 24:17–27, 1998a.

Peter R. Wurman, Michael P. Wellman, and William E. Walsh. The Michigan Internet AuctionBot: A configurable auction server for human and software agents. In *Second International Conference on Autonomous Agents*, pages 301–308, Minneapolis, 1998b.

Håkan L. S. Younes, Michael L. Littman, David Weissman, and John Asmuth. The first probabilistic track of the international planning competition. *Journal of Artificial Intelligence Research*, 24:851–887, 2005.

Citation Index

Subject Index

Made in the USA
Monee, IL
05 November 2026

67811377R00138